American Imperialism
Viewpoints of United States
Foreign Policy, 1898-1941

*Reproduced with the cooperation of the
Hoover Institution of War, Revolution and Peace,
Stanford University, Stanford, California*

THE LOOTING OF NICARAGUA

Rafael De Nogales

ARNO PRESS & THE NEW YORK TIMES
New York ★ 1970

Collection Created and Selected
by
CHARLES GREGG OF GREGG PRESS

Reprinted from a copy in The New York Public Library

Library of Congress Catalog Card Number: 70-111726
ISBN 0-405-02041-4

ISBN for complete set: 0-405-02000-7

Reprint Edition 1970 by Arno Press Inc.
Manufactured in the United States of America

THE LOOTING OF NICARAGUA

General Rafael de Nogales, from a photograph taken during the World War, when he served as Inspector General of Turkish Cavalry.

THE LOOTING OF NICARAGUA

by
RAFAEL DE NOGALES
Author of "Four Years Beneath the Crescent," etc.

ILLUSTRATED

NEW YORK
ROBERT M. McBRIDE & COMPANY
MCMXXVIII

COPYRIGHT, 1928,
BY ROBERT M. MC BRIDE & COMPANY

First Published, January, 1928

PUBLISHER'S NOTE

This history of the exploitation of Nicaragua by American capital backed by American arms is offered by the publishers in the interest of fair play. That General de Nogales, himself a distinguished citizen of our sister-republic Venezuela, should write with fiery zeal, should display certain prejudices common to his race, is readily understandable. The nations of Central America have felt the heel of the oppressor.

It is our belief that the statements contained in this book are, without exception, based upon fact. Thus, it will be obvious to the reading public that the broad distribution of the work is a matter of the first importance to the people of the United States. At a time when our Government is conducting a war in Nicaragua; when American boys are being killed on foreign soil in the furtherance of heaven knows what imperialistic project; when the Monroe Doctrine and the well-worn slogan of "manifest destiny" are once again being dusted off in the sacred halls of the State Department with an eye to possible future use, it is, in our opinion, necessary that the widest publicity be given to every aspect of the Nicaraguan situation. As the plain statement, then, of a Latin-American, a trained military observer's first-hand report, this book is offered to the citizens of the United States.

CONTENTS

Chapter I 1
    Latin America Contrasted with the United States — What Americans Generally Are Led to Believe About Latin Americans — The Wave of Hatred and Distrust — Albert H. Putney on Nicaragua — President José Santos Zelaya and Secretary Knox — Adolfo Diaz and the Estrada Revolution — President Madriz and the Beginning of American Armed Intervention — First American Loan Forced on Nicaragua — Nicaragua Opposes Loan Project — Diaz Appointed President — The Mixed Claims Commission — Unlawful Sale of Canal Zone by Diaz to the United States — United States Senate Refuses to Ratify Knox-Castrillo Treaty — Beginning of American Financial Rule — The Tthelburga Loan.

Chapter II 17
    The New Nicaraguan Constitution — General Luis Mena Opposes American Interference and Fights Diaz — Election Frauds in 1912 — Nicaraguan Government a Family Affair — The National Bank and Nicaraguan R.R. Scandal — Americans Control Coffee Market — The New Currency System and Its Drawbacks — Economic Loss Through American Financial Intervention — Misery and Emigration — Vice-President Martinez — Repurchasing of Controlling Stock in Bank and R.R. — Election of 1924 — Extension of Contract — Chamorro Rebellion.

Chapter III 30
    Description of Nicaragua and Its People — Its Geography and History — William Walker, the Buccaneer and First Tool of Dollar Diplomacy in Nicaragua — The American Armed Interventions of 1912 and 1927, and Some of Their Disastrous Results.

Chapter IV 43
    Leaving New York for Nicaragua to Investigate the Situation — Visiting Friends in Washington En Route —

viii   CONTENTS

Arrival in Mexico City — Colonel Edward Davis and Ambassador Sheffield — The Soviet Minister — Two Birds with One Shot — The Powerful C. R. O. M. — Senator Wheeler Speaks — Plans of the Oil Kings and Their Allies for the Dismemberment of Mexico.

Chapter V 63

From Mexico City to the Coast — Disheveled Vera Cruz — Mexico's Need — By Train Across Tehuantepec — A Prince Turns Planter — At the Headquarters of the Nicaraguan Nationalists in Guatemala City — Conduct of Certain United States Ministers — A Motion Picture Show and a Show of Rage — Departure for Costa Rica — Passing Over an Old Battle-ground — A German ex-Secretary of War — Costa Rican Feeling Against the United States — Colon: What They Think in Panama.

Chapter VI 84

My Arrival at Puerto Cabezas — Dr. J. B. Sacasa and His Cabinet — Pleasant Intercourse with Lt.-Commander Bischoff and United States Navy Officers — The Father of Dollar Diplomacy — Some of H. O. Arguello's Written Statements About Wall Street's Activities in Nicaragua.

Chapter VII 105

Copies of Documents, Proving the Similarity of Views of Several Prominent North and Latin-American Statesmen and the Majority of the Honest American Press, in Regard to the Nicaraguan Imbroglio.

Chapter VIII 130

The Diaz-Chamorro Gang's Hold on the Conservative Party — How the Solorzano-Sacasa Coalition Government Was Formed — Reasons Why Sacasa Appointed Moncada Secretary of War — Moncada's Lurid Career — Beltran-Sandoval and the "Machete" Revolution — Sacasa's Letter Intercepted by Chamorro — Consequent Failure of the Expedition Under Irais' Command — Sacasa at Last Arrives in Nicaragua.

Chapter IX 146

The Campaign of the Nicaraguan Constitutionalist Army from the Battle of Laguna de Perlas up to the Armistice at Tipitapa.

CONTENTS

Chapter X 168
General Beltran-Sandoval's Report — Sacasa's Government, as the Constitutional Régime, Fully Acknowledged by Latin America — North American Outlaws in Nicaragua Not Arrested by the Marines — Who Asked for American Protection? — Letters from Prominent Foreigners, Both British and American, Testifying to the Conduct of Sacasa's Troops — Marines Cracking Safes and Forcibly Entering Homes — Dollar Diplomacy and the Peonage System.

Chapter XI 190
I Leave Puerto Cabezas for Managua — By Motorboat, Barge and Canoe Up the Rio Grande — A Pair of German Military Trousers Rouses Suspicion — A Wrecked Safe — How Laborers Who Demand More Pay Are Answered in the Banana Country — Ancient Indian Inscriptions on the River Rocks — Opportunities for Legitimate Business in Nicaragua.

Chapter XII 210
San Pedro; a Concrete Example of the Ruin Which Dollar Diplomacy Has Wrought in the Interior — A Spanish-American Frontiersman — By Canoe Up the Tuma and Willike Rivers — Seven Weeks in the Heart of the Jungle — How I Became a Marked Man — Dodging Bandits and Deserters — The Clever Ruse of the Bandit, Rodriguez, to Get My Rifles — Indian Medicine — Hunting Pigs, Tapirs and Jaguars — A Black Tiger — The Glamor of the Jungle — Matagalpa at Last.

Chapter XIII 228
The Golden Alligator Remains Unseen of Man — A Friendly Deserter Warns Me in Time of Impending Capture by Conservatives — Some Proclamations by General Moncada and Admiral Latimer — Sandino Answers a Captain of Marines — Moncada Betrays the Army Under His Command — Mr. Stimson Represents President Coolidge — Moncada Bargains with Stimson Behind Closed Doors.

Chapter XIV 250
From Matagalpa to Managua — How Long Hate Can Last — Report of the Pan-American Federation of Labor

CONTENTS

— H. Blanco Fombona Gives a Series of Shameful Facts About the American Occupation in Santo Domingo.

Chapter XV 277

Double Jobs for Correspondents — Something About the New Loan — A Repulsive Farce About a Crucifix — Pertinent Remarks by Carleton Beals, S. Guy Inman and Senator Shipstead — The Terrific Slump in U. S. Trade with Latin America — Something About Hatred and a Few Suggestions for Its Cure.

Sources of Information 301

ILLUSTRATIONS

General Rafael de Nogales . . . . *Frontispiece*	
	PAGE
U. S. Chargé d'Affaires, Mr. Dennis, Adolfo Diaz and Emiliano Chamorro at Managua, Nicaragua . .	8
Nicaraguan Constitutionalist mountain artillery . .	9
Breastworks constructed with mahogany logs, Puerto Cabezas, Nicaragua	32
Rear Admiral Latimer, U. S. N.	33
The Author, Dr. Juan Bautista Sacasa, and Dr. Cordero Reyes, at Puerto Cabezas, Nicaragua	88
Some of the dead, after the fight at Puerto Cabezas, Nicaragua	89
Chinandega, Nicaragua, after its partial destruction by American bombing planes	136
Nicaraguan Constitutionalist machine gun detachment .	137
Nicaraguan woman conscripts in Adolfo Diaz's Conservative Army	176
Victims of the American fliers at Chinandega, Nicaragua	177
Victims of the American fliers at Chinandega . . .	177
The Author at his arrival at Matagalpa, Nicaragua .	192
Some of the victims of the massacre of El Guayabo, La Cruz, Nicaragua	193
General Augusto Sandino, Commander of the Nicaraguan Constitutionalist Army	240
American Sailors awaiting attack of General Sandino's forces, Nicaragua	241

THE LOOTING OF NICARAGUA

THE LOOTING OF NICARAGUA

Chapter I

Latin America Contrasted with the United States — What Americans Generally Are Led to Believe About Latin Americans — The Wave of Hatred and Distrust — Albert H. Putney on Nicaragua — President José Santos Zelaya and Secretary Knox — Adolfo Diaz and the Estrada Revolution — President Madriz and the Beginning of American Armed Intervention — First American Loan Forced on Nicaragua — Nicaragua Opposes Loan Project — Diaz Appointed President — The Mixed Claims Commission — Unlawful Sale of Canal Zone by Diaz to the United States — United States Senate Refuses to Ratify Knox-Castrillo Treaty — Beginning of American Financial Rule — The Ethelburga Loan.

ALIKE in being new nations shaped by conditions of the western hemisphere, essentially alike in their passion for freedom and for daring, the peoples of Latin America and of the United States are nevertheless essentially unlike in temperament as well as in most of their traditions. The causes of the dissimilarities must be taken into consideration in seeking a sound basis for understanding.

The United States were once a British colonial possession. Here men of England's best, intelligent, liberty-loving, resourceful, vigorous in mind and body, adventurous, planted settlements, established law and society in conformance with the principles of English civilization and the Anglo-Saxon temperament; and, in due time, because of the influences of their environment, because they were Americans, separated from Britain and established themselves as a new and individual nation.

To the south of them was a vast tract of country comprising Mexico and Central America, and, southward still, a great continent; and this combined territory had been colonized by another race, the Latins, and, with the exception of Brazil, by one Latin people, the Spanish. In this enormous domain, or about three-fourths of the New World, the culture, the speech, the law, society, and ideals were Spanish; and they had been established there by hardy, venturesome, resourceful men. The best blood of Spain flowed in the veins of the Conquistadores, many of whom sought not only gold in the colonies but freedom from the restrictions with which life was circumscribed at home. In due time they, also, threw off the political yoke of the mother country, as the British colonists had done to the north of them. Theirs was the harder task; because the Spanish system, unlike the English, had not schooled the colonies in self-government and coöperation; because no European powers lent them aid as France and Spain aided the Americans; and because they had also to contend with the opposition of their Church which was more firmly entrenched in the land, as well as in the loyal faith of the people, than was the imperial power of Spain. They achieved the seemingly impossible. And, in time, what had been a vast colonial possession became a number of republics, each independent and self-governing, liberal in aim and endeavor, hoping and working toward progress for all its citizens, Latin in its speech and traditions and in its cultural ideals. We Latin Americans are an individual and new nation, compounded of heredity and environment. We are ourselves; content to be so, without either an inferiority complex or an intolerant demand that our nearest neighbors to the north shall resemble us. We recognize that, like ourselves, the people of the United States are the products of heredity and environment; a different stock shaped by different surroundings, conditions and climate.

As a step towards mutual understanding, then, it should be borne in mind that our twenty republics, with the possible exception of Panama, do not owe their independence to the United States, but to themselves. Also, that if only a few of these republics have kept pace with the United States in industrial development the lagging is due, in part, to the long struggle against a retrogressive ecclesiasticism and in part to climatic conditions. The tropical climate does not permit a man of the educated classes to do manual labor in a factory or on a farm; as he can easily enough in the United States and in temperate Europe. The Americans and other aliens in the tropics do not attempt it. In the lowlands, or torrid zone, of our republics, which means from fifty to seventy per cent of their territory, only peons can work ten hours a day under the broiling sun and live. No other demand is made on their energy; whereas much more is demanded as the social and national contribution of the man of higher intelligence and culture. Quickly grasping this essential fact of life in the tropics, the Conquistadores settled on the high plateaus and in the mountain regions where the temperate climate allowed them to do their own farming. This is also the reason why most of our principal cities and towns are situated from three thousand to ten thousand feet above sea level. Not man but the sun differentiates the races that people our globe. If the Spanish had settled "These States," and the English had colonized Latin America, conditions in each territory would still be as they are. Look at Argentine!

The sun creates, and it maintains the character of what it creates, even when political bonds loosen or change. Porto Rico is as Latin as it was thirty years ago when the United States took it over. Cuba is as Cuban to-day as it ever was, despite the Platt Amendment. Why then should any one marvel that little Nicaragua clings to her Spanish civilization, resents American marines, and fights to hold her independence, which she in no way owes to the United States?

Of these things pertaining to Latin America, apparently, the average American neither thinks nor cares to think. Why should he bestir himself to ask questions about what his government and certain American financiers are doing in Nicaragua; or whether their actions there are in keeping, morally, with America's high claims to "spiritual leadership" of the world? Nicaragua is only a dwarf compared with the United States.

Still, even a flea-bite in an elephant's ear is likely to cause infection if not properly treated. The infection in this particular case is already apparent. It is spreading rapidly, not only over Central America but also over all the Latin countries. The average American citizen may not know it, but it is a fact that little Nicaragua has roused a wave of sympathy and admiration throughout the world. /She is acclaimed in the press of several lands as the "little Belgium" of our hemisphere. /

For most Americans a championship prize-fight seems more important than the news about Sandino and his handful of barefooted soldiers fighting for

THE LOOTING OF NICARAGUA

the very existence of their plucky and chivalrous little country. And why should they worry, after all? Is not the State Department attending to all that? Have they not been informed time and again by the most reputable papers of the country that Nicaragua is a country which does not deserve to be free because she cannot take care of herself? Have not the Nicaraguans been fighting among themselves for the last twenty years, just for the love of fighting—being people who enjoy a fight better than a meal? Did not the American advisors have a terrible time straightening out their finances, and the American marines in trying to make them behave? Did not Adolfo Diaz ask for American protection? *And did he not get it?* What else do they want?

These and several other questions are precisely the ones which I intend to answer in this book to the best of my knowledge, because I think that it is about time. /I do not consider it right or necessary that North and Latin Americans should continue to live/ like dogs and cats for the sake of a few financiers who, by keeping the American public in ignorance of what is really going on there, are driving things to an extreme. /The end will be an incurable hatred, and perhaps the ruination of the two billion dollar trade between the United States and our twenty Latin American republics./

North and Latin America cannot afford to be enemies because we need one another and cannot get away from one another even if we try. We are like Siamese twins. They too have their petty quarrels every once in a while, but that is about all they can do. We must be friends. But the only way for us to become friends is to know each other. Real friendship and good fellowship between North and Latin America cannot come if certain financial interests continue to succeed in keeping the American people in ignorance about what they are *really* doing south of the Rio Grande and, particularly, in Nicaragua.

There is no doubt that the American intervention in Nicaragua is not, as some people believe, a local affair only, but one which involves the future of eighty millions of Latin Americans, with the forces of American imperialism arrayed on one side against the welfare of our twenty Latin-American republics on the other. Basing her views on the American Administrations since the days of the Panama scandal, Latin America has come to feel that it is hard to find in most United States governments anything but selfishness, imperialistic political aims and insane ambitions blended with possibly willful ignorance of facts. Out of this mistrust, engendered by the different United States Administrations, the Latin-American people cannot help looking with a lively admiration at Mexico because she has enacted and enforced laws to her liking, which are adapted to her necessities and conducive to her advancement. Mexico, who abolished slavery fifty years before the Civil War, whose religious legislation of 1859 was copied by France in 1905, and whose economic emancipation was embodied in her Constitution drawn up in 1917, has won, at once, the ardent loyalty of Latin America and the hatred of the financial imperialists. What tragedy can result from financial and political intrusion upon the rights of a fearless proud people is readily to be observed in the south. A sister republic, insignificant in size, weakened by four hundred years of fanaticism, and by exploitation and revolution, is in the ring to-day confronting the mightiest power on earth.

Mr. Albert H. Putney, during an address which

THE LOOTING OF NICARAGUA

he delivered before the People's Reconstruction League on December 11, 1926, said that the attitude taken by the United States toward the rival governments of Nicaragua is of an importance which can hardly be overestimated. He pointed out other matters of exceptional interest. Such as the importance which the State Department has, in the past, attached to American investments in Nicaragua; which is shown by the fact that between the years 1909-12 the United States took an active part in the deposition of four Presidents in Nicaragua before it succeeded in finding one who measured up to its requirements.

It is interesting to note that this president, who proved entirely satisfactory to both the State Department and the financiers in New York, was the same Diaz whom the department again recognized as the president of Nicaragua after his sudden election by a fake Congress to fill a vacancy which really did not exist. The present chapter of the relations of the United States with Nicaragua began in 1909 with the downfall of President José Santos Zelaya.

Santos Zelaya had committed the indiscretion of trying to cancel the concession of the La Luz and Los Angeles Mining Company, in which, according to the noted Venezuelan writer, Horacio Blanco Fombona, ex-Secretary-of-State, Philander Knox, was the principal stockholder, while a nephew of his was the manager of the Company in Bluefields and was, therefore, also the "boss" of Adolfo Diaz. At that time Diaz was acting as a minor clerk at a salary of twenty or twenty-five dollars a week in this concern. The revolution of General Estrada, with Emiliano Chamorro as Commander-in-Chief, broke out against Zelaya. Adolfo Diaz financed it immediately with six hundred thousand dollars cash, which he had apparently saved out of his twenty-five dollar a week salary! Shortly after the outbreak of this revolution, the United States broke off relations with Zelaya on December 1, 1909. This act on the part of the United States caused the resignation of Zelaya, who turned over the presidency to Dr. José Madriz. But Secretary Knox seems not to have been satisfied yet. Apparently at his instigation Zelaya was hounded. Porfirio Diaz, then President of Mexico, in a gesture much to his credit, gave shelter to President Zelaya on the Mexican cruiser *Zaragoza,* which took him to Mexico.

Dr. Madriz, the Vice-President, who was one of the most popular and respected men in the country, became president. He had been a member of the Central American Conference in Washington in 1907 and had served as a Judge of the Court of Justice of Central America. When he assumed the presidency the revolution was about to collapse. The forces of Estrada were quickly driven back to Bluefields, where they were on the verge of capture when the United States Government declared the neutrality of Bluefields, denounced the Nicaraguan blockade of that port as illegal, and ordered the American warships to convoy merchant-ships through the blockade. Assisted in this way by the United States, the revolutionary forces of Estrada were able to withdraw their army from Bluefields; and, with the additions to their forces which resulted from the prestige of American support, Emiliano Chamorro, on August 19, 1910, was able to inflict a decisive defeat on President Madriz, who resigned on the following day. The United States Government then instructed its Minister to Panama to proceed to Nicaragua; and, on October

U. S. Chargé d'Affaires, Mr. Dennis (left), Adolfo Diaz (center) and Emiliano Chamorro (right) at Managua, Nicaragua.

Nicaraguan Constitutionalist mountain artillery.

27th, on board an American warship, an agreement was reached between the American Minister and the five Conservative leaders, Estrada, Diaz, Mena and the two Chamorros. This agreement included provision for the recognition, by the United States, of the new government and the acceptance by Nicaragua of an American loan on terms very advantageous to the lenders; and also a provision that the president and vice-president at the next election should be chosen from among the five Conservative leaders!

In January, Estrada was recognized by the United States, and negotiations for the loan were at once begun. As soon, however, as the proposed terms of the loan became known, such general indignation broke out in Nicaragua, even among several Conservative leaders, as to endanger the continued existence of the Estrada government. The newly appointed American Minister in Managua, Northcott, on March 9th, cabled Secretary Knox that it seemed impossible to secure the ratification of the proposed loan by the Assembly. Mr. Northcott also informed Secretary of State Knox, "The natural sentiment of an overwhelming majority of Nicaragua is antagonistic to the United States; and, even with some members of Estrada's cabinet, I find a decided suspicion, if not distrust, of our motives." On March 27th, he supplemented this by writing that "President Estrada is being sustained solely by the moral effect of our support, and the belief that he would unquestionably have that support in case of trouble."

These reports from the American Minister at this time, a man who was, of course, entirely in sympathy with the policy of the United States Government, would seem clearly to prove that the Liberals were in an overwhelming majority in Nicaragua. Additional evidence may be found in a statement in a letter written by the Hon. Elihu Root, at that time in the United States Senate, to the effect that three-fourths of the inhabitants of Nicaragua belonged to the Liberal party. The letter, addressed by Senator Root to Senator Fuller, on January 5, 1915, reads as follows: "Reviewing the report of the Commander of our forces in Nicaragua, I find the following: 'The present government of Nicaragua is not in power by the will of the people; the elections were in their greater part fraudulent,' and in a former report he says that the Liberal party, that is, the opposition party, 'constitutes three-fourths of the inhabitants of the country.' From this report and others, which have accidentally reached my hands, I have come to the conclusion that the present government, with which we are negotiating this treaty, is in power because of the presence of the United States troops in Nicaragua."

A few months after Estrada had been elected president, he dismissed one of the members of his cabinet, an act in accordance with the laws of Nicaragua. The American Minister in Managua objected to it. Estrada energetically protested against the United States Minister's interference in affairs which concerned only the Executive and on May 5th, he turned over the presidency to Adolfo Diaz.

When on March 9th, Minister Northcott cabled Secretary Knox that it seemed impossible to secure the ratification of the proposed loan by th National Assembly, Mr. Knox disregarded that statement and cabled in reply that steps must be taken at once for the promulgation of a decree authorizing the loan and for the establishment of a Claims Commission to pass upon American claims against Nicaragua. Two of the three members of this commission were to be citizens of the United States! Such a procedure is almost without precedent! In the case of a commission to pass upon the claims of one country against another, it is the established custom for one commissioner to be appointed from among the citizens of each country, and the third commissioner to be the citizen of a neutral country. The Mixed Claims Commission was proclaimed by the President on February 27th and ratified by part of the Assembly on May 17th. By this time the opposition to the American program in Nicaragua had become almost universal.

As soon as Diaz became president, he negotiated the sale of the Nicaraguan Canal Zone to the United States Government for three million dollars. He only received part of the money, however. He could not draw the balance without special consent from the United States Government. The treaty regarding the canal bears the name of the Chamorro-Bryan Treaty, because Emiliano Chamorro was at that time Nicaraguan Minister to the United States.

Blanco Fombona, who, by the way, is a political writer of no small importance, claims that the treaty not only endangered the independence of Nicaragua, but also deprived Costa Rica, El Salvador and Honduras of certain water-rights which these three republics owned in the San Juan River and Fonseca Bay. He also states his belief that the United States and Adolfo Diaz were deliberately and cynically trying to cheat those three republics.

In order to have the Nicaraguan Congress approve the Chamorro-Bryan Treaty, Adolfo Diaz had it read in English to a crowd of Senators and Congressmen whom he had picked out previously and purposely because they did not understand a word of

English! Despite this linguistic precaution, American marines were stationed around the Congress building in order to prevent "outsiders" from entering before the treaty had been properly accepted. Simultaneously with the Chamorro-Bryan Treaty the Diaz-Chamorro clique submitted to the American Government an amendment similar to the Platt Amendment in Cuba, which happily the United States refused to consider.

According to the Cana-Jerez Treaty between the two republics, neither Nicaragua nor Costa Rica can dispose of her rights to the navigable waters of the San Juan River without *mutual agreement!* Diaz did not consult Costa Rica before he sold to the United States Nicaragua's rights to this waterway. By doing so he handed the American Government a goldbrick; and another one when he sold them the right to establish a naval base in Fonseca Bay without previously consulting Honduras and El Salvador as, by treaty, he was honorably obliged to do. Diaz also fooled the American Government when he sold them a lease of ninety-nine years on the Big and Small Maiz Islands for "coaling station purposes," because the ownership of these two islands is still in dispute, Colombia claiming them. These facts go to show that the Chamorro-Bryan Treaty is absolutely worthless. It could not stand the test of any honorable court of arbitration! If the United States was not fooled, then her State Department planned to trample underfoot the rights, not of Nicaragua alone, but of all Central America.

In the meantime heavy clouds were gathering in the political sky of Nicaragua. The situation from the viewpoint of the American Government did not seem to improve under the Diaz administration. On

May 25, 1911, the American Minister notified Washington: "Rumors have been current that the liberals are organizing a concerted uprising all over the country with the declared object of defeating the loan. It is difficult to estimate how serious a measure this might be if well organized and led, as the liberals are in such a majority over the conservatives. I therefore hasten to repeat my suggestion as to the advisability of stationing permanently, at least until the loan has been brought through, a war vessel in Corinto."

Mr. Knox replied to this information from the American Minister by instructing him that Diaz should not be permitted to resign, that he should receive renewed assurances of the support of the United States, and that a United States warship had been ordered to Nicaragua. On June 5th, the Minister sent another report to the effect that President Diaz had no personal following and that his only support arose from the friendship of General Mena. On June 6th, Mr. Knox signed the Knox-Castrillo Treaty which, to the everlasting credit of the United States Senate, it must be said, that body refused to ratify.

The main object of the Knox-Castrillo Treaty had been to lay the foundation of a loan to Nicaragua by American financiers. The failure of the Senate to ratify the treaty did not prevent the making of the loan.

On September 1, 1911, a contract was entered into between the government of Nicaragua, the *United States Mortgage and Trust Company,* as *Trustees,* and *Brown Bros. Company and J. W. Seligman & Co.,* as *Fiscal Agents.* It should be mentioned in this connection that all through the period of American financial intervention in Nicaragua an effort has always been made to have an American company act as an intermediary between Nicaragua and the American company which makes the contract, for the purpose doubtless of creating an excuse for paying an extra commission. Here the main use of the *Trustees* was the chance thus afforded for paying them a commission on the bonds to be sold by the Government of Nicaragua to the *Fiscal Agents*.

At the time of the date of this contract (Sept. 1, 1911) the total debt of Nicaragua, both domestic and foreign, was only about seven and a quarter million gold dollars, and from that sum should really be deducted nearly two million gold dollars representing the portion of a loan to Nicaragua by English bankers, which these bankers still kept in their possession. To refund this debt, and to pay the claims against the Nicaraguan Government which were to be fixed by the Claims Commission—on which the United States was to have two of three members—the total of these claims being estimated in advance as likely to amount to between three and three and a half million dollars—it was proposed to issue bonds to the amount of fifteen million dollars to be secured on the customs of Nicaragua. The Fiscal Agents were to have the right to present a list of names to the Nicaraguan Government, from which the Collector General of Customs should be appointed.

With this security the bonds should be of the gilt-edged order, but the Fiscal Agents were given the option (on their side they promised nothing!) of taking twelve million dollars' worth of the bonds at ninety and one-half per cent. Furthermore the bonds were to be redeemed at a premium of two and one-half per cent. The Trustees were to be paid three per cent commission on all the bonds sold, including those which the Fiscal Agents chose to take under their option. The Trustees were to receive all the proceeds of the bonds, as well as certain existing assets of the Nicaraguan Government, and were to pay off the debts of the government and the awards of the Claims Commission.

The agreement on September 1, 1911, contained a clause embodying a somewhat startling method of determining the credits and liabilities of the Trustees. The largest claim against the Nicaraguan Government was based upon the bonds of the *Ethelburga Loan*. The total amount of these bonds was one million two hundred and fifty thousand pounds; but the English bankers, who had made the loan, had retained possession of three hundred and eighty-nine thousand, three hundred and seventy-five pounds. It was now agreed that this sum should be turned over to the Trustees. In determining the amount of assets which should be given by Nicaragua to the Trustees to enable them to pay the loan, the English pound was reckoned on the basis of four dollars and eighty-eight cents. But in determining the charge to be made *against* the Trustees for the three hundred and eighty-nine thousand, three hundred and seventy-five pounds, turned over to them, the English pound was reckoned at three dollars and eighty-eight cents! The Trustee thus made instantly a profit of one dollar to the pound on this sum of three hundred and eighty-nine thousand, three hundred and seventy-five pounds. Altogether the various costs of the proposed methods of refunding would amount to considerably over forty per cent of the existing foreign debt of Nicaragua.

For some reason, however, the European creditors of Nicaragua, on this occasion, did not take kindly to the efforts made by the United States, avowedly on their behalf. The Ministers to Nicaragua from Great Britain, France and Germany protested against submitting the claims of the citizens of these countries to a commission composed of two citizens of the United States and one Nicaraguan! The Government of Nicaragua then appealed to the United States for aid and counsel. On November 10, 1911, Mr. Knox wrote to the American Chargé in Managua: "The Department is not disposed to counsel the Nicaraguan Government to resist the demands of European countries through diplomatic channels for the direct settlement of its claims; but if the Nicaraguan Government, of its own initiative, should decide that European claimants must first exhaust the remedies afforded by the Nicaraguan Courts or other local tribunals, including the Claims Commission, the Department believes that international law and practice afford ample precedents therefor."

Chapter II

The New Nicaraguan Constitution — General Luis Mena Opposes American Interference and Fights Diaz — Election Frauds in 1912 — Nicaraguan Government a Family Affair — The National Bank and Nicaraguan R.R. Scandal — Americans Control Coffee Market — The New Currency System and Its Drawbacks — Economic Loss Through American Financial Intervention — Misery and Emigration — Vice-President Martinez — Repurchasing of Controlling Stock in Bank and R.R. — Election of 1924 — Extension of Contract — Chamorro Rebellion.

IN the meantime the Constituent Assembly of Nicaragua was considering the Nicaraguan Constitution which was adopted shortly afterward. The United States State Department at once objected to Articles 2 and 55 of the Constitution, which read as follows:

"Article 2—The sovereignty is one, inalienable and imprescriptible, and resides essentially in the people from whom the officials, provided for by the Constitution and laws, derive their powers. Consequently, no compacts or treaties shall be concluded which are contrary to the independence and the integrity of the nation, or which in any way affect its sovereignty, except such as may look toward *union with one or more republics of Central America.*"

"Article 55—Congress alone may authorize loans and levy direct or indirect taxes; any authorities are prohibited from negotiating the former or levying the latter without its permission, save the exceptions provided for in the Constitution."

Vigorously and repeatedly attempts were made by the American State Department to prevent the promulgation of the Constitution without the changes demanded in the name of the American investors. The Assembly, however, (January 12, 1912) promulgated the Constitution and attacked American interference in the following decree: "The Constitutional Assembly, considering that the Chargé d'Affaires of the United States has given evidence of exceptional interest, as was manifested by Dr. Suarez, the President of the Assembly, in delaying the promulgation of the Constitution until the arrival of Mr. Weitzel, the new Minister who in all probabilities bears instructions from his government to make the amendments thereto:

"Considering that this interposition of the Chargé d'Affaires of the United States carries with it, in effect, an insult to the National autonomy and the honor of the Assembly:

"Considering that, above all, it is the duty of the Assembly to preserve the dignity and decorum of the nation and the good name of this august body; . . . Decrees:

"Article 1—That the Constitution elaborated by the present National Constituent Assembly be published by proclamation or in the *Official Gazette,* or in any newspaper of the republic.

"Article 2—That the Junta Directiva of the Assembly be commissioned to take the necessary steps to cause this decree to have effect from date, by publishing said Constitution in this city. Given, etc."

Because of this action, the Assembly was at once declared to be dissolved by President Diaz! The Assembly had previously elected General Luis Mena for the office of president during the following term.

THE LOOTING OF NICARAGUA 19

Mena had been one of the original leaders of the revolution but, when the test came, he was found to be too good a patriot to become a party to the exploitation of Nicaragua. Diaz ordered the arrest of General Mena, who escaped to Masaya, convened the Assembly and organized a government. Public opinion in Nicaragua was so overwhelmingly in favor of Mena and the Assembly that the conservatives were soon driven back into Managua. The rule of Diaz would soon have been over had it not been for the very active interference of the United States.

In the report of the United States Secretary of the Navy for 1913 the story of American intervention is told in great detail and with much pride. Eight war vessels, one hundred and twenty-five officers and two thousand six hundred enlisted men took part in the campaign "and participated in the bombardment of Managua, a night ambuscade in Masaya, the surrender of General Mena and his rebel army at Granada, the surrender of the rebel gunboats *Victoria* and *Ninety-Three*, the assault and capture of Coyotepe, the defense of Paso Cabillos bridge, including garrison and other duty at Corinto, Chinandega and elsewhere."

Particular attention was given to the fact that "the most notable event during this campaign was the assault and capture of Coyotepe, resulting in entirely crushing the revolution and restoring peace in Nicaragua; this assault, lasting fifty-seven minutes, under heavy fire from the rebel forces, before the position, which was considered impregnable by the federal forces, could be taken."

The military intervention by the United States resulted in turning the control of Nicaragua completely over to the Conservatives. Diaz issued a proclamation disfranchising all those citizens of Nicaragua who had supported the Assembly, leaving only a comparative handful of voters in the country. In Leon, one of the two largest cities of Nicaragua, only eighty out of its fifty thousand inhabitants were allowed to vote during the election of 1912! American marines were also kept in the country and, during the next three presidential elections, they took an active part, not only being stationed at the polls, but also doing electioneering for the candidates favored by the New York investors! The natural result was the easy election of the Conservative candidates—Adolfo Diaz in 1912, Emiliano Chamorro in 1916, and Diego Chamorro in 1920.

How completely the Government of Nicaragua had become a family affair in 1921 is shown by the following list (prepared by the Pan-American Federation of Labor) of office-holders at that time:

President of Nicaragua, Diego Manuel Chamorro
Minister of the Interior, Rosendo Chamorro
Minister at Washington, Emiliano Chamorro
President of the Congress, Salvador Chamorro
Counselor of the Treasury Department, Agustin Chamorro
Chief of Police in Managua, Filadelfo Chamorro
Chief of the Military Fortress of Managua, F. Bolanos Chamorro
Director of Internal Revenue, Dionisio Chamorro
Chief of Police in Corinto, Leandro Chamorro
Chief of the Army for the North Zone, Carlos Chamorro
Consul in San Francisco, Cal., Fernando Chamorro
Consul in New Orleans, La., Agustin Bolanos Chamorro
Consul in London, Pedro C. Chamorro

THE LOOTING OF NICARAGUA

The reader will note that there are just thirteen in the list. Thirteen seems to have been the lucky number of the Chamorro family, but it was a very unlucky number for Nicaragua.

During all this period the financial control of Nicaragua remained in the hands of a small group of New York capitalists. While the American firms mentioned in the contract of September 1, 1911, only loaned six million dollars to the Nicaraguan Government, instead of the twelve millions contemplated by the contract, and although the Knox-Castrillo Treaty was never ratified, the American investors were given all the advantages and concessions proposed by the treaty and contract. In particular they were given fifty-one per cent of the stock of the National Bank of Nicaragua and fifty-one per cent of the stock of the railroad, together with complete control of the Board of Directors, and the right to name all the important officials. The number and salaries of such officials were very largely increased. All of the government funds were deposited in the Bank of Nicaragua, and the bank, instead of paying any interest to the government on such deposits, actually received a payment of one per cent of the deposits for taking care of them, and a further one-half per cent for all money paid out by the bank on behalf of the government.

The salaries of government officials were paid by the bank. What this amounted to was that the bank, which was completely controlled and mainly owned by Americans, received one and one-half per cent on practically all the revenues of Nicaragua, besides the free use of the government money deposited with it.

The New York banking concerns, in control of the Bank of Nicaragua, controlled also the coffee market by means of an institution which they owned and which was called the Compania Mercantil de Ultramar. Their system was very simple. The bank would advance money to the coffee growers at the rate of ten to eighteen per cent a year, with the understanding that their crops would have to be sold to the Compania Mercantil de Ultramar for a price lower than the market quotations.

During the period when these same interests controlled the railroad not a mile of new track was built, although the extension of the railroad had been one of the main reasons stated for the creation of the fiscal agency. Not a single new engine was bought and few, if any, new cars. On the contrary, when the railroad was returned to the Nicaraguan Government during the administration of President Martinez, the Chinandega-El-Viejo branch—which had been turned over to the Management Corporation of Baltimore in good order—was absolutely useless, almost non-existent. So was the Monkey Point branch on the Atlantic coast. Of several steamers belonging to the Railroad Company, only one was left.

It should not be forgotten that the Management Corporation was getting fifteen thousand dollars a year for managing said railroad. They also had the right, according to report, to buy for, and sell to, the railroad company rolling material and other equipment at a price stipulated by themselves. Almost one-half of the gross receipts of the railroad were paid out in dividends, and the operating expenses of the road were increased from the equivalent of about thirty thousand dollars gold a year to about three hundred and fifty thousand dollars gold! No wonder the bankers were so anxious to retain control of the railroad!

THE LOOTING OF NICARAGUA

A change in the currency system was effected in such a way as to permit large commissions and other profits to American investors, and it resulted in almost completely ruining the business of the country. In 1912 the currency of Nicaragua had amounted to sixty-seven million pesos in paper currency. This was superseded by an issue of about three and one-half million gold cordovas (a cordova being the equivalent of an American dollar), the ratio between the cordova being fixed at twelve and one-half to one. This had the effect of reducing the total currency by about one-third. The normal result of the reduction of the total amount of currency in the country is to reduce prices, but the reduction in prices was far less in this case than the increased value of the money. It is also worthy of note that this reduced the currency to about three or four cordovas per capita, an exceedingly stringent economical condition.

After the change in currency the lowest coin in existence was worth twelve and one-half centavos of the old currency. As a great many articles used by the poorer people had previously sold for less than twelve and one-half centavos there was at once a very serious increase in the cost of living to the poorer classes.

Again, prior to the change of currency, the custom duties had been fixed on a gold basis, the law provided that paper money might be received in payment at the ratio of five to one. The establishment of the gold standard at the rate of twelve to one ratio had therefore the manifest effect of immediately increasing all customs duties one hundred and fifty per cent with an accompanying increased cost of all imported commodities.

The general effect of the change of currency was

24 THE LOOTING OF NICARAGUA

to bring about a very great increase not only in the cost of living, but in rates of interest (twenty-four per cent and even thirty per cent), and a great increase in the high salaries, particularly those received by Americans, and a small increase in wages. So bad did the condition of the people become, that, for perhaps the first time in the history of Central America, there was a large emigration from Nicaragua.

When in 1923 the new president, Martinez, called upon the leading citizens of Nicaragua for their opinions as to the results of American financial rule in Nicaragua, the following detailed statement as to the losses occasioned by such rule was sent in reply by Señor José Castellon, a financial expert and economist of Nicaragua:

Loss in the sale and the repurchase of the railroad (the fifty-one per cent interest in the railroad was sold to the bankers in 1912, and after ten years repurchased for double the original price. No improvements or extensions having been made during this time) .... $	2,485,182.16
For increase in railroad passenger and freight rates over the old ones	3,286,419.75
For increase in government fixed expenses	11,156,016.23
Civil wars and exactions (most of these should properly be classed as payments of alleged losses to favorite partisans)	8,836,723.31
Moral sufferings (alleged losses to favorite partisans)	5,000,000.00

THE LOOTING OF NICARAGUA

Expenses in collection of customs over old rate	$596,502.77
Salaries, Mixed Commissions, High Commissions and Credit Commissions	206,237.06
Commissions to bankers	852,262.22
Undue interest to bankers	437,039.39
Profit to bankers from Emery Claim	443,461.85
	$33,309,842.72

The same gentleman also prepared the following table showing a portion of American gains from such control:

Net profits on purchase and sale of railroad stocks	$2,485,182.16
For commissions from government	852,262.22
Undue interest	437,039.39
From Emery Claim, net profits	443,461.85
	$4,217,945.62

Plus

Increased railroad rates	$3,286,419.75
Increased cost of customs collections	596,502.77
Salaries, Mixed and High Commissions	206,237.06
	$8,307,105.18

The tide of fortune had at last turned in favor of Nicaragua, with the elevation of Vice-President Bartolome Martinez to the presidency in 1923, upon the death of President Diego Chamorro.

While Martinez had been elected as a conservative, he belonged to what might be called the left wing of that party; and he was a good enough patriot to feel alarmed and indignant at the condition into which Nicaragua had fallen. He wisely concluded that the chief cause of the misery of Nicaragua was the control of the railroad and bank by New York financiers; and he succeeded in negotiating and consummating the repurchase of these properties.

The presidential election of 1924, the fairest which has taken place in Nicaragua for a generation, was won by a combination of Liberals and anti-Chamorro Conservatives: Carlos Solorzano being elected president, and Dr. Juan Bautista Sacasa, vice-president.

Although the American investors had completely sold out their interests in the bank and railroad, and had been paid in cash and had realized a large profit on their investments, they were very loath to give up the control of these properties with the accompanying salaries and commissions.

The American officials of the companies attempted to persuade the people that the companies would collapse without American supervision. It is reported that the American President of the Bank of Nicaragua made the statement, at the annual meeting of the corporation, that he had been requested by President Martinez of Nicaragua, through the Nicaraguan Consul in New York, to remain in office at a salary of five hundred dollars a month. The consul denied having made any such request.

During the control of the bank by the New York interests, a permanent fund of two million dollars and, in addition, a fluctuating balance, had been kept by the National Bank of Nicaragua in the Bank of Central and South America, in New York. The Bank of Central and South America was largely owned and controlled by the same New York interests who owned

THE LOOTING OF NICARAGUA

the stock in the Nicaraguan companies. No interest had been paid on these accounts.

In 1925 the Bank of Central and South America was sold to the Royal Bank of Canada. After the repurchase of the outstanding stock of the bank and railroad by the Government of Nicaragua, President Martinez had their boards of directors changed, both, however, remaining American corporations. Among the Nicaraguans who had been added to the new board of directors were Dr. Timoteo Seydel Vaca and Mr. Torribio Tijerino, who demanded that interest be paid on the balances in New York. After a careful investigation it was found that the Royal Bank of Canada offered a higher rate of interest than any other bank in New York. Accordingly the funds of the National Bank of Nicaragua were left there, and began to draw interest. Thereupon, the charge was made and circulated, by those opposed to the control by Nicaragua of her own property, that leaving this balance in a British bank was a sign of hostility toward the United States.

In September the board of directors of the Nicaraguan railroad voted to cancel the contract with the Management Corporation by which said corporation acted as agent for the railroad at a salary, as I said before, of fifteen thousand dollars a year and two per cent commissions on all purchases. This cancellation was to take effect in October. Thereupon, it is charged, an agent of this company went to the State Department and received permission to send a cablegram to the United States Minister in Nicaragua in the private code of the State Department. (This statement has been corroborated by officials of the State Department upon inquiry by the Nicaraguan Minister.) It is further charged that this message was transmitted by the United States Minister to the President of Nicaragua with the statement that it came in the secret code of the State Department; from which statement the natural inference would be that the American State Department had a special interest in the matter. The President of Nicaragua, Carlos Solorzano, therefore, cabled to the directors in New York to extend the contract for one month. Upon the receipt of this cablegram one of the Nicaraguan directors asked one of the American directors why an extension for one month was so important. The reply was that much could happen in a month.

Within a week came the Chamorro rebellion!

Under these circumstances the Nicaraguan liberals claim that this rebellion was instigated in New York for the purpose of keeping the control of the bank and the railroad (although all the stock in these companies had already been bought and paid for by Nicaragua) in American hands; and to prevent an audit of the account between the bank and the Government of Nicaragua.

No sane person who knows the facts of the case, can doubt that Chamorro and Diaz are the real rebels in Nicaragua!

The *Nation* may not be altogether wrong when it says in an editorial of July 27, 1927: "Murder is the fit word to describe the action of the United States in Nicaragua. The United States created the anarchy which she is now trying to suppress. When the Constitutionalist forces had substantially reconquered the country, American marines retook it for the Conservatives, and to-day they are doing police work for a government which would collapse in sixty seconds if the American forces retired. When President Coolidge's personal envoy, Henry L. Stimson, threatened

THE LOOTING OF NICARAGUA

forcibly to disarm the Constitutionalist forces in May, one Nicaraguan General, Sandino, retired to the hills and kept up the fight. Undoubtedly he has the sympathy of the vast majority of his countrymen. A general, who at the head of five thousand barefooted Nicaraguans defies the United States, commands our respect. When William Green, President of the American Federation of Labor, protested to Secretary Kellogg, that official replied that Sandino's men were 'outlaws.' What law excuses the use of American marines on Nicaraguan battlefields or of American bombing planes for mass Murder?"

Chapter III

Description of Nicaragua and Its People — Its Geography and History — William Walker, the Buccaneer and First Tool of Dollar Diplomacy in Nicaragua — The American Armed Interventions of 1912 and 1927, and Some of Their Disastrous Results.

THE ignorance which prevails in the United States in regard to Nicaragua is astonishing when we consider that Nicaragua has been so prominently in the public eye of the world during the last two years: and that she must, perforce, become of greater international importance because she owns the water rights of the future canal, which will so greatly benefit, not only herself and the United States, but all Latin America and, in some degree, the rest of the commercial world also.

Where is Nicaragua? What is its geographical significance? What is its political history? What does it produce? And what are the commercial potentialities of this little country which has been well called the "treasure box" of Central America? Who are its people?

Nicaragua lies, east and west, between the Caribbean Sea and the Pacific Ocean; it is bounded on the north by Honduras, and, on the south, by Costa Rica. Its territory comprises about fifty thousand square miles; and its climate is tropical, being pleasant and healthful on the higher lands, and hot in the lowlands. Of the seven or eight hundred thousand inhabitants, the majority are criollos, that is of mixed Spanish and Indian blood. Among the aristocratic and cultured

THE LOOTING OF NICARAGUA 31

classes, sometimes the blue blood of the first Castilian and Galician *Conquistadores* is mingled with the blood of the proud Indian races of the past; those Aztec and Mayan peoples whose ancient inscriptions and pictures, chiseled on huge blocks of basalt along the banks of the upper Rio Grande and its tributaries, still testify of old faiths and past glories. The foreign population, chiefly of the commercial classes, is largely German, English and American. The only remaining Indians who date back to the conquest are the Sumas, or Caribs, and the Mosquitos, natives of the Mosquito Coast. They have a strong negroid strain due to intermarriage with runaway slaves from Jamaica and elsewhere who found a sure refuge in Nicaragua. With the exception of the latter tribes, who have been partly christianized by the Moravians of Bluefields, and the foreigners of Protestant faith, the Nicaraguans profess the Roman Catholic religion. The influence of the Catholic faith, combined with the economic fact that the agricultural areas are very equitably distributed among the people, are powerful arguments against the wild claims of the American yellow press to the effect that Nicaragua is a hot-bed of radicalism or "bolshevism," even if bolshevism were not utterly at variance with the Latin temperament. The Mosquitos and Sumas still roam the jungles, as their ancestors did, living on the abundant natural supply of fish and game.

Nicaragua forms an irregular equilateral triangle. Its base on the Atlantic coast extends about three hundred miles from Cape Gracias a Dios to Grey Town, or San Juan del Norte as it is now generally called. The apex of the triangle is the Coseguina volcano overlooking Fonseca Bay on the Pacific side. The Mosquito Coast—that is, the north and central sections of the Atlantic littoral—is a low, swampy, monotonous shore with lagoons, estuaries and fringes of reefs and islets, cut by the Segovia, Grande or Atlamara, and Escondido rivers. The principal towns and harbors on the Atlantic are Bluefields at the mouth of the Escondido, La Barra at the mouth of the Grande, Gracias a Dios, Puerta Cabezas, and Prinzapolca. On this coast, and inland, sending their exports by way of these harbor towns to the world outside, are the plantations of the Coyumel Banana Company, the timber tracts of pine, mahogany and cedar belonging to the Bragman's Bluff Lumber Company and other timber companies and the famous Pis-Pis mining district in which is the La Luz and Los Angeles mine. Grey Town at the mouth of the San Juan, south of the Mosquito Coast, was a prosperous center in the days of President Zelaya. To-day it is in ruins. Its condition is but one evidence of the disaster wrought in Nicaragua by the sordid political régimes of those pseudo-presidents who have been jockeyed into power by the unscrupulous agents of Dollar Diplomacy, backed up by United States marines. Look at Grey Town and see there Nicaragua in miniature! The ruin is symbolic of the whole country: a country once prosperous and progressive and independent of all external control, but now retrogressive and miserable as the result of seventeen years of "intervention," and the political machinations and wholesale plundering under Dollar Diplomacy's dummies, Estrada, the two Chamorros and, now, Adolfo Diaz. Puerta Cabezas, the headquarters of the Bragman's Bluff Company, came into the news prominently this past year as the capital of Dr. Juan Sacasa's government.

Along the two-hundred-mile stretch of bold rocky

Breastworks constructed with mahogany logs, Puerto Cabezas, Nicaragua.

Rear Admiral Latimer, U. S. N.

THE LOOTING OF NICARAGUA

Pacific coast, Nicaragua has only three real harbors, Corinto, Brito and San Juan del Sur. The country here is a series of isolated igneous peaks connected by low ridges. Between Coseguina, two thousand eight hundred and thirty-one feet high, in the extreme north west, the chain runs to the foot-hills about the headwaters of San Juan river in the southeast, thrusting skyward here and there the cones of El Viejo (five thousand eight hundred and forty feet), Momotombo (four thousand one hundred and twenty-seven feet) and Masaya, which has had frequent eruptions, and the two island mountains of Ometepe and Madera in Lake Nicaragua. In 1835 Coseguina flamed with such tremendous fury for four days and nights that volcanic dust and ashes fell in a vast circle, as far north as southern Mexico, as far east as Jamaica, as far south as Bogotá. Ometepe disgorged molten lava for a week in 1883. There are low peaks in this range which still emit sulphurous smoke and vapors and, at night, burn a lamp of bluish flame to light the fierce four-footed travelers of the countryside.

The accumulated flow of this great watershed pours into Lake Managua and Lake Nicaragua which are connected by the Penaloya channel. Lake Managua is thirty miles long and from eight to sixteen miles in breadth. Lake Nicaragua, one hundred miles long and forty-five miles wide at its widest point, is the largest body of fresh water between Lake Michigan and Lake Titicaca on the Peruvian border. Steamers ply on both lakes, but the channel is not navigable because of the Tipitapa falls some fifteen feet high. Because of these falls, the future canal will not pass through Managua but will empty into the Pacific at Brito twenty miles west of the old town of Granada.

The San Juan river, which drains Lake Nicaragua, is only ninety-six miles long; the principal mouth of its wide delta is called the Colorado entrance. In old chronicles we read that several deep water craft, coming from Spain at the time of the Conquest, sailed up the San Juan river and Lake Nicaragua as far as Granada. I am afraid those old chroniclers must have been misinformed for they do not mention the five rapids of the San Juan river, insurmountable except by shallow-draft river boats, and seeming to represent the last remnants of the connecting range, or ridge, which, millions of years ago, was leveled by the erosive action of the waters of San Juan, thus causing the severance of the main Cordillera and the Cordillera de los Andes in Panama. The uniform tableland, which slopes away by degrees from the main Cordillera toward the Mosquito Coast, has been changed by fluvial action into the many plateaus, ridges and isolated hills characteristic of the jungle section of Central Nicaragua. The easternmost of these lone ridges, or extinct volcanoes, is Mount Musun, which stands out solitary at the headwaters of the Williki river, surrounded by an ocean of deep green virgin forests; and, in fancy, embellished by the legends of past civilizations.

Coffee, bananas, rubber, mahogany, cedar, pine, and many other products of her seemingly inexhaustible forests, as well as cattle, and gold and other precious metal of her mineral belts, have earned for Nicaragua her luring reputation of being the treasure box of Central America. She is part of the bright golden wedge between two Americas.

Nicaragua was discovered and fully explored between the years of 1502 and 1522 by the Conquistadores who were mainly attracted by her enormous mineral wealth. Not satisfied with the rich crop of gold dust and nuggets which her rivers used to yield in those days, they drove tunnels and sank shafts into the outcroppings of the Segovia and Pis-Pis mineral belts, thus opening up mines by the score, by means of the "enforced labor system" which they had imposed upon the Indians. They went even so far as to look for precious metals in the depths of the Masaya crater, whose molten lava they had mistaken for gold!

Attracted by her wealth, buccaneers and pirates of all nationalities soon commenced harassing the Spanish settlers along the Atlantic coast of Nicaragua. Drake is supposed to have paddled up part of the Segovia river, sacking and burning the numerous mining camps along its lower course; while others even managed to go clear across, to the Pacific Coast, on their plundering expeditions.

The Indians along the Atlantic littoral, who had been vainly trying to shake off the Spanish yoke, joined hands with the English buccaneers. The buccaneers furnished them with arms and ammunition in order to keep them in rebellion. Allowing for their less sophisticated era, their methods did not differ much from the methods of the present day Dollar Diplomacy in Central America, and especially in Nicaragua.

With the help of hundreds of runaway slaves, proceeding from the Antilles, and the protection of the English buccaneers, who were using them with a view to driving a wedge across the Spanish Main and separating Central from South America, the Indians kept up a guerrilla fight for years among the thick forests of the marshy lowlands; until the Spaniards, tired at last of trying to hunt them down in those inaccessible jungles, abandoned the Atlantic coast to its fate and concentrated their energies on the development of the western settlements, situated around the lakes and along the Pacific Coast, from Corinto down to San Juan del Sur.

Thus started the British protectorate of "Mosquitia" or the Mosquito Coast, which lasted about two hundred years (1655-1850).

The first step taken by the English government in order to exercise control over Mosquitia was the founding of a Chartered Company (1630), whose mission it was to settle that narrow strip of territory fronting the Caribbean Sea and stretching inland for about forty miles. The seizure of Grey Town by the Mosquito Indians (with English support) in 1848, came near to causing a war between England and the United States; for the possession of Grey Town and the mouth of the river San Juan would have put the English government practically in control of the water-rights of the future interoceanic canal.

The result of this clever move on the part of England was the Clayton-Bulwer Treaty, by which both Great Britain and the United States bound themselves *not to colonize, fortify nor exercise dominion over any part of Central America.* This agreement was later superseded by the Hay-Pauncefote Treaty. In 1859 Great Britain delegated the protectorate of the Mosquito Coast to the republic of Honduras. This step caused great dissatisfaction among the Indians, who revolted, with the result that on January 28, 1860, the suzerainty over the entire Caribbean Coast was transferred, by the Treaty of Managua, to Nicaragua, with the understanding that the Indians should be granted autonomy in the Mosquito reservation and that they should be ruled by a native Chief. When the first Indian *cacique* died in 1864, the Nicaraguan government refused to recognize his successor. After much parleying it was finally agreed that the reservation should be governed by an elected chief, aided by an administrative council at Bluefields. But after fourteen years of almost complete autonomy the Indians voluntarily surrendered their privileged position; and, on November 20, 1894, the Mosquito Coast was formally incorporated in Nicaragua.

During the three hundred years of Spanish colonial rule in Nicaragua, her peace was hardly ever disturbed, except by the inroads of marauding bands of buccaneers. In 1821 she obtained her independence; and in 1823 she joined the Union of Central American States and remained a part of it until 1839, when the Union was dissolved.

During these first eighteen years of her independent life there were armed conflicts between the Liberals, who had their headquarters in Leon and who stood for religious liberty and the rights of man, and the Conservatives, who made their headquarters in Granada and insisted on keeping up the old Spanish colonial rule with its accompaniments of religious intolerance and plutocratic nepotism. The antagonism between these two principles is the real reason of the many revolutions which have taken place, during the last century, not only in Nicaragua but practically all over Latin America. Most of our republics have finally succeeded in shaking off the shackles of fanaticism and have gradually fallen in line with the rest of the constitutionally organized commonwealths of western civilization. If Dollar Diplomacy had tried to force itself upon those republics with the aid of the United States Government's armed interventions, as in Nicaragua, the republics would never have been able to achieve their aim, but on the contrary, they would surely have perished in the swamp of graft and political corruption in which all those nations which follow the principles of Dollar Diplomacy are bound to be sucked down sooner or later.

Only three years after her separation from the Union of Central American States, Nicaragua was once more plunged into fratricidal war by the presence of an ambitious Jack of all trades, a low grade foreign adventurer named William Walker. After trying his luck unsuccessfully as a shyster-lawyer, medicine doctor and newspaperman in California, Walker finally made up his mind to make some quick money in Latin America, even at the expense of his religion and his nationality. In his mad endeavor to seize political power in Nicaragua, he did not hesitate for a moment in shedding, like a soiled shirt, his American citizenship, nor in becoming a Roman Catholic. He realized that it paid better to be a Catholic than a Presbyterian in Central America. No wonder that he wound up by being known all the way from Mexico down to Panama as "the king of tropical tramps"—a phrase which, on our lips, is not one of romance but of obloquy and contempt.

Having failed in his triple profession as a lawyer, doctor and newspaperman, he joined a filibustering expedition to Sonora, Mexico, in 1855, which, however, did not turn out successfully. The fact that his aim was forcibly to convert the Mexican State of Sonora into a "slave state," goes to prove that he must have been backed by "black ivory" interests in the United States. In the following year, that is in 1856, he embarked with a force for Nicaragua, probably with the premeditated intention of holding up the Accessory Transit Company, an American corporation in which Commodore Cornelius Vanderbilt owned the

THE LOOTING OF NICARAGUA

controlling interest. It seems that as the commander-in-chief of the army of Patricio Rivas, whom he had practically installed as president, he did not have much difficulty in realizing his intentions, especially since he had been amply supplied with funds, arms, and ammunition, by two of the stockholders of the company, who were anxious to take the controlling interest away from Vanderbilt. Violating international law and using an authority which he had usurped, he confiscated, in the name of the government of Nicaragua, the wharfs, warehouses and river steamers of the Accessory Transit Company. Thus Walker is seen in historical perspective as the first hired tool of Dollar Diplomacy and also as the first "agent provocateur" of American armed intervention in Nicaragua. On September 22, 1856, he went even so far as to repeal the law prohibiting slavery in Nicaragua; which had long been in force in that country. And, that same year, the Democratic National Convention in the United States passed a resolution expressing its sympathies with Walker *for his efforts to regenerate Nicaragua!* Though the cynicism of that seems too gross even for a smile, let us not be surprised if, one of these days, some other National Convention passes a resolution expressing sympathy with, and admiration for, Dollar Diplomacy for its unselfish efforts to regenerate Nicaragua over again!

As a result of Walker's outrageous behavior he was run out of the country. After three years of unsuccessful efforts to return to Nicaragua, he was finally taken prisoner by the Honduran Government and executed in Truxillo, on September 12, 1860. So did a cheap and venal scoundrel come to a just end.

After twenty years of armed disputes, as the result of the seed of corruption which Dollar Diplomacy had sown in Nicaragua by means of its hired tool, the buccaneer William Walker, the much disputed presidential chair was occupied by General Zavala who brought Nicaragua to a high degree of prosperity. During the administration of Dr. Cardenas who was elected in 1883, President Barrios of Guatemala tried to unite the Central American states under one flag, with heavy bloodshed as a consequence. Shortly after the election of President Roberto Sacasa, in 1889, Guatemala, Honduras and San Salvador again tried to unite. As in indirect consequence of their failure to establish the Union, Sacasa was overthrown; and in 1894 President José Santos Zelaya, the Porfirio Diaz of Nicaragua, came into power. He ruled Nicaragua (as a dictator, it is true, but a benevolent and progressive one at that) until 1909; when, as stated before, he was practically forced by American pressure to resign because he had ordered the revision of the titles of the La Luz and Los Angeles Mining Company, in which—as has been stated in a previous chapter—ex-Secretary of State, Philander Knox (at that time in office) was one of the main shareholders.

The American Consul at Bluefields had advance information of the revolution and, in his notification to the State Department, came within two days of prophesying exactly when it would begin. This, coupled with the fact that the United States broke off relations with the Zelaya government almost immediately after the outbreak of said revolution, at least suggest that the resignation of President Zelaya was practically forced upon him by American interests, to prevent at any cost—even by means of American armed intervention, if necessary—the revision of the possibly illegal titles of the La Luz and Los Angeles Mine.

THE LOOTING OF NICARAGUA 41

The present day chapter of the relations between the United States with Nicaragua began, therefore, in the year 1909, which witnessed the close of the long rule of President Zelaya.

During the Zelaya administration, Nicaragua had been a prosperous and highly progressive country. Her railroad was built in those days; steamers were plying the waters of the Managua and Nicaragua lakes. The Mosquito reservation was incorporated into the republic. The mahogany, cedar, and other woods, as well as rubber and other concessions of great value, were being exploited in accordance with the law. The gold mines were flourishing as never before, even in the old colonial days. Cattle, coffee, bananas, were being exported in large quantities. Even in the smallest hamlets, hidden in the jungle wilderness, public schools were established; and missionaries were at work civilizing the wild Suma Indian tribes. A strict moral code was being enforced. The public moneys, which, according to members of Vice-President Sacasa's Staff, have been employed, during the last sixteen years, in building up Jesuit and other merely clerical establishments, were being used in those days to maintain public and parochial *schools* all over the country. The expenditures in the year of President Zelaya's administration, when they were the largest, were less than three quarters of a million gold dollars; while the total debt, both domestic and foreign, hardly exceeded seven million gold dollars.

Such were the conditions in Nicaragua in those happy days when Nicaraguans were managing their own country; before the vulture buried its beak in her throat, to suck the lifeblood out of her body.

It is an incontestable fact that American intervention in Nicaragua, since 1909, has set that country back both morally and materially. During this period, as in the days of the buccaneer, William Walker, Dollar Diplomacy has resorted to its favorite expedients of bribery, threat, and misrepresentation, in order to keep the honest American citizen from knowing the truth about what is really going on in Nicaragua. In Nicaragua, in short, sinister Big Business and sinister politics are achieving the ends which they have also tried in vain to achieve in Mexico for a long time. Mexico is resolved to be blotted off the map rather than to become a second Nicaragua.

However, while there is life there is hope. And our Latin ideals of liberty and happiness are alive still in Nicaragua. The final chapter of American Dollar Diplomacy in Nicaragua has not been written yet, and there is many a slip between the cup and the lip! The facts that the conservative renegade, whom the too tolerant Sacasa foolishly appointed commander-in-chief of the liberal army, José Maria Moncada, betrayed the cause of Nicaraguan Liberalism by tricking fifty per cent of the forces entrusted to him into surrendering their arms, in the hope that American influence would appoint him President of Nicaragua next year; and that Vice-President Sacasa tacitly concurred in Moncada's action, do not imply by any means that Nicaragua has lost its independence. Among other factors, which will have their say in that matter, are two which must be reckoned with seriously. These are General Augusto Sandino, backed by the sympathies of ninety per cent of the Nicaraguan people; and the Nicaraguan Labor Unions, who are a hard-headed lot and who will not surrender, nor rest, until Nicaragua's independence is fully restored, and the American marines are withdrawn from Nicaraguan soil.

Chapter IV

Leaving New York for Nicaragua to Investigate the Situation — Visiting Friends in Washington En Route — Arrival in Mexico City — Colonel Edward Davis and Ambassador Sheffield — The Soviet Minister — Two Birds With One Shot — The Powerful C. R. O. M. — Senator Wheeler Speaks — Plans of the Oil Kings and Their Allies for the Dismemberment of Mexico.

WHILE I was in New York during the winter of 1926-27, I read a newspaper report of the discussions of the Nicaraguan situation, in Congress and the Senate, which quoted a representative as saying: "If Admiral Latimer, instead of following orders, were doing in Nicaragua what he is now doing there, on his own account, he would deserve to be courtmartialed and shot on the spot." A few days later I was talking about this report with acquaintances in the Newspaper Club. Some one remarked, "Rats! That was settled long ago. Things were getting too hot in Mexico; so Dollar Diplomacy has probably promised to leave Mexico alone for a while if it is given a free hand in Nicaragua. That's all!"

This remark intrigued me. It seemed to shed a light. It helped to bring my deep interest in the Nicaraguan struggle to a head. I determined to go to Nicaragua at once, in order to make as thorough an examination of the situation as possible; I say "as possible," because, at that time, Mr. Henry Stimson had not performed his tender offices, as the quite Extraordinary Envoy of this government, which resulted in the disarming of the constitutionalist forces.

The troops of the Liberals and the troops of the Conservatives were still fighting each other, fighting, that is, wherever the United States Marines could not penetrate to declare the spot a neutral zone and thereby rob the Liberals of their victories. The lines of guerrilla warfare are uncertain; and a conscientious observer, such as I wished to become, would find no neutral zones marked out conveniently for him in penetrating Nicaragua in search of information. There would be difficulties between me and the facts I sought to learn. But I resolved to try my luck! Next evening the Newspaper Club of New York was to celebrate its famous "Old Timers' Night"; and I had been looking forward to it. Nevertheless in the morning I packed my trunk, so eager was I now to be off, and left for Nicaragua via Mexico, Guatemala, Costa Rica and Panama.

I stopped a day in Washington, D. C., to talk with Senator Borah; the Mexican Ambassador, Sr. Tellez; President William Green of the American Federation of Labor; Mr. Kalish, editor of the *Army and Navy Journal*, and Dr. Gil Borges, Secretary of the Pan-American Union. Two days later I crossed the Rio Grande and after another day or two I arrived in Mexico City, where I had the pleasure of meeting my old friend and gallant foe, Lieutenant-Colonel Edward Davis, D.S.M., D.S.O., formerly American military observer with Lord Allenby's forces, and at the time of my visit American Military Attaché in Mexico, and where I also had the honor of meeting and being the guest of Ambassador and Mrs. Sheffield in the American Embassy.

During my stay in Mexico City I had also the satisfaction of meeting Her Excellency, Mrs. Kolonday, Soviet Minister to Mexico, who expressed her great regard for the American people and denied that her government had ever tried to incite Mexican public opinion against the United States, or to influence the Calles administration in any way. She claimed that such attempts would be necessarily fruitless for the reason that the Mexican Government was based on socialist ideas; while the Soviet Government was based on syndicalist principles. Mr. Leon Haykis, secretary of the Soviet legation and an old personal friend of mine, also went to the trouble of explaining this point to me very thoroughly. I feel convinced that a great injustice has been committed against Mexico by certain important newspapers in the United States which have rashly published stories to aid Dollar Diplomacy in representing Mexico as a hotbed of radicalism. No wonder that not only in Latin America, but throughout much of the civilized world the American press is supposed to be in the pay of the Big Interests.

I am firmly convinced that if the Associated Press and some of the leading American papers took the trouble to examine the personal records and business connections of some of their representatives in Latin America, and particularly in Mexico and Nicaragua, they would discharge those men instantly. Thus they could easily undo many a wrong which they have done to those countries; and by cleaning house themselves, they would incidentally help the United States to avoid future international complications directly affecting the two-billion-dollar trade between North and Latin America—for the saying goes that he who sows the wind is bound sooner or later to reap the whirlwind. There are certain laws of nature which no nation, not even the United States, can interfere with without suffering the consequences. Germany is proof of that. There is no such thing as a *small enemy!* The smaller the snake, the stronger, as a rule, is the effect of its poison!

That insignificant group of isles, called Great Britain, for instance, which has succeeded in destroying one after another the Napoleonic, German, Austrian, Russian, Turkish and Chinese empires, by means of coalitions—because they were in her way—because they threatened to deprive her population of its daily bread!—might not have much difficulty in bringing about, some day, a coalition against the United States, which has become a far bigger menace to British interests abroad than Germany ever was. Oceans are no longer obstacles, in our day. In another thirty or fifty years from now—to judge by the way aerial navigation is progressing—the combined air forces of Europe and Asia might gather in, relatively speaking, a few hours and reduce to ashes the principal cities of the United States. They could also starve the American people by means of blockades similar to those which decimated the Germans during the World War.

The days of splendid isolation are gone! In olden times it took centuries to build up empires and centuries to destroy them. In modern times, empires, and particularly industrial and commercial empires, like Germany for instance, which it took only decades to build up, can be destroyed almost overnight. There should be a special warning in this to the United States, whose strength is not based on tradition but upon wealth only. This apparently healthy country carries already in its system the deadly germs of radicalism and race prejudice which have been, in other nations, invariably the forerunners of disaster. But it is not only Dollar Diplomacy which is leading the United States, slowly but surely, toward destruc-

THE LOOTING OF NICARAGUA 47

tion by the universal hatred which it is provoking. No! There is also that other factor, those one-hundred-per-cent-American-Make-the-Eagle-Screech fanatics who, through crass ignorance, keep on helping Dollar Diplomacy abroad, and radicalism at home, to prepare the ground for a future coalition against their own country by those people and nations who fear American industrial and commercial competition. This includes the millions of Asiatics who resent the exclusion of their territorials from the United States and will never rest until the barrier of race prejudice has been done away with. This means that there are breakers ahead of the United States which the American people will only be able to avoid by using common sense in their home politics and by keeping their hands off Latin America.

There will probably be many persons who will consider my statements exaggerated. However, let us take Germany as an example who, despite her tremendous military power and without having to contend with the serious problems of radicalism and race prejudice which continue to confront the United States, was finally brought to her knees because she believed she was strong enough to consider treaties as scraps of paper. Her callous attitude, based on her wealth and power, was much the same as that of the United States in Nicaragua, where the American Government broke faith by recognizing and materially supporting the Adolfo Diaz régime, notwithstanding the treaty which it had signed with the Central American countries not to recognize a government resulting from a revolution! By this action the American Government has not only disgraced itself but has also laid the foundation for future international complications. By treating international compacts as scraps of paper the United States Government has put itself morally on the same level as the government of the former German Empire. Does the United States Government think that it can make an exception of Nicaragua because Nicaragua is small? Nicaragua is a member of the League of Nations which is controlled by England, France and Japan; by the three biggest political and commercial rivals of this country to-day. And always there is Russia! These are matters which are being freely discussed all over the world. Except in the United States. It is in the interest of Dollar Diplomacy not to let the American people know the truth about what is really going on south of the Rio Grande.

But it is not yet too late for Americans to know and to act. That is the reason why I am writing this book,—to remind the average, honest, American citizen of the fact that there will never exist real friendship between North and Latin America, but on the contrary, that the abyss will be growing deeper and wider all the time, so long as the American people allow Dollar Diplomacy to continue in control of the American political mechanism and the American Army and Navy south of the Rio Grande.

One of the most serious problems of the United States is her relations with Mexico.

Many books have been written in the United States about Mexico's past and present history, but few of the authors have given a clear statement of the cause of contention between these two countries.

It should not be forgotten that when General Porfirio Diaz first got into power, some fifty years ago, he was only backed up by the liberals, while the conservatives, who outnumbered them three to one, controlled seventy-five per cent of the cultivable ground

THE LOOTING OF NICARAGUA 49

and therefore the revenues of the country; for in those days Mexico was almost entirely lacking in railroads, modern industries, etc. The régime of Porfirio Diaz was consequently only nominal. The first serious reactionary movement was bound to make an end of it without great difficulty. Happily for him and his partisans, some Wall Street financiers conceived the idea of bringing about an alliance between Diaz, who controlled the army and had therefore the power, and the conservative party (to which belonged also the Clergy) who owned practically seventy-five per cent of the republic and, besides, almost entirely controlled the labor market through the "peonage" system of the old colonial days. This coalition, backed up by the large investments of Wall Street, was bound to produce big profits. The American speculators saw that they would reap not only the legitimate profits which such investments would produce in a rich and almost virgin market like Mexico, but also the additional profits to be derived from cheap labor. It is an established fact that the Mexican peon who was getting in those days across the line, that is on the American side of the Mexican border, one or one and a half dollars a day for a ten-hour day's work, was receiving for the same amount of working hours *on the Mexican side* only twenty-five cents gold a day. Investing money in Mexico at that time was almost equivalent to shooting two birds with one shot; for, as long as Porfirio Diaz remained in power, the system of "enforced peonage" was kept up, religiously, by both the Mexican and American capitalists in their factories, plantations, mines, etc. And why not? Was not Porfirio Diaz their business partner? Were not he and his confederates getting the lion's share of the winnings? Why was he keeping a large army of *rurales,* if not for the purpose of helping them to pile up their millions at the expense of the blood and tears of hundreds of thousands of underfed and underpaid Mexican *peones* and their families? The duty of those *rurales* was by no means that of tin soldiers, but of regular bloodhounds. Every time a *peon* escaped from the factory, ranch or mine, no matter if it belonged to a native or an American capitalist, the *rurales* were promptly summoned and the run-away *peon* was brought back in chains, or was shot down like a dog if he attempted to resist the law; for the *peones* were not considered, during the Diaz régime, as human beings but as chattels belonging to the plantations, etc., where they were born or employed. They were doomed to remain working there all their lives, until they died, and so were their sons and grandsons, for a paltry salary of twenty-five cents gold a day; which was never paid out to them in cash but in provisions or deadly liquor. As soon as a Mexican or a foreigner dared to mention the sacrilegious word "labor reform," he was promptly spirited away, never to reappear. Those were certainly happy days—in fact the *golden era* of Dollar Diplomacy in Mexico . . . now gone, never to return!

In those glorious days of business partnership between Wall Street, Porfirio Diaz and the land barons, it would have amounted almost to an insult to ask the Clergy and the landed proprietors to register inventories or to pay any except nominal taxes on their industrial, rural or urban properties. Were they not partners of the President? If he did not pay taxes, why should they?

Thus Porfirio Diaz and his partners, the land barons, the Clergy and Dollar Diplomacy, were getting richer every day, and the country was developing rapidly in a material way; while the proletariat, comprising over eighty per cent of the population and composed chiefly of millions of Indian *peones* and their families, was being kept in bondage, underfed, filthy, ignorant. They lived the lives of slaves and died the death of worn-out beasts of burden. Congress was a farce. Senators and representatives were chosen by the President among the political sympathizers of the "system." They were professional "yes men." The laws were made by Porfirio Diaz himself. He would not consult any experts. He was the law and the law was he! No wonder that the oil and land laws, which he had decreed solely for the purpose of protecting his own interests and the investments of Dollar Diplomacy, had to be revised by the present administration in order to safeguard the national interests, as every independent country has the right to do.

When Dollar Diplomacy invested several hundred million dollars in Mexico, during the Diaz régime, it knew perfectly well that those laws, which had been promulgated by Porfirio Diaz to protect their joint interests, were based on the famous "two birds with one shot" system and would have to be changed therefore sooner or later. These laws had been forced on the country by the dictator and they endangered the sovereignty of the Mexican republic. Anybody with any common sense at all in Mexico, as well as abroad, knew that the feudal system of Porfirio Diaz, which suited so well the purposes of Dollar Diplomacy, was bound to collapse on account of the increasing discontent of the labor classes which, despite all the efforts of the Diaz administration and Dollar Diplomacy to keep them in bondage, were gradually waking up. Numerous members of the upper classes, even among Diaz's own partisans, gradually commenced realizing, also, the impending danger of foreign intervention—as the only means whereby such a monstrous régime could be kept up indefinitely.

The unsuccessful uprising of General Ricardo Flores Magon in 1909, also called the "socialistic revolution," was the first thunderbolt which struck the Diaz-Dollar Diplomacy régime from a blue sky and set the ball rolling. And when General Francisco Madero rose in arms, a year later, against the Diaz administration, the social hurricane broke loose with such vehemence that it obliterated almost immediately not only the Diaz régime but also the hateful "system," by which Dollar Diplomacy had been enriching itself for almost thirty years. If there are, therefore, any claims to be made in the case of Mexico, these ought not to be presented by Dollar Diplomacy to the Mexican Government, but by the *Mexican people* against Dollar Diplomacy and its accomplices in the different American administrations for the lives of those hundreds of thousands of Mexican *peones* (before the Madero revolution); and for the lives of free Mexican citizens, during the ten or twelve years of revolutions after Madero's death. For those revolutions were launched in many cases, and in all cases were materially supported, by the "agents provocateurs" of Dollar Diplomacy in the vain hope of restoring the old system of the Porfirio Diaz régime.

The efforts of Dollar Diplomacy to bring about the restoration of the old system had, however, the effect of a boomerang for, instead of succeeding in enslaving again the unhappy Mexican proletariat, as in the old days, it forced the laboring class to organize legally, as the powerful C. R. O. M., or Confederacion Regional Obrera Mexicana (with a membership

THE LOOTING OF NICARAGUA

of about two million) affiliated with the Pan-Ameri-Federation of Labor. The C. R. O. M. instead of receiving orders from Dollar Diplomacy is now dictating them. The tables have been turned! Here is a case where the hunted have become the hunters, and where right has turned out to be mightier than might itself.

Among the friends of Dollar Diplomacy who have apparently contributed most toward the bitterness between the Mexican and American peoples, which were really born to be friends, instead of enemies, ranks uppermost Mr. Henry Lane Wilson, former American Minister to Mexico. With a view to substantiating this statement (for I wish not to injure any one unjustly) I submit an extract taken from a criticism of Mr. Wilson's Memoirs which was recently published by Mr. Carleton Beals in the book review section of the *Nation:*

". . . Mr. Wilson's analysis of the Diaz régime is exceedingly superficial, and though he remarks that fully eighty per cent of the population 'was without an abiding place except by sufferance,' he shows no sympathies for the struggle of that eighty per cent for liberation; nor does he for one moment feel, let alone understand, the great forces sweeping Mexico; nor does he at any point mention, let alone grasp, the magnitude of the problems represented by the destructive conflict between modern industrialism, represented by American capital, and the semi-feudal system south of the Rio Grande. Nor does he, in the midst of his bombastic concern for American property, reveal the scandalous manner in which many of the American concessions were illegally or unjustly acquired, or make known the exaggerated and questionable character of some of the claims he pressed, not diplomatically but irritably and angrily. Certainly, Mr. Wilson was not expected to reveal *his backdoor connections, via his brother, with the associates of the Guggenheims (smelter competitors of the Madero family),* or tell of the clique of Cientifico grafters with whom he hobnobbed, or give the true composition of the adulatory Committee of the American Colony which whitewashed him.

"Mr. Wilson wishes, above all, to exonerate himself and Huerta of the oft-repeated charge of not having taken proper steps to safeguard Madero's life. The officer of the guard, when Madero was shot down, was promptly promoted; Huerta perpetrated other savage assassinations. As to Mr. Wilson, in a most trying moment of Madero's career, the ambassador seized upon a doubtful rumor that the government intended to arrest and execute the ex-President Francisco de la Barra, and insultingly sent a hostile note of warning. De la Barra's safety was none of Mr. Wilson's business; but in the case of Madero, Wilson had grave and direct responsibility, since he had, through the Spanish Minister, asked the President (Madero) to resign and so became sponsor for Huerta's treason. But in a crucial hour a note requesting that Madero's life be respected—scribbled by Wilson's wife on a visiting card—sufficed. So much confidence had Wilson in the drunken assassin newly at the helm, and in ladies' visiting cards! Wilson, at the tearful importunity of Madero's wife whom he told 'that Madero was a very wicked man!', later made two lukewarm efforts, and while he easily saved the lives of associates of Madero,—the latter, shortly after Wilson received Huerta and his brummagem crew under the American Embassy roof in a blaze of festive lights, and Stars and Stripes, to

THE LOOTING OF NICARAGUA

determine the personnel of the new cabinet—Madero went down to a vilely treacherous death. Mr. Wilson might have made a good engraved card ambassador to Diaz; as poison cup ambassador to Madero he helped spill years of bloodshed across Mexican history."

Instances like that (of corrupt representatives) I could cite by the dozen. And, although it is not my intention to volunteer any advice for the benefit of the American Government, I cannot help mentioning that the voluntary or involuntary wrong committed by the various American administrations, since the days of Roosevelt, in not properly examining the *private records and business connections* of their diplomatic representatives in Latin America, specially in Mexico, Central America and the Antilles, has been the cause not only of serious moral and material losses to those countries, but also of much bloodshed. No wonder that public opinion all over Latin America continues to accuse the American Government of criminal neglect, to say the least, and even of having supported Dollar Diplomacy in Haiti, Santo Domingo, Mexico and Central America almost entirely for its own political purposes at home. In order to explain this statement, which some people may consider rash and unwarranted in the extreme, I will translate back into English the following letter written by William Jennings Bryan which was published in *El Mundo* of Havana on January 22, 1915:

"MY DEAR MR. VICK:

"Now that you are in Santo Domingo and have familiarized yourself with the situation over there, I wish you would let me know of the political jobs which become vacant so that I can reward our democratic friends in the United States for 'their services rendered.' Every time you hear of a vacancy please let me know. You, as an experienced politician, ought to realize how valuable are the services of all those friends of ours who have taken part in our electoral campaigns and how hard it is sometimes to find adequate positions for all of them. I do not know to what extent a knowledge of the Spanish language will be required in order to hold such positions. Do not fail to let me know the necessary conditions as well as the amounts of the salaries and the exact date when these positions shall become vacant. Sullivan will arrive there (in Santo Domingo) very soon. You and he will be able to introduce all the necessary reforms, etc. The more I treat with him the more I am convinced that he will be a regular Johnny on the spot, and will do whatever he is ordered to do.—W. J. BRYAN."

"I understand," says H. Blanco Fombona, in commenting on this letter, "that Mr. Bryan is supposed to be an honest politician. Look at how little is required in the United States for a man to be considered an honest politician!"

In order to show what kind of men these American politicians were who were given government positions in Santo Domingo, at the expense of the Dominican revenues, Blanco Fombona mentions the following incident. . . . "Dr. Rodriguez Estalot, a distinguished Spanish physician, in charge of the Sanitary Department, was suddenly dismissed and substituted by an American. In the first days of August this substitute arrived and was carried ashore, to the Hotel Inglaterra, paralyzed drunk! . . . and after another month he was carried again aboard a ship and sent

THE LOOTING OF NICARAGUA

home, still in the same condition in which he had been taken ashore; he had not been sober during those thirty days even for an hour!"

Now, coming back to Mexico—and to show that my views are not merely those of a biased alien—I will reproduce a few extracts taken from a speech which Senator Burton K. Wheeler, of Montana, delivered at Ford Hall, Boston, Mass., on March 6, 1926. They read as follows:

". . . In the case of Mexico, our State Department has not yet ventured anything like so far into the field of action as it has done in Nicaragua. Its warlike attitude toward our nearest neighbor on the south has chiefly manifested itself in unmannerly and accusatory and threatening language and what might be called military demonstration on the far-off horizon and on the upper air.

"What is the main trouble in Mexico? Church in the picture!

"I know the situation in Mexico is not quite as simple as it seems to be to the ordinary American observer in Nicaragua. In Mexico there is a church—a lot of churches—in the picture. And that fact has complicated the Mexican question in the minds of many Americans.

"Churches are supposed to simplify things, to make them run smoothly. But sometimes (so the incontrovertible facts of history teach us) they have complicated things. They have been the cause, innocent or otherwise, of political rough houses in many lands.

"If you read the history of England, Germany, Italy, France, the Philippine Islands, you cannot fail to realize that the clash between the State and the Church, which is taking place in Mexico, has taken place in many other countries. It is no part of my business to-day to undertake to weigh the rights and wrongs in this religious issue in Mexico, or in any other country in which it has arisen. History tells us that when the clash comes, whether it come in England, in Italy, in Germany, in France or in Mexico, feeling runs high, blows are struck that it takes many generations to heal, and both the State and the Church come in for much sharp criticism.

"In passing by this perplexing phase of the Mexican question, which I merely mention and have no thought of discussing, I venture two remarks: (1) sooner or later every political state will declare war against any group within the state, whether ecclesiastical or other, that undertakes to shape the state for its own ends—complete separation of state and church is bound to come. (2) No state has yet been able to carry through its whole program during its fight against the church. In the end some more or less satisfactory compromise is effected. However much for a time it may think it is desirable to do so, the state cannot kill the church or put it out of business. Sooner or later every secular reformer who sets out with that idea will learn what Bismarck, the Iron Chancellor of Germany, learned; that is, that it cannot be done, and that it is the part of wisdom not to push the experiment too far. I deplore the unwisdom that does so at the high moral cost of wholesale or petty persecution.

"But this church question is not a *casus belli* so far as our State Department is concerned. From the viewpoint of Mr. Kellogg and Mr. Coolidge the trouble down in Mexico has to do solely with oil— profane oil—not holy oil. If you ask—Whose Oil? the answer is, Doheny, Sinclair and Mellon's oil!

"Here are the figures: The total acreage under oil

development in Mexico is 28,493,914. The total acreage for which concessions have been asked in compliance with the Mexican constitution and land laws is 26,833,335. The total acreage refusing to apply for permits is 1,660,579. The percentage of this defiant acreage owned by Doheny, Sinclair and Mellon is eighty-seven and nine-tenths.

"It is said, with much show of reason, that the titles to much, if not the whole, of this acreage which has refused to comply with the Mexican laws are defective, and that *that* is why Messrs. Doheny, Sinclair and Mellon, with aid of their friend at court, Mr. Kellogg, have undertaken to run a bluff on the Mexican Government.

"Possibly there are many Americans who in the absence of proof would be inclined to give the Mellon land titles the benefit of the doubt. There are very few Americans with sense enough to come out of the rain who would feel that way about the Doheny and Sinclair titles. Their malodorous reputation is too well established. It is something like that of the city of Cologne, where Coleridge says he detected 'Seventy stenches, sharp and well defined, and several stinks!'

"These two American oil magnates have left little room for doubt in any intelligent American mind that, in their effort to acquire oil lands, they never let a little obstacle like fraud or corruption stand between them and their objective.

"Let me sum up what I mean.

"Reduced to the simplest terms, the Kellogg-Coolidge policy has led to armed intervention in Nicaragua in behalf of an American-made puppet-president foisted upon the people against their own will for the simple reason that he is ready, at whatever cost to Nicaragua, to serve the New York bankers who are, and for seventeen years have been, mercilessly exploiting Nicaragua under the ægis of the State Department.

"And further, this policy, unless it is altered or abandoned, will lead to armed intervention in Mexico in support of the dubious claims of Doheny, Sinclair and Mellon. That is to say, the people of the United States will be invited to wage war, declared or understood, against the people of Mexico in behalf of these three distinguished, disinterested American patriots!"

Mr. Carleton Beals indicates the special line of action which some of these "patriots" have been taking secretly for about fifteen years. In an article entitled "Who Wants War With Mexico?" published in the *New Republic,* April 27, 1927, Mr. Beals says: "This is not the first time Mexican imbroglios have involved harmful secret documents, forged and authentic. During the past fifteen years, there have been, and there now are, elements in the United States which have schemed for the dismemberment of Mexico. In governmental archives and in other quarters exists documentary proof of their activities. . . . Both private interests and public officials have, time and again, in almost every period, connived to obtain additional strips of Mexican territory. Former Ambassador Henry Lane Wilson cynically outlined the proper process in the *World Outlook* some five years ago. Roughly, the plan is, first, to cut off northwest Mexico, including the entire petroleum area, either annexing it to the United States, or creating a frank protectorate; second, to precipitate intervention in Mexico proper in order to impose a puppet-president —a la Diaz in Nicaragua; third, to foment an independent Maya state in southeast Mexico, which will ultimately form part of a Central American union under our hegemony."

Here I think I may insert, without going outside the range of this subject, that there are evidences that certain American Oil interests in Venezuela are laying similar plans for separating the chief petroleum-bearing region of my country from the republic. All the territory of Central America, with the "independent" Maya state on the north and the oil province of Venezuela (equally "independent"?) on the south, would give this sinister partnership of Big Business and Big Stick Politics a roomy sphere in which to operate and to loot. To be sure there is British Honduras—an interloping midget posed along that profitable line of march. But no doubt ways could be found to get rid of it. One who is aware of these "dismemberment" plans, and has watched for some years how the base is being laid for them, not unnaturally queries whether the demands recently made (at Geneva) on Britain in the conference on naval reduction, were not in part inspired by the desire to thoroughly safeguard Dollar Diplomacy in its present and future programs in Central America, Mexico and Venezuela. But Mr. Beals has more to say:

"During the Villa-Carranza period, this plan (for Mexico) was actively though secretly pushed. Some years ago, I went over a sheaf of letters extracted from the files of one of the oil companies by a relative of the vice-president, documents which he declared he subsequently turned over to the Mexican Government. These were letters from Teapot-Dome principals; letters from Central America *on Consular paper;* letters *on State Department paper;* letters from prominent American lawyers (one of whom desired to have charge of the legal reconstruction of Mexico when the plan was a *fait accompli*)."

Mr. Beals' aim is the same as mine: to lay the facts before the American people. As an American he has faith in the underlying sound sense, honesty and fair play of the majority of the men and women in this country, his compatriots. I have the same faith; as a Latin-American who has known all classes of Americans in the large cities, the villages, the ranches, in camps and barracks, from New York to San Francisco, and from New Orleans to Nome. I am writing this book because I have that faith.

Chapter V

From Mexico City to the Coast — Disheveled Vera Cruz — Mexico's Need — By Train Across Tehuantepec — A Prince Turns Planter — At the Headquarters of the Nicaraguan Nationalists in Guatemala City — Conduct of Certain United States Ministers — A Motion Picture Show and a Show of Rage — Departure for Costa Rica — Passing Over an Old Battle-ground — A German ex-Secretary of War — Costa Rican Feeling Against the United States — Colon: What They Think in Panama.

AFTER a week's stay in Mexico City, where I also met Dr. Pedro Cepeda, confidential agent of Dr. Sacasa, I continued my trip south by way of Vera Cruz, where I spent another week in company of my old friend, Baron Gerhart von Bredow and his wife, who were returning to Germany after a visit to Central America. They insisted on my going home with them. The temptation was great, to tell the truth, for I knew from frequent experiences how pleasantly the days can pass at Castle Bredow within easy reach of Berlin. However, I had to decline their invitation regretfully. It still seemed clearly my duty to go to Nicaragua so that, afterwards, I could tell the people of the two Americas the result of my investigations. Instead of a book perhaps this is really only a *potpourri,* since it contains, along with my personal observations, a compilation of the numerous written materials which I managed to gather in the sweat of my brow and in some lively peril during my travels through Nicaragua. It would be foolish to write about such a stormy subject as *contemporary Nica-*

ragua only from hearsay. One is always safer in being able to produce the documents.

There is hardly a state in the Mexican Union, except Oaxaca perhaps, which has suffered so much as a consequence of civil wars, since the fall of Porfirio Diaz, as the State of Vera Cruz. It does not seem to have recovered yet from the effects of the rabble dictatorship which ravaged it four or five years ago, despite all the efforts of its late military governor, General Arnulfo Gomez, who succeeded, it is true, in reëstablishing order in its principal cities, such as Jalapa, Cordova and Vera Cruz, but failed to do so in the rural districts.

One result of the bad state of affairs, of course, is banditry all over the state and misery and discontent in the populous centers, such as the city of Vera Cruz, for instance, where it is said hardly anybody pays his rent and where five and ten *pesos* gold pieces have become almost as rare as grizzly bears in the State of Ohio. Since the days of the old régime when Mexico started neglecting her agriculture and cattle raising in order to further her oil industry, the country has been going from bad to worse. It has been only playing the part which Dollar Diplomacy intended it to play in order to weaken its backbone, which, of course, is agriculture, for oil is not a real, but a temporary, asset only, much the same as "black-ivory" used to be in the Southern States before the Civil War.

The city of Vera Cruz which only a few years ago was still a very busy place, despite the many revolutions which ravaged it on account of its being the only outlet to the sea for the greater part of central Mexico, is to-day a dead town—ruined and destitute! Its harbor is practically empty six days out of every week—and so is its treasury—and so are the hearts of its inhabitants. Only when you mention to them the good old days, when the State of Vera Cruz was still being ruled by men of substance, do their sour faces temporarily light up. But soon that dull and stolid look of despondency settles again, and on they pass . . . brooding, yes, brooding all the time . . . but about what? That is precisely the question—about what?

The same thing happens elsewhere in Mexico.

After drawing my own conclusions I am of the opinion that when a country, rich in agriculture like Mexico, is forced to import provisions and even eggs, it must be a sick country. What Mexico really needs to-day is, in my estimation, less *hypothetical political pedagogism,* which I think has inspired the attempt to grapple with too many problems at once without a clear perception of their ramifications. There is need for another man such as President Juarez, wise enough to postpone some of his dearest interests, and to realize that Mexico will be going to the dogs very soon unless strong means are taken at once to eradicate partisan favoritism, mob-rule, illiteracy and banditry.

A two days' journey by train across the Isthmus of Tehauntepec and down the Pacific Coast was slightly enlivened by the presence of the military escort which was constantly on the outlook for bandits. After an unexpected delay near San Jeronimo on account of one of the engines having jumped the track, apparently for no reason but pure fun, I finally arrived about midnight, covered with smoke and dust, at the Mexican-Guatemalan frontier. This frontier line is a river about a quarter of a mile wide which I was obliged to cross, that same night together with my luggage, in a crazy canoe, in order to catch the train for Guatemala City. It was not so bad on the Mexican side, where I had to have my passport viséed only by the Mexican emigration authorities and the Guatemalan Vice Consul, and to have my luggage reviséed at the Customs House. But on the Guatemalan side, in the hamlet called the City of Ayutla, I went (and I hope for the last time in my life) through an ordeal of red tape, compared with which the "after revolution" chicane system in Berlin was only child's play! All I remember (and I am an old campaigner) is that at about three A.M., after having pulled out of bed numerous authorities, including the military commander of the place, to visé my passport, I finally landed with my luggage on an ox-cart at the depot where my traveling companion, Mr. Rene Picado of Costa Rica, had already preceded me.

After a hasty cup of coffee which we managed to purchase from some gaudily attired Indians who were dog-trotting along the dusty road toward the marketplace, carrying lighted torches, and with enormous loads of earthenware strapped to their backs, we boarded the Guatemala Express at four o'clock in the morning and disappeared in the jungle of the coastal region. At six A.M. the sun began to rise like a disk of gold behind the somber pyramid of the Santa Maria volcano, and one hour later we reached the famous highlands of Central Guatemala, studded with coffee farms and occasional emerald green patches of sugar cane.

Sitting next to me was a very tall, slim, blue-eyed German coffee planter in shirt sleeves and riding breeches. His saddlebags seemed to be the only luggage he was carrying with him. We took covert glances at each other, as people do, who are thinking

THE LOOTING OF NICARAGUA 67

"Where have I seen you before?" I was always aware of his furtive look, now at my unshaven face, now at my dust and mud-covered khaki shirt and riding breeches. Incidentally Rene Picado called me by my name. On hearing it, the giant's light-blue eyes lit up for an instant and his lean hand, wearing the signet ring of the Hohenzollerns, shook, nervously, the ashes off his cigar. That anonymous traveler was no less than Prince Sigismund of Prussia, the most sensible Hohenzollern who ever rode a horse or stood on his own legs without the need of a crutch. For immediately after the War, he burned his bridges and went to Latin America, as we like to say in this hemisphere, "to make a man of himself."

Late that night we arrived in Guatemala City and, after driving for a mile or so over its gayly lighted main street, Sexta Avenida, we stopped and made ourselves at home in the Hotel Central, which was also the headquarters of the Nicaraguan Nationalist party in Guatemala. There I met among other revolutionary notables, Dr. Julian Irias, the leader of the unsuccessful expedition to Coseguina, in August, 1926, which really started the ball rolling. Dr. Irias impressed me very favorably personally, though he had the disadvantage of being a *rather* heavy and continuous drinker. This may have accounted in part for the failure of his expedition which had been entrusted to him by Dr. Sacasa, despite the fact that there were available in Guatemala Generals Teofilo Jiminez and Horacio Portocarrero, both younger and far abler soldiers than Julian Irias. If it had not been for Dr. Sacasa's unwise selection of a commander the Constitutionalist revolution would have been an absolute triumph from the start and many, perhaps thousands, of lives, which were lost through Sacasa's lack of judgment, would have been saved. The rank and file certainly pay for it when their superior officers are appointed for political instead of military reasons.

I found Guatemala a happy and prosperous country, as compared with its situation four or five years ago, when I visited it last. General Orellana, the late President, had made good after all despite all prophecies to the contrary and despite the fact that he had risen to power by means of a revolution. Dollar Diplomacy tried its utmost to obstruct his way, for, in a prosperous Guatemala, there was very little chance for its type of "shady business." But Orellana stood pat and outwitted, time and again, the American Minister who, according to public opinion, had tried to control him, in the habitual manner of some (not all) American diplomatic representatives accredited to the Central American Governments, Panama and the Antilles.

There is Mr. Dennis, for instance, late American Charge d'Affaires in Nicaragua, who, during the Corinto Peace Conference, last year, went to the extreme of trying to ram the recognition of the fake Diaz régime down the throats of the Constitutionalist Delegates by threatening that unless they did recognize Diaz the Liberal party would not get into power again in Nicaragua for the next ninety-nine years! A similar case is that of Mr. Francis White, formerly in charge of Latin-American relations and to-day Assistant Secretary of State in Washington, D. C., who, according to a story published in the New York *World* of August 24 or 25, 1927, has been trying to cow the Panama Delegates by threatening that, unless they accept the new treaty as it stands, they may find some day that the United States will have to occupy the Canal Zone. That seems to have been also the habitual system with a certain Mr. G., in Honduras, who, after mixing cocktails for years, as a bartender in Tegucigalpa, was suddenly elevated to the dignity of American Minister in that same locality ... evidently not without special reasons! ... for an old hand in the cocktail mixing business like Mr. G., was undoubtedly able to mix also some homebrews of a certain "brand," perhaps not exactly to the liking of those down whose throats they were to be forcibly poured.

Coming back to Orellana I wish to state that, according to what I heard from different sources, the American Minister to Guatemala never let him out of sight, constituting himself almost his shadow—a regular leech and self-invited guest at all occasions—even during Orellana's private parties. But all that did not help much, for Orellana was a strong and able man, and Guatemala progressed during the four or five years of his administration.

The second evening after my arrival I went with a friend to a moving picture theater. On the program was a film representing President Orellana or his successor, President Chacon (I do not remember which), with the *adhesive American Minister* standing alongside of him. No sooner had it been projected than a rain of empty bottles and other missiles hit the screen —accompanied by deafening howls from the whole audience, which commenced breaking chairs, tables, in fact everything that came handy, in order to throw them at the picture. The frightened operator, after ducking a couple of dozen times for dear life, finally managed to turn off the current and to project another picture of Orellana, or Chacon, without the American Minister sticking to him. That saved the day. Yet the spectators were not satisfied until some patriotic film had been displayed, whereupon they applauded and hurrahed until the ceiling threatened to come down on us. I mention this case to show what disgust and rage the sight, only, of anything connected with the American Government provokes in Latin America, because of the meddlesome character of some of its diplomatic representatives, and the ruthlessness of Dollar Diplomacy. Latin Americans suppose that these evils are sponsored by the American people, evidently because the American public does not seem to object, since it does not end these wrongs.

In those days I was told the real reason of ex-President Estrada Cabrera's downfall by one of Estrada Cabrera's former confidential agents, a Guatemalan diplomat. It seems that because the Germans owned (and still own) most of the biggest coffee plantations in Guatemala and therefore controlled the coffee market in that country, they had been (and they continue to be) a thorn in the flesh of Dollar Diplomacy. During the World War Guatemala had been asked to declare war on Germany, which she did, of course, in order not to lose her markets in the United States. Consequently, among other German property, all German coffee plantations were confiscated. After the War, Dollar Diplomacy proposed to the Guatemaian Government to buy those plantations. Estrada Cabrera at first objected. When he finally acquiesced, it was too late, for the Germans, having got wind of it, took certain steps which finally wound up by causing the downfall of Estrada Cabrera and led the new government to return to them their confiscated property—inclusive of their coffee plantations—despite all the efforts of Dollar Diplomacy to the contrary.

General Chacon, who used to be Orellana's right hand man and succeeded him in the presidency after

THE LOOTING OF NICARAGUA 71

his death, inherited a rather difficult job, for he too is constantly dogged by that same adhesive American Minister who, according to reports, is doing the work of both a detective and a bully. So much so that when, in the spring of 1927, the Secretaries of State of Honduras, El Salvador and Guatemala assembled in order to bring about *closer relations* between the three countries, the American Minister (according to the Managua press), had the Guatemalan Secretary of State, Mr. Matos, promptly removed from office by exercising pressure on President Chacon. However, even that did not help much, for a treaty was signed shortly afterwards, whereby Guatemala, El Salvador and Honduras agreed to work together in all matters concerning their foreign relations. One of the results of the treaty was that a threatened litigation between Honduras and Guatemala, on account of some tract of territory along their frontier, was luckily averted.

Notwithstanding this happy circumstance the feeling continues running high, in fact *very* high, against the American Government among the population of those countries, because everybody realizes that what the American Government has been doing and continues doing in Nicaragua, it will probably try to repeat also in their countries. And as none of them desires to become another Nicaragua, it is no more than natural that they should first band together and then commence looking abroad for allies.

When I passed through Guatemala four or five years ago I heard from several labor leaders that, because of the misery which was rife at that time in Nicaragua, due to unbearable oppression, they had addressed themselves by wire or cable to both Secretary Hughes and Mr. Gompers, then president of the American Federation of Labor, protesting against their deplorable state of affairs; but that neither Secretary Hughes nor President Gompers had taken the trouble of even acknowledging the receipt of their message. It did not surprise me that Secretary Hughes should decline to stoop to answer the message of a mere labor organization (and Guatemalan at that!). But it certainly alarmed me to hear that Mr. Gompers had acted likewise. I am sure that William Green, the present head of the Federation, would never have committed such an error. That is why I, immediately after my arrival in New York, published in the New York *Tribune* of April 8, 1923, a letter of which the following is an extract:

"The only way by which trouble in Central America can be averted is for Congress to send a Labor Delegation to the scene of the impending trouble, *for the majority of the Latin Americans refuse longer to trust the average American politician!* This delegation, by examining the *real* conditions existing in Central America, may be able to prevent the trouble.

"Referring to the Central-American Conference, which was brought to an end on February 7th, I feel skeptical as to the benefits therefrom accruing to this country. At the Conference fifteen documents were signed and among other measures an agreement was reached authorizing the United States to delegate fifteen citizens to serve on the Central-American Tribunal, together with thirty members to be appointed by the five Central-American Republics. This means *that the United States maintains over a thirty per cent interest in the financial and political management of Central America!*

"Viewing the situation from another standpoint—

that is, from the standpoint of eighty millions of Latin Americans—the results achieved by the conference are merely a repetition of the Panama Canal scheme, the only difference being that, instead of Colombia, this time Costa Rica, Honduras and El Salvador, as well as Guatemala, are concerned. They claim their share in the Bay of Fonseca and the benefits of the transcontinental waterway of Nicaragua which Spain did not bequeath to Nicaragua alone, but to all of the five republics.

"It is a popular belief in Latin America that conditions in the five republics are identical with those existing in Colombia during the Roosevelt administration, and that the government of Chamorro and Company in Managua owes its maintenance solely to the bayonets of the American Marine Corps stationed in that country. Should the marines be withdrawn it seems certain that the Chamorro Government would be overthrown within twenty-four hours, to be replaced by a new government, representative of practically the whole of the Nicaraguan people. *Should this transpire, the Chamorro-Byran Treaty of 1914 would be abrogated and another treaty promulgated with the rightful claims of Costa Rica, Honduras, El Salvador and Guatemala, which the Chamorro Treaty has unjustly and entirely ignored!*

"In order to render the situation more intelligible I consider it my duty to mention that the members of a certain group of financiers have created a state of affairs bordering on anarchy all over Central America and Mexico. They have gained control, among other things, of coffee production in Nicaragua by forcing the larger plantation owners, through a ruinous currency system, to sell to them most of their valuable plantations. They also, through a concession granted

74 THE LOOTING OF NICARAGUA

them by the Chamorro Government, have gained control of transportation and of the customs house for an indefinite period of years.

"I am of the opinion, therefore, that an uprising in Central America, and especially in Nicaragua, can be averted only by recalling the American marines stationed in Managua. In this way only can Central Americans ever enjoy the benefits of self-government, which under existing conditions they cannot hope for.

"RAFAEL DE NOGALES,
"Citizen of Venezuela."
New York, April 8, 1923.

It is impossible to discuss Nicaragua intelligently without including Mexico and Central America as a whole, for their history, both past and present, and their material and ethnical development are so closely related that their solidarity as a Latin Block, from the Rio Grande down to Panama, instead of decreasing will keep on increasing all the time, despite the strenuous efforts of Dollar Diplomacy to prevent it. *Financial shackles and political muzzles but strengthen their racial solidarity!*

It would have been an easy matter for me to go to Nicaragua by way of El Salvador and Corinto. But in that case I would have been only another one in that flock of dupes who used to spend their days sitting in easy chairs in the Club Internacional of Managua, sipping cocktails, having their hands manicured, smoking cigarettes, while the press agents of Dollar Diplomacy (some of whom had business affiliations with Adolfo Diaz) dished out to them the usual slush or *fixed news*—which they immediately cable to the newspapers of the United States. Instead I decided to get into Nicaragua quietly by its back door—with a flashlight and a chisel, if you want to put it that way—in order to find out the facts. Having been informed at the last minute that a German boat, bound for Puerto Limon, Costa Rica, was scheduled to leave on the following day (this was about noon) from Puerto Barrios, on the Atlantic Coast, and that the first-class tickets had been sold out, I had my passport viséed by the Costa Rican Minister immediately and, with a letter of introduction from the German Legation for the captain of the steamer, I left that same day on a special train, chartered by the Sinfonia Costarricensa, which was due to arrive that afternoon or night in Guatemala City on its way to Puerto Barrios. The seventy or eighty members of the Symphony who had gone broke in Mexico were hurrying home for fear of getting stranded also in Guatemala. Their special train was therefore bound to reach Puerto Barrios in time. And it did. But how! I will never forget it!

Some way or other I managed to purchase a ticket —for there is always a way—and as soon as the train steamed into the depot I sneaked into one of the coaches with a handbag or two, and curled up behind the big drum, which was in a corner. There was hardly standing room in the cars. The drum was large enough to give a small man a feeling of security. I went to sleep. But somehow the conductor discovered me—probably because I was snoring—and asked me rather roughly: "What are you doing in this car, if you please?"

"How dare you ask me such a question?" I answered, putting on a face like Mascagni or Richard Wagner.

"Then you are a member of the orchestra, I suppose?" he insisted.

"You ask *me* that," I replied haughtily. "Do you not see my big drum right here?" I gave it a bang which could be heard for miles around!

"Oh! Then you are the famous So-and-So?" respectfully naming I know not what celebrity. "I beg your pardon, Señor." Making a deep bow, he departed. I turned over and never woke up again until we arrived at Puerto Barrios next morning.

While trying to get into the steamer I was stopped at the head of the ladder by one of the officers. My white shoes, hat and palm beach suit must have been a sight after that all-night sleep on the dirty floor of the car, which was filled most of the time with a thick cloud of smoke and dust.

"Where is your ticket, sir?" he asked me sharply.

"I have no ticket, they were sold out when I tried to purchase one in the city yesterday. Could I not get one on board?"

"There is no room left in the first class," he snarled, "you better go to steerage! . . ." But, oh, wonders! No sooner had he glanced at the headlines of my letter of introduction when he, too, was all smiles, and the captain, probably to show special courtesy to me, had one of his officers move on the double quick in order to give me his cabin. Such is life. It is always better to get in through the back door and walk out through the front door, than vice-versa. To be sure!

That day, after supper, when the stars began to glow in the evening sky and the blue mountain ranges of the Honduran Cordillera turned purple beneath the dying rays of the sun, I happened to look south and noticed far, far away, the dimly sparkling lights of Puerto Cortes . . . those same lights for which I once had been anxiously on the lookout many years ago, when, as a boy of twenty-two, I had proudly

THE LOOTING OF NICARAGUA 77

crossed the blue, churning waters of the Caribbean Sea at the helm of the little schooner *La Rosa* in which I was conducting a load of guns and ammunition to my friends in the Santa Rita district near the Guatemalan frontier! I could not help remembering with a certain sadness how we sailed like a phantom ship past the lighted wharf of Puerto Cortes, which was fairly bristling with bayonets, and how we finally landed our cargo safely west of Amoa! . . . And how my small band of men kept marching silently, one night after another, over those purple mountain ranges . . . until, one day, a government force destroyed our little convoy after a ferocious struggle! . . . And how I had been left for dead, lying on my face, on the hill . . . And the weird sensations of coming back to consciousness and feeling the buzzards nibbling at my blood-soaked hair! . . .

Next morning, or a day after, while walking up and down the deck with a German scientist whom I had met on board, I noticed a funny-looking chap sitting at a table all by himself. He was over six feet tall and dressed in white. His legs were normal so far as width was concerned. His corpulence really began at his hips and went on, increasing in alarming proportions, toward the top. His stomach stood out like a juvenile balloon. With his white, short-cut hair, his gray clipped mustache and his little piggy eyes, peering out of his soggy face, he was the true type of the German bartender or master butcher. Indeed, when he donned his gold-rimmed spectacles, one would say, "Ah! there is a prosperous brewer who has risen from the ranks!" Both of his arms were extended, half-moon fashion, around a stein of beer standing on the table in front of him. Through the stolid, cynical, even brutal expression of his puffed-up face stole once in a while that contented smile, so characteristic of the low-born German when he realizes that his stomach has been satisfied. I could not help feeling repugnance at the sight of that man. Still, he interested me. I asked my companion who he was. Whereupon he immediately introduced him to me . . . "Herr Reichs—etc., etc., Noske!"

So this was Noske! That ex-Secretary of War of the German Republic (and ex-corporal of the German Navy) who betrayed his oath and his flag in Kiel, by revolting and sacrificing his superiors, the brave German Naval Officers Corps, to the infuriated rabble; and who, afterwards, during the Spartacist Revolution, had his former comrades mowed down with machine guns, like a pack of dogs. All this, in his hungry endeavor to become a "Herr So-and-So," equivalent to a "bourgeois gentleman," which seems to represent the ideal of every German parvenu. No wonder that I felt repugnance at the sight of that specimen of "modern German officialdom" who, after the World War, plunged the dagger into Germany's back in order to elevate themselves and enslave their country for generations to come. How I pitied my former German war comrades who, during the Spartacist Revolution, in order to save their country from total ruin, had to recognize as their superior this bloodhound and moral freak.

At our arrival in Puerto Limon I found out with regret that no gasoline schooners were expected to leave for Puerto Cabezas for quite a while. So I went to San José de Costa Rica in order to consult with Dr. Clodomiro Urcuyo, the confidential agent of the Constitutionalist Government of Nicaragua.

In Costa Rica as in Guatemala and, practically also in the whole of Central America, as I said before, feeling was running very high not only against Dollar Diplomacy but also against the American Government. Public demonstrations were being made all over the country. Even the legislative body addressed itself to the rest of the Latin-American republics on behalf of Nicaragua. The banana companies (which a noted Austrian traveler had compared a few years ago to a giant octopus, stealthily extending its tentacles over the coasts of the Caribbean Sea in order to strangle the life out of the Central American republics, Santo Domingo, Haiti, etc., and which are considered, therefore, by those countries to be the forerunners of Dollar Diplomacy) were seemingly delighted when Mr. Jimenez assumed the Presidency of Costa Rica. The Costa Ricans themselves, however, soon changed their minds as to the advisability of having elected him. They came near stoning him when he dared only to insinuate that he was thinking about whether it might be convenient or not to recognize the fake Diaz régime in Nicaragua! It may be added here, too, that the late President of El Salvador (another tool of Dollar Diplomacy) who sold to the Diaz Government a considerable amount of war material, to be used against the Nicaraguan Constitutionalists, has been practically run out of the country.

In San José I had the pleasure of meeting among other old friends of mine, General Pinaud, Colonel Noriega, Colombian Chargé d'Affaires; and Father Maehler, of the Order of the Paulists, who served with us as army chaplain in Mesopotamia during the World War.

I have heard lately, with considerable concern, that the next victim of Dollar Diplomacy is probably going to be Costa Rica on account of her water-rights in the

San Juan River, of which she does not intend to let go except on terms which *fully guarantee her independence!* As such terms would not be helpful to Dollar Diplomacy's Central-American policy, I would not be surprised if ex-President Tinoco or some other adventurer of his caliber, backed up by American marines, should start "something," and very soon, in Costa Rica, even at the expense of a few thousand lives, if necessary. Latin-American lives do not matter!

One evening, while I was with Col. Noriega in the Teatro Nacional, Dr. Urcuyo rushed up and told me that if I went immediately to Puerto Limon and embarked for Panama, I had a chance yet of catching up with the motor-schooner *La Linda* which was expected to leave Colon almost any day for Puerto Cabezas. There was my chance!

Three days later I landed in Colon, but *La Linda*, due to counter orders, was forced to remain there for another week, and so was I, of course. I took advantage of this forced delay, naturally, in order to look over the situation, talk with old friends, and gather reliable information.

I heard bitter complaints about the means being used to enforce the new treaty on the unhappy people of Panama. Coercion is by far too mild, in fact, too decent, an expression to be used in connection with this latest example of highbindery. According to what I heard in Colon, most, maybe even all, the Panama laborers employed in the Canal Zone had been dismissed and replaced by colored laborers from the West Indies, as a punishment—because the Panama National Assembly had refused to swallow that monstrous treaty which, according to the Panama Delegates, to whom it had been submitted, is imperialistic, high-handed and one-sided in every respect. They claim that they protested against its imposition as long as they could, but finally the treaty was virtually rammed down their throats. What a crime! To deprive perhaps thousands of honest laborers and their families of their daily bread in order to force a friendly people to its knees, because it has dared to stand up for its rights and for its freedom! I hardly remember to have read anything so low and so cowardly before in the history of the world!

Dissatisfied with the articles which made Panama virtually a vassal state of Dollar Diplomacy, the delegates served notice last fall that they would demur at signing the treaty *which had been drafted almost entirely by the War Department!* When the day came for the final meeting with Mr. Francis White, now Assistant Secretary of State, who was then in charge of the Latin-American Relations, White, according to the delegates, told them that they either sign or they might find some day *that the United States would occupy the Canal Zone and seize by force what the Panamans were being asked to yield in the treaty!*

The Municipal Council of Colon condemned the treaty, and the Panama Chamber of Commerce cabled Senator Borah, Chairman of the Senate Foreign Relations Committee, asking him to make the treaty the subject of a senatorial investigation.

At any rate, the upshot is that it is very doubtful whether the Panama National Assembly in its forthcoming session will ratify it. It is useless for the State Department to try to appease the Panamans by promising to restrict the *American Commissaries,* over which Panama merchants have been bitterly complaining on the ground that these American agencies sell in a way that makes it impossible for the Panamans to compete. It is also significant that during the last meeting of the Pan-American Federation of Labor a resolution was presented and passed, if I am not mistaken, to the effect that the Panaman laborers who had been dismissed from the Canal Zone should be reinstated in their former positions.

One of the many factors which have contributed powerfully toward making the Panamans lose faith in the United States is a certain adventurer by the name, I believe, of Mr. March, who willfully instigated and fanned the rebellion of the Tules, or San Blas Indians, against the Government of Panama (February 19-22, 1925) which resulted in the massacre of about a dozen or two Panaman gendarmes, most of them college youths.

It is also significant that it was the United States cruiser *Cleveland* which was rushed to the scene ahead of the Panama punitive expedition, and took Mr. March to the Cocos Naval Base, I think, protecting him thus from the drastic action which otherwise would have been taken against him by the Courts of Justice of Panama. I do not remember having heard that March was punished by the American Government for that massacre in Panama. In fact, was he not presently bamboozling the American press and public with some diseased albinos whom he introduced as the (legendary) White Indians of South America?

The Panamans have not forgotten either how, during a concert given by a Japanese military band in the Plaza of Panama City, some five years ago, the Americans of the civil and military services saluted when the Japanese and American national hymns were played, but none of them saluted or even rose to his feet while the Panama hymn was played. The Japanese were strongly of the impression that the

Americans wished the Panamans to understand that they had no right to have a national hymn of their own. I was present at that concert so I am not speaking from hearsay.

Before closing this chapter I wish to call the attention of the American public to the fact that the city of Colon has a colony of about one thousand Chinamen; Panama City has about four thousand, and the whole Republic of Panama has no less than ten thousand Chinese citizens, most of them natives of Hongkong or Southern China and members of the Kuo-Ming-tong, which means of the anti-foreign Nationalist Party in China. Besides the ten thousand Chinamen, there are said to be about eight thousand East Indians and six thousand Japanese in Panama, or from twenty to twenty-five thousand Asiatics, as compared with the American garrison of the Canal Zone which probably does not exceed eighteen thousand men.

With over twenty thousand Asiatics at the very doors of the Panama Canal is it wise of the United States Government to keep on oppressing the people of Panama? There is no such thing as a small enemy! A small nation, holding a strategic position, is likely to become over night a formidable foe if driven to despair. Belgium proved that!

It never pays to play the bully, for some day, usually when you least expect it, somebody comes around and calls the bluff!

Chapter VI

My Arrival at Puerto Cabezas — Dr. J. B. Sacasa and His Cabinet — Pleasant Intercourse With Lt.-Commander Bischoff and United States Navy Officers — The Father of Dollar Diplomacy — Some of H. O. Arguello's Written Statements About Wall Street's Activities in Nicaragua.

SOMETIME about the latter part of March I took passage for Puerto Cabezas on the sixty-ton gasoline schooner *La Linda,* Captain Surgeon; and on the third day, about noon, we sighted the Mosquito Coast, like a dark green shadow along the western horizon. After a while the towers of a wireless station commenced to rise slowly above that gloomy screen of everglades, announcing that we were approaching our goal, the little town and harbor of Puerto Cabezas, at that time the seat of Vice-President Sacasa's Government.

The trip had been everything but pleasant, to me at least; for the malodorous company of my fellow travelers, all of them negro laborers from the West Indies, contracted by the Bragman's Bluff Lumber Company, had not contributed to the well-being of my olfactory nerves nor heightened my appetite.

An hour later we sighted the three smokestacks of the Lumber Company, belching forth black clouds of smoke, and after a while, also silhouetted on the evening sky, the roofs of the Company's buildings, then its mile-long wharf. Alongside the wharf, two white fruit steamers were loading bananas from a halting train while, a few hundred yards away, surrounded by a swarm of schooners and other coasting craft, the

United States gunboat *Tulsa* and a torpedo-destroyer were gracefully riding at anchor.

We were not allowed to land until next morning for some reason or other. I took advantage of this circumstance to have the captain announce my arrival to Dr. Sacasa.

Next day, while I was chatting with an American sentry on the wharf, Col. Zacarias, the Liberal military governor of Puerto Cabezas, came to greet me, and, an hour later, I hung up my hammock and made myself at home in the house of a German merchant by the name of Mr. Wendt. He and Mr. Fuchs, who also owned a big store in town, took care of me from that day in a really magnificent way. Their ice boxes were constantly filled with fresh imported Lager, and they were not stingy about it either. Wendt, Fuchs and the veteran Mr. Rossmann were respectively the president and the first and second vice-presidents of the "Deutscher Verein," which was not much of a Verein if you consider that it consisted only of six members—four Germans and two Austrians. But though small in numbers, they were certainly living up to their old German traditions of a hospitable and happy life.

At about 11 A.M. I went to call on Vice-President Sacasa, who received me courteously and invited me to return that same afternoon to drink a glass of champagne with him and the members of his Cabinet. I could see that Sacasa was a gentleman so far as social standards are concerned, but, of course, it takes more than a day to penetrate a man's mind. The impression made by his personality and good breeding was very favorable. However, I did not feel that I had been in the presence of a strong, decisive character. Perhaps I am over quick to suspect insincerity wherever I see signs of the, after all, quite common capacity to wobble. A sincere weak man is no use at the top of the line anywhere. It is his weakness, not his sincerity, which he will display at crucial moments. Out of that flawed timber is the whole school of "well-meaning" professional politicians made. I had an uneasy feeling that Sacasa belonged to that school.

That uneasy feeling which took hold of me when I first shook hands with Vice-President Sacasa (for unless he resigns he will remain, until January 1, 1929, the legally elected Vice-President of Nicaragua!) turned out later not to have been altogether unjustified for, from what I learned in Managua and Guatemala, Dr. Sacasa has not been always the zealous defender of the Nicaraguan Constitution which he appeared to be at that time. The following extracts taken from an article which was published in the *Excelsior* of Guatemala on July 15, 1927, go to show very plainly that Dr. Sacasa became Vice-President solely because he befriended the conservative President, Bartolome Martinez, in a crucial hour. Without President Martinez's *official support* Dr. Sacasa would probably never have been elected Vice-President; because he was not a big enough man for that job, according to public opinion in Nicaragua.

Here are the extracts from the *Excelsior* to which I refer:

"In November, 1923, Dr. Sacasa, together with six liberals and six conservatives, proposed and tried to force the reëlection of President Bartolome Martinez, although he knew very well that such an act was contrary to the Nicaraguan Constitution. He even agreed with his twelve companions to submit the case (that is, this flagrant case of breach of the Constitution) *to the consideration of the American Government!* Notwithstanding he did not hesitate for a minute, later on, to head the so-called Constitutionalist Government.

"While being Vice-President of the Republic, Dr. Sacasa never moved a finger or even protested *in any way* when President Carlos Solorzano (under pressure from the usurper Emiliano Chamorro) asked the United States Government *not* to withdraw the American marines from Nicaragua, nor did he *even try, for a moment,* to go to Solorzano's rescue, despite all the efforts of the Labor party which fairly *beseeched* him to do so, and even offered him all the necessary money, arms and ammunition to organize an army of volunteers. [This is supported by a verbal statement to the same effect made recently to me, in New York, by Mr. S. de la Selva, Secretary of the Nicaraguan Labor Union.]

"After his arrival at Puerto Cabezas, as announced by a cable transmitted in February, 1927, Dr. Sacasa made declarations by which he practically recognized the validity of the Byran-Chamorro Treaty, and, as early as December, 1926, he had practically and tacitly agreed already also to the establishment of Admiral Latimer's neutral zones.

"In December, 1925, Dr. Sacasa went to Washington, D. C., where he remained until May, 1926, *soliciting the favor* of the United States Government, despite the fact that that same American Government continued forcibly intervening in Nicaragua.

"The reason why Sacasa remained idle in Guatemala from May until November, 1926, was because he was apparently obeying orders from Dollar Diplomacy *not to go to Nicaragua to establish a Constitutionalist government!* This assertion has been verified by a detailed exposition to that effect which the rebel general Beltran-Sandoval published, in June last, in the Liberal paper *La Noticia*, of Managua. Beltran-Sandoval said among other things . . .: 'Shortly after our arrival at La Barra, and after having discussed the matter thoroughly with the generals, Moncada and Carlos Pasas, I went by way of Puerto Barrios to Guatemala City in order to convince Dr. Sacasa of the necessity of his going to Puerto Cabezas to establish a Constitutionalist government. I explained to him the way the revolution was progressing and the great advantages which it would derive from the establishment of such a government. But Dr. Sacasa would not listen. He was apparently too busy trying to adjust matters in a peaceable way. All my efforts to convince him were absolutely useless, despite the fact that all Nicaraguan Liberals resident in Guatemala agreed with me that the establishment of a Constitutionalist government on Nicaraguan soil was absolutely necessary. Seeing that I was only wasting my time, I returned to La Barra.'"

The preceding statements indicate that Dr. Sacasa's later efforts to defend the Constitutionalist Government should not be taken too seriously and, therefore also, that he is not the man who can throw the first stone at President Carlos Solorzano for having asked the American Government *not* to withdraw the marines from Managua. Solorzano was forced to this step by the usurper, Emiliano Chamorro, who, entrenched in the fortress of Tiscapa (and in order to extort new decrees, to his liking, from President Solorzano), used to have the electric lights of Managua turned out at night, and infantry and artillery fire opened on Solorzano's presidential mansion, killing

The Author (left), Dr. Juan Bautista Sacasa (center) and Dr. Cordero Reyes, at Puerto Cabezas, Nicaragua.

Some of the dead, after the fight at Puerto Cabezas, Nicaragua.

passers-by and other innocent people of the neighborhood by the score. Solorzano, so as to stop the bloodshed, finally had to sanction, one after another, the numerous decrees which that pet of Dollar Diplomacy, Emiliano Chamorro, kept on extorting from him in that cowardly way. Through all this, Vice-President Sacasa, without ever thinking of going to Solorzano's rescue, remained tranquilly in Leon, talking about politics. Not much wonder that Solorzano, tired of waiting for Sacasa to act, threw up the sponge, resigned at last and went away, leaving Emiliano Chamorro in possession of the country.

Under such circumstances it is not at all surprising that José Maria Moncada (who is in reality only a newspaperman posing as a soldier) should have taken, later on, all the advantage he could of Dr. Sacasa's lack of character in order to feather his own nest. He did this by betraying and sacrificing the Liberal army—which Sacasa had entrusted to him—in the hope that Dollar Diplomacy would appoint him President of Nicaragua at the next "election"—during which American troops, as usual, would guarantee impartiality and no corruption!

When I went back to Dr. Sacasa's headquarters that afternoon I was presented by him to the members of his Cabinet. Among them I was most favorably impressed by the Secretary of State, Dr. Leonardo Arguello, who was a noted physician as well as a well-known writer, and by the Secretary of Foreign Affairs, Dr. Rodolfo Espinosa, who was also a physician, distinguished in his profession, and of some renown as an orator. Dr. Espinosa has spent part of his life in Europe and in the United States. Either of these gentlemen would have made, I imagine, a far better president than Dr. Sacasa. But fate willed it differently, maybe for the good of Nicaragua, for, with the fall of Sacasa's Government, a new Nicaragua has been born. Traitors and tricky politicians of the old school, like Moncada, Diaz and Chamorro, who look out only for their own personal interests, are being supplanted rapidly by disinterested patriots like General Sandino, for instance, who scorn political jobs and graft, but love their country dearly and are ready to fight and die, if necessary, on the battle field or on the scaffold for its independence.

That is what the new Nicaraguan Nationalist movement stands for! It is men of this sort whom Dollar Diplomacy will have to face in a near future, not only in Nicaragua but all over Central America and the Antilles, for Labor and the intellectual elements in these countries are rapidly combining, because they realize that such is the only means of saving their republics from the talons of Dollar Diplomacy.

The remaining members of Dr. Sacasa's Cabinet were:

Dr. Arturo Ortega, lawyer, Secretary of Finance
Dr. Onofre Sandoval, lawyer, Secretary of Public Works
Dr. Modesto Armijo, lawyer, Secretary of Public Instruction
Dr. J. Ramirez Brown, lawyer, Subsecretary of Foreign Affairs
Dr. Antonio Flores Vega, lawyer, Subsecretary of State
Don Julio Portocarrero, economist, Subsecretary of Finance
Dr. Arturo Baca, lawyer, Subsecretary of War
Dr. Ramiro Gamez, M.D., Subsecretary of Public Works

Don Hernan Robledo, author, Subsecretary of Public Instruction
Dr. Manuel Cordero Reyes, lawyer, Secretary to the President
Don H. Ofilio Arguello, writer, Counselor to the President

Among these gentlemen, several of whom belong to the old aristocracy, there was not a single one who did not receive me as a friend, who did not open his heart to me. Some of them I met again afterwards in Guatemala, when they had exiled themselves once more, voluntarily, rather than submit to that perfect rubber stamp of Dollar Diplomacy, that arch-enemy of their country, Adolfo Diaz.

However, it is not only of Dr. Sacasa's Cabinet and the rest of the members of his Staff in Puerto Cabezas that I retain the kindest recollections. There were others who treated me royally and like a friend. These were the officers of the American Landing Forces, L. B. Bischoff, Lt.-Commander, U. S. A., E. C. Robbins, First Lt., U. S. M. C., the Ensigns A. Cunningham, M. R. Patterson, W. E. Terry and F. S. Wither, Paymaster. I am still keeping as a souvenir the first invitation they sent me. It said—"If you should be at leisure, the Commanding Officer and Officers of the Landing Force would enjoy having you lunch with them to-day. March 21, 1927."

From what I could see, the conduct of the officers and men of the American Landing forces in Puerto Cabezas, at the time I was there, was absolutely correct. I never heard even the slightest complaint. I never saw a drunken sailor or marine. Commander Bischoff and the other officers were also exceedingly considerate toward Dr. Sacasa, although they never addressed him as President or Vice-President, but simply as Dr. Sacasa. Real prohibition was enforced in Bischoff's headquarters. I never tasted or saw there a drop of liquor.

The behavior of Commander Bischoff, his officers and men, who were only doing their duty under orders, was a new proof to me that it is unjust to hold the United States Army and Navy in general responsible for the crimes committed by certain American Military Authorities in Haiti, Santo Domingo, and elsewhere. The responsibility for those deplorable crimes lies, in my estimation, not so much with the army or navy men who committed them but with their Commanding and Superior officers who, instead of submitting them immediately to a regular court-martial, used leniency where they should not have used it, and even tried to whitewash them so as to keep public opinion in the United States from knowing the real facts. This whitewashing or suppressing process was on in Haiti when Senator King was refused admittance to that country, because he intended to conduct some investigations, as I understand it.

Such misplaced leniency has been the real cause of the unsavory reputation which attaches to the American Marines and, therefore, also to the United States Army and Navy, not only in Latin America, if particularly there. Such leniency is, I venture to say, not only unsoldiery but also anti-patriotic in the extreme. The discipline of Lieutenant-Commander Bischoff's men at Puerto Cabezas proves again that when the officers are right so are the men.

From the written information which I managed to gather not only in Puerto Cabezas but afterwards also in Managua and abroad, I have the impression that if it had not been for the boundless ambition of the late American Secretary of State, Mr. Philander Knox, Dollar Diplomacy would never have been able to raise havoc with poor Nicaragua (both morally and materially) the way it has done during the seventeen years of American armed intervention. The following data, taken mainly from the records of the State Department, are self-explanatory. Anybody can understand why H. Blanco Fombona and other noted Latin-American and European writers and publicists have christened Secretary Knox "the Father of Dollar Diplomacy."

1907—Central American Court of Justice created under joint auspices of United States and Mexico.

1909, October 7th: American Consul at Bluefields, Nicaragua, wires State Department that "a revolution will start in Bluefields on the 8th," that the revolutionists "propose to protect the property of foreigners," and that General Emiliano Chamorro (who, with J. J. Estrada and Adolfo Diaz, the latter secretary at one thousand five hundred dollars per year of an American mining company, was to lead the revolution) has just "landed secretly from Costa Rica."

October 12th: Consul wires State Department that the revolution occurred on the 10th; that "foreign business interests are enthusiastic," that "immediate reduction of tariff is assured," also the annulment of "all concessions NOT OWNED BY FOREIGNERS!"

December 1st: Secretary Knox withdraws recognition of the Nicaraguan Government, stating "that the government of the United States is convinced that the revolution represents the ideals and the will of a majority of the Nicaraguan people more faithfully than does the government of President Zelaya."

December 16th: President Zelaya resigns, naming Madriz, also of the Liberal party, to succeed him.

1910, May 16th: Madriz' armed forces, having swept all Nicaragua, call upon Estrada to surrender his last stronghold at Bluefields.

May 16th (the same day!): U. S. S. *Paducah* declares Bluefields a neutral zone.

May 31st: United States prohibits interference with American ships carrying arms to Estrada in Bluefields; insists that Customs duties be paid to Estrada faction, not to Madriz.

August 20th: Madriz resigns; Estrada enters capital and declares himself President; his first official act is to cable Secretary Knox that the victorious party "entertains warm regard for the American people."

September 12th: Estrada promises to ask for an American loan.

October 11th: Department of State *offers aid* in securing loan from American bankers, *suggests foreign control of customs* and *offers* service of *confidential financial agent!*

October 18th: Thomas C. Dawson arrives as special Agent of the United States.

October 27th: "Dawson Pact" signed on board United States battleship by Nicaraguan conservative leaders, promising loan, American Customs control and a Claims Commission—one member to be appointed by Nicaragua, two by United States—to settle American claims against Nicaragua; and agreeing upon election of Estrada and Adolfo Diaz as President and Vice-President.

After reading the preceding lines anybody, with no matter how little common sense, ought to be able to see the cat in the bag.

In order to show that the successors of Secretary Knox, both Republican and Democrat, have been faithfully following the KNOX DOCTRINE, I reproduce the following statement of Dr. T. S. Vaca, published in the Philadelphia *Record* of January 8, 1927 . . . "When presidential elections were about to be held in Nicaragua, in 1916, B. F. Jefferson, American Minister at Managua, called into conference the leaders of the political parties opposed to the Diaz administration and informed them *that no candidate for the presidency would be acceptable unless he personally agreed to abide by certain propositions!*—and in view of this the several parties decided to withdraw from the presidential elections. This was precisely what the American Minister desired in order to leave a clear field for the official candidate, Emiliano Chamorro, who had no followers outside the Diaz administration."

As the object of this book is to let North and Latin America know not only my own viewpoint of the Nicaraguan imbroglio, but also the opinions of others who know just as much or more perhaps than I do about that complicated question, I am going to set down certain parts of an outline of Nicaraguan history which was furnished to me in Puerto Cabezas by Mr. H. Ofilio Arguello, a graduate of Columbia University and counselor to Vice-President Sacasa:

"Inasmuch as the attention of Latin America and of the whole world has been focused upon Nicaragua during the last few weeks, and that the majority of the United States papers have so nobly come forward and aided their readers in forming an opinion of the salient facts of the Nicaraguan controversy, I shall be as brief as possible and only give a general résumé of so-called *Dollar Diplomacy,* from its inception and its injection into Nicaraguan politics, up to the present day. Its effect upon the present generation is clear, and it will have a far-reaching, disastrous effect for innumerable years to come on the friendly relations that Latin-American countries have done their best to cultivate with the United States in the past three decades, and which the United States has done its best TO NULLIFY THROUGH A FOREIGN POLICY THAT HAS BEEN NEITHER CONSISTENT NOR JUST to the weaker nations which it seeks to control and to bend to its will, as though they were merely vassal states whom it can rule and tread upon, as it sees fit, whenever political advantages or commercial expediency demand it.

"Secretary of State P. C. Knox was the father and sponsor of DOLLAR DIPLOMACY as applied to Nicaragua. For some obscure reason, which is commonly believed throughout Central America to have been his financial interest in the La Luz and Los Angeles Mining Co., whose headquarters, in 1909, were in Bluefields, Nicaragua, he decided to establish a Conservative Government in Nicaragua, instead of the Liberal one, and he used Adolfo Diaz, who was an insignificant employee of the La Luz and Los Angeles Mining Co., to further his plans of conquest. Diaz at that time was being paid the paltry salary of one thousand five hundred dollars per annum, but he blossomed forth as a millionaire overnight, for he advanced to Juan B. Estrada, who had risen in arms against the Nicaraguan Government of President Zelaya, the sum of six hundred thousand dollars, which was spent for war equipment, materials and payrolls of the Estrada Army. The Estrada rebellion was defeated throughout the county and finally reduced to the town of Bluefields; but, when this port was surrounded by land and blockaded by sea, Secretary Knox sent warships from the United States, landed marines, declared Bluefields a 'neutral zone' to protect, as he

THE LOOTING OF NICARAGUA

stated, 'American lives and property' WHICH HAVE NEVER BEEN IN DANGER. By the use of these unfair means and devious methods he kept the Estrada-Diaz revolution alive and threatened to land ten thousand marines more if he deemed it necessary. After six months of ineffectual fighting against the Conservative friends and tools of Secretary Knox, backed by the naval forces of the United States, the Liberal government finally gave up and the Conservatives seized the country and have remained in power ever since that time against the will of an overwhelming majority of the Nicaraguans. Marines were also landed on the Pacific Coast and sent to Managua, capital of Nicaragua, ostensibly as a guard for the American Legation, but, in reality, because the puppet Conservative government forced upon Nicaragua by Secretary Knox *was, is and always will be* unpopular and *intensely hated* in Nicaragua. These American marines have been, ever since that time, the mainstay and raison d'être of the Conservative governments which have succeeded one another in Nicaragua.

"General Juan Bautista Estrada, who was the first president inaugurated under the rule of the marines, was soon kicked out of the presidency, and Adolfo Diaz, Secretary Knox's former employee and willing tool, became the president instead. Under his master's orders he transferred the bank and the railroads owned by the Nicaraguan Government to a banking syndicate in New York controlled by J. and W. Seligman & Co., and by Brown Brothers & Co., both well-known banking firms in Wall Street. The Foreign Debt of Nicaragua was at the time approximately thirty-four million PAPER PESOS which, converted into gold currency, would amount to a little over three million dollars ($3,000,000.00). Conservatives like to boast of how they have made Nicaragua progress, have paid the foreign debt, etc. Nothing can possibly be further from the truth; Nicaraguans know it. Nicaragua, under the Conservative régime of the past sixteen years, *has gone back at least half a century.* Public schools, which had been established by the Liberal governments through the entire country, have been closed wholesale, *and the money formerly devoted to public instruction is used to subsidize Jesuit schools, and parochial schools owned, controlled and supervised by Jesuits and Catholic priests* in three or four of the largest cities in the country. Concessions of an utterly ruinous character have been given time and again by the Conservative governments to powerful American companies, which have merely exploited the natural resources of the country for their own benefit without any advantage whatsoever to Nicaragua. These concessions, however, have been the price which the banking interests, controlling the Conservative governments of Nicaragua, have exacted from all of them, *threatening them with the withdrawal of the marines which would have meant their downfall within a few days.* And this price has been gladly and gratefully paid by the Conservative governments, in their eagerness to remain in power, regardless of the consequences which the country has had to bear and suffer through so many long years.

"The threat of the marines, who have been mounting guard at the American Legation since 1909, and of the many more thousands which could be rushed to Nicaragua on a minute's notice, has, logically, meant practical slavery to the free-born citizens of Nicaragua, who are not allowed to protect themselves in any way nor to express their will at the polls which are controlled by the Conservatives and supervised by the United States Marines.

"Doctor Solorzano's and Dr. Sacasa's advent to the Presidency and Vice-Presidency as the result of a coalition government, which defeated the Conservatives by an overwhelming majority at the elections held in 1924, was hailed by the Nicaraguan people as the dawn of a new era. Conservative administrations had caused *more than thirty thousand Nicaraguans to emigrate* to Central America in order to escape persecutions, exactions and imprisonment. Unfortunately Nicaragua was sadly disappointed in its expectation of fair play. The Government of the United States and the State Department had deliberately decided to continue their traditional policy and were backing the Conservative party. Emiliano Chamorro, head of the Conservative party, under the guidance of the notorious Adolfo Diaz, who is looked upon as the 'brains' of the Conservative party on account of his connections with the banking firms of Wall Street, bribed his way into the fortress of Tiscapa in Managua, which was in the custody of his friends, compelling Carlos Solorzano, the president, to come to terms with him, and by force became the military dictator and virtual ruler of the country toward the end of 1925. He sent two thousand men to Leon, where Vice-President Sacasa made his home, with the order to bring him back dead or alive, so as to make him also resign. Dr. Sacasa managed to escape, fortunately, and went by way of El Salvador and Guatemala to Washington, D. C., where he stated his case in writing to all the governments of Central America, and to the American Government, which had sponsored the Treaties of Peace and Amity signed by the

Republics of Central America in Washington, in February, 1923.

"Dr. Sacasa made his home in Washington, D. C., from December 25 to May 26, hoping that the *'moral pressure,'* which the American Government asserted was being brought to bear on General Chamorro would reëstablish constitutional government in Nicaragua and restore him to his country as the legal President, since Carlos Solorzano had been forced to resign his post as president. But Chamorro only laughed when 'moral pressure' was talked of in his presence. He stated repeatedly that he did not care whether the United States ever recognized him or not.

"The wrongs that the Nicaraguan people had suffered and continued to suffer under the Conservative governments supported by the United States had been so unbearable that the reign of terror inaugurated by General Chamorro could not last. 'Moral pressure' having proved a miserable failure, the Liberals rose in arms and wired to President Sacasa in Washington (in May, 1926) to assume the Presidency and lead them to victory. The first attempt was unsuccessful because Dr. Sacasa was utterly unprepared and unaware of what had been going on during his absence,— WHILE HE WAS PATIENTLY WAITING IN WASHINGTON, D. C., for the effect of the so-called 'moral pressure,' which the American Government seemed to think sufficient to solve the problem, but which General Chamorro sneered at and ridiculed in Managua. A second uprising in August, 1926, met with success on the Atlantic Coast of Nicaragua, and the Chamorro forces were routed from every place on the coast with the exception of Bluefields, where the American Government promptly established a 'neutral zone' before the Constitutionalist army, busy at other points, could

THE LOOTING OF NICARAGUA

capture it from Chamorro. The whole country, although ill equipped for war on the Pacific slope, rose against Chamorro when they heard of the Constitutionalist triumph on the Atlantic Coast.

"General Chamorro, who could not get along indefinitely without the recognition of the American Government, called into consultation his guide, philosopher and friend—Adolfo Diaz—and a brilliant plan, which was probably hatched in Wall Street and put forth by Diaz as his own, was discussed. Chamorro was to resign in favor of one of his friends, and his friend, in turn, would resign and hand the presidency of Nicaragua to Adolfo Diaz, who, with the aid of the Wall Street bankers, would be able to bring enough pressure to bear upon the government at Washington to receive recognition in a short time. And exactly what J. and W. Seligman & Co. and Brown Bros. & Co. had planned, *to again enslave the Nicaraguan people,* has happened, according to schedule. Chamorro resigned the 'de facto' government to Senator Sebastian Uriza and, within a few days, Uriza, after Congress and the Supreme Court had been tampered with, so that they would not interfere with these illegal proceedings, handed the presidency to Adolfo Diaz, the intimate friend and inside partner of the Wall Street bankers. Secretary Kellogg, who must have followed step by step this devious process, who received written memoranda and protests advising him of all that was being done in Nicaragua, whose sources of information must be better than those of the average citizen—in spite of the weighty evidence presented to him against the crookedness of Diaz and Chamorro, and of their Wall Street allies and friends—*promptly recognized Adolfo Diaz* as the legitimate President of Nicaragua. Mr. Kellogg has thus betrayed the trust and implicit faith that Nicaraguan citizens had put in him, but he has also betrayed the faith of the American people whose love of justice and fair play has raised such a storm of protest in the newspapers of the United States for several weeks.

"In the meantime the banker friends of Adolfo Diaz had not been idle. They had taken particular pains to guard what they considered as their own interests first, and those of their tender protégé, Adolfo Diaz, also; naturally enough they expect juicy contracts, exceedingly profitable concessions and other trifles of that nature from him that will enable them to clip coupons for years at the expense of the Nicaraguan people whom they look upon as serfs or slaves. By means of wires which those bankers, through long years of practice, are able to pull without attracting too much undesirable public attention, they managed to have the Navy Department of the United States send six warships, six destroyers, etc., to Nicaragua, and to land hundreds of marines at Puerto Cabezas, Rio Grande, Bluefields and several other places along the Atlantic and Pacific Coasts, where they might be needed in order to protect their friend and associate, Adolfo Diaz, and, especially, to intimidate by a display of tremendous force the Constitutionalist army which had been winning victories during two months wherever they had met the Diaz forces.

"These methods, which are so manifestly unfair and virtually amount to a declaration of war on the Constitutionalist Government, did not seem sufficiently effective since this policy of intimidation was decided upon and, within the last few weeks, in order to hamper the Constitutionalist forces, the marines seized by force at La Barra two million rounds of ammunition and seven hundred rifles belonging to the Constitutionalists and deliberately dumped them into the Rio Grande so as to deprive the Nicaraguan Liberals of their precious war materials, and leave them at the mercy of the Diaz forces. Moreover the United States Navy has established a blockade of the Atlantic littoral (which is held by the Liberals), and several war vessels continue cruising up and down the coasts of Nicaragua to prevent war materials, provisions and even medicines for its hospitals from reaching the Liberal army. The marines went even further. On December 23d, a force of marines (about five hundred) surrounded the house where Dr. Sacasa and his Cabinet had their headquarters, disarmed them and the few who were with the President as his guard of honor, *and ordered Dr. Sacasa and his friends to leave Puerto Cabezas within six hours!* Dr. Sacasa refused, of course, to obey such an order which was given him verbally by a representative of Rear Admiral Latimer. The officer who made this notification was *Captain Lewis of the cruiser Cleveland* and he stated that *Admiral Latimer had received instructions from the government in Washington to oust Dr. Sacasa and the Constitutionalists from Puerto Cabezas!* A very significant fact that ought to be taken into consideration is that *whenever an Admiral or any officer of the naval forces of the United States does or attempts to do anything that is illegal or unjust,* as in the case just mentioned, they may state and do state *verbally* that they have received orders from the American Government or from the Department of State, *but they invariably refuse to give these notifications in writing* as should, and would, be done in every case by diplomatic representatives of the United States Government, whose places these Admirals or officers of the

Navy are supposed to fill. Those of us who have been privileged to witness some of these outrages sincerely believe that the officers did not receive instructions from the Government in Washington, and that they are trying by means of bluff, coercion and intimidation to help Adolfo Diaz and his friends, the bankers of Wall Street, for their own exceedingly personal and none too disinterested reasons!"

Chapter VII

Copies of Documents, Proving the Similarity of Views of Several Prominent North and Latin-American Statesmen and the Majority of the Honest American Press, in Regard to the Nicaraguan Imbroglio.

IN the September (1927) number of *Current History* I read, with amazement, the following lines in an article by Mr. William Jennings Price, former United States Minister Plenipotentiary to Panama, whom *Current History* considers, apparently, an *authority* on Nicaraguan affairs, since it publishes his essay in its September number, which is dedicated *exclusively* to Latin America:

"Referring to the recent strife in Nicaragua, there appears in the *Congressional Record* of last session the following observations quoted from Col. Weitzel, former American Minister to that Republic: 'One who is not a deserving Democrat may, perhaps, be permitted to say in justice to Mr. Bryan that if the Senate had accepted his amendment (*adding a provision like the Platt Amendment*) to the Nicaraguan Canal Treaty, the Nicaraguan problem would have been settled without bloodshed.'"

Now let us see what Mr. H. Ofilio Arguello has got to say, in his letter of March 20, 1927, to Senator Burton K. Wheeler about that same Col. Weitzel, ex-American Minister to Nicaragua.

"Puerto Cabezas, March 20, 1927.
"Hon. Burton K. Wheeler, Esq., etc.
"The brilliant, masterly speech which you delivered in the United States Senate on January 26, 1927, on

behalf of the sovereignty and people of Nicaragua has been translated into Spanish, and it will be soon reproduced in the press throughout the breadth and length of Latin America.

"You have analyzed the policy, or, rather, the lack of any definite policy, towards Latin America with uncanny accuracy and have placed the blame for it where it belongs, i.e., on the shoulders of the Department of State and the New York banking groups which manipulate it and direct its policies. It would be interesting to know how many of the members of the Department of State (Latin-American Division) have, at some time or another, been employed by the banking syndicates of Wall Street, and how many former employees of the Department of State *have been taken care of* by the banking firms of Wall Street after their usefulness as Dollar Diplomats in Washington had ceased. No one who has kept in touch with events in Latin America in the last twenty years can doubt that the banking firms of Wall Street and the Department of State in Washington have worked in perfect harmony for the purpose of forcing the peoples of Central America to accept whatever 'government' the Wall Street firms decided should rule each and every one of these countries." [1]

Mr. Arguello goes on to say that the American Minister to Nicaragua was well rewarded by the conservative party of that country for services rendered to them at the time when Dollar Diplomacy commenced to exert its active influence in Nicaragua and continues:

"Mr. Weitzel is still (naturally) an ardent advocate

---

[1] I am in possession of a copy of this letter also signed by Mr. H. O. Arguello, given to me for the purpose of having it published.

of Dollar Diplomacy, and he made a speech about six weeks ago, published in a New York paper, heartily approving and defending the attitude of the Department of State.

"He has had several worthy successors at that post, but the 'king-maker,' Lawrence Dennis, is undoubtedly the crackerjack of them all. Although Mr. Dennis was supposed to preside at the Corinto Peace Conference, what he really did was to aid and abet the Conservative Delegates in their stubborn attitude not to accept any of the peace proposals made by the Liberal Delegates, and to stand pat on the formula 'Adolfo Diaz or nothing.' He is directly responsible for the failure of the Peace Conference of Corinto. It is ludicrous for us to learn through the newspapers that this same Mr. Dennis has tendered his resignation as Dollar Diplomat and qualified his resignation with the statement that 'only rich men receive favors at the hands of the Department of State.' Although there is every reason to believe that the Conservatives, whom he has served so well in Nicaragua, have rewarded his zeal and devotion to their 'Cause,' it is the general opinion in Latin America that a man of his caliber cannot very well be spared by the bankers and that he will land some nice position in Wall Street before long. [This appears to have happened.]

"In spite of all the 'neutral zones,' forces of occupation sent to cities to enable Diaz to muster larger forces against the Liberals while the American marines hold the cities for him, and all the hindrances and hostilities which have been specially devised to help Diaz, the Liberals have continued their advance and severely defeated the Diaz forces wherever they have met them, capturing from them enormous quantities of machine guns, ammunitions and stores. The

Liberals are now less than forty miles from Managua, where Diaz is guarded by American marines and upheld by the Department of State and the American Minister, Mr. Eberhart. When Diaz' Army is routed, as it surely will be within the next few days, the American marines will probably take the field against the people of Nicaragua and crush the so-called 'rebellion' for Diaz, the Department of State and for Brown Bros. and Seligman & Co. of Wall Street. [The outcome was as herein predicted.]

"The American Minister in Managua has declared that the marines will not interfere with Nicaraguans in their military operations against Diaz 'unless they are attacked;' but those of us who have had experience with the subterfuges of Dollar Diplomacy feel certain that this unqualified 'unless they are attacked' will, in the end, mean just this: a group of Diaz soldiers will be carefully instructed to approach some American Detachment either in the outskirts of Managua, Masaya, Chinandega or Leon, fire a few shots in the air, or, if it is thought necessary, right at the marines, and run away to avoid capture. This 'attack' will naturally be played up to beat the band; it will be cabled to all the newspapers of the United States, to the Department of State and the Navy Department, and the excuse that 'American forces have been attacked by Liberal rebels' will then furnish the desired pretext for the marines to be ordered to take the field and one more glorious page in the history of Dollar Diplomacy will have been written after two or three thousand Nicaraguan citizens, who have dared to oppose the Diaz-Wall Street-Department of State combination, have been mercilessly killed, in their own country, by the marine forces of the United States. This method was successfully adopted in 1912 and practically the same technique was followed by the forces who attacked General B. Zeledon at Coyotepe, in Masaya, and annihilated four hundred Nicaraguans who were defending their sovereignty against the same traitor, Adolfo Diaz, aided and abetted by the Department of State."

I am wondering why the September number of *Current History,* which has several critical studies of the Nicaraguan situation, does not include a single line written by a Nicaraguan, leaving the task of writing these essays almost entirely to former employees and dignitaries of the American Government and the Department of State! Let us hope that this curious omission on the part of *Current History Magazine* has not been intentional for, if so, it might be misconstrued, to its detriment, by public opinion in Latin America.

Another statement which I wish the American public to read is the following letter, which Mr. H. Ofilio Arguello addressed on February 19, 1927, from Puerto Cabezas to the *Baltimore Sun:*

". . . If in the Department of State in Washington, Secretary Kellogg and other high officials really do not know what DOLLAR DIPLOMACY means for these Latin-American countries, in spite of all the agencies at their command through which they can receive truthful reports, then the most charitable thing we can think of them is that they are utterly ignorant men, unfit to occupy the high positions that the American people have entrusted them with, and the conclusion is that they could not profitably manage even a grocery store or a butcher shop.

"If, on the other hand, we start from the opposite premise and take it for granted that Secretary Kellogg and the officials of the State Department are well acquainted with all the humiliations, all the atrocities, which have been perpetrated on our defenseless countries in the name of the United States of America, and that they not only know about them but that they approve of them and actually order them to be committed, then you can draw your own conclusions about what we think about the Department of State, Mr. Kellogg and the Government of the United States, which is owned, directed and run for the exclusive benefit of banking firms in Wall Street. In the case of Nicaragua, J. & W. Seligman & Co. and Brown Bros. & Co. are the guilty parties.

"What possible excuse can be offered by the Department of State for the hasty, ill-advised recognition of the notorious traitor, Adolfo Diaz, who had betrayed Nicaragua in 1909 and helped those same banking firms to loot the Nicaraguan Treasury? Who but an imbecile could possibly consider the fraudulent 'election' of this same Adolfo Diaz as the expression of a majority of the Nicaraguan people? Why should the Department take up Diaz's claims so vigorously, and try to force the Nicaraguan people to accept him as President, when they have been fighting, after exhausting all peaceable means, to reëstablish constitutionality in their country?

"What is the price that Diaz has paid or promised to pay to the banking group which controls the American Government for their unconditional support? Does it not seem strange that the American Government should send enough destroyers and warships to Nicaragua, in order to uphold Diaz, to bombard and lay waste all the ports of Central America in less than two days?

"Can anybody blame Nicaraguans for their sus-

THE LOOTING OF NICARAGUA

picion that the Admiral in command of all these naval forces is merely a more direct representative of the banking interests and that he gets secret instructions from his principals in Wall Street? What kind of a diplomat can a naval officer in command of thirty or forty war vessels make, anyway? Where do naval officers study diplomacy and what do they know about matters of state?

"Can a man who has either ordered, or at least tolerated, the illegal seizure of two million cartridges and seven hundred rifles belonging to the Nicaraguan Constitutionalists, who oppose Diaz, and had them dumped into the Rio Grande without any formalities of any kind, be considered a 'diplomat' in any sense of the word? Could you or anybody else in this world think that he could qualify as an 'arbitrator' between the two contending parties in Nicaragua, after committing this act of vandalism which practically amounts to an act of war? And still, the Department of State in Washington proposes that this man 'arbitrate' and decide as their representative in Nicaragua. Can anything be more asinine?

"All the actions of the United States naval forces in Nicaraguan waters at present cannot be misconstrued. They have been sent with the express purpose of supporting the traitor, Diaz, in the presidency of Nicaragua, against the wishes of Nicaragua itself. And if we do not accept him, we are led to believe that marines will be landed in sufficient number to crush all opposition to this plan. This will mean the murder of thousands of Nicaraguan citizens who are fighting for their freedom, for their right to rule themselves. But the American bankers do not stop at murder. They did not stop at murder in 1912, to uphold this same traitor Diaz, and they 'got away with it' at that time. Why should they not do it again? Are there not enough marines at their beck and call to force as many presidents as they may need down people's throats in Central America?

"But the end is not yet. The people of Nicaragua have been trodden upon long enough and they would rather die than bear it any longer. Everybody in Nicaragua surmises that this lull, this breathing spell, will not last long. Wall Street and the Department of State are merely waiting for Congress and the Senate to adjourn early in March and then they will surely wreak their vengeance on Nicaragua. They will try to teach Nicaraguans who their master is. Senators and Congressmen in the United States have such an obnoxious habit of asking questions about affairs that do not concern them. And the worst of it is, you cannot shut them up. They are immune, even from the Department of State, even from Secretary Kellogg. But Wall Street is wise and can wait. As soon as Congress adjourns they will make the next move. And then, if the newspapers of the United States do not keep up the fight and keep on stirring up public opinion, the fight for freedom in Nicaragua will be irreparably lost and another period of at least twenty-five years of political and economic slavery will have begun for this unfortunate country.

"In the end, two or three decades hence, poetic justice will be done in so far as Latin America is concerned. The American people, as such, have no quarrel with any of the Latin-American countries. The American Government which should represent the American people (but it doesn't) has no quarrel with Latin America. In fact, the best interests of the American people and Government demand that friendship, good will and reciprocity be carefully cultivated

THE LOOTING OF NICARAGUA

for the sake of the immense markets of Latin America. But the banking firms of Wall Street, which control the American Government at the present time, are not looking into the future. They want immediate profits, they demand large profits, they must have dividends every three months from their *investments* in Central and South America to satisfy their avarice, their greed. What difference can it make to them that their policy is unprofitable in the long run? That it will kill the markets of Latin America for the United States in the near future? Who is worrying about world markets, anyhow? Is it not better to make a nice pile during your life-time and enjoy it while you can, than to worry about political, economic or military problems that may come up after you are dead and gone?

"And that is exactly what is going on in Central and South America at present. DOLLAR DIPLOMACY *is killing the goose that lays the golden eggs!* DOLLAR DIPLOMACY has instigated, aided and abetted every revolution, every coup d'état, every kind of treason in Latin America in the last twenty-five years. DOLLAR DIPLOMACY is creating hatreds and animosities for the United States wherever it is being applied. DOLLAR DIPLOMACY has made fortunes for a few private individuals and has made of 'diplomatic representatives' of the United States in Central America a bunch of grafters who work for their own profit and who offer and take bribes wherever they find it profitable to do so. DOLLAR DIPLOMACY is nothing but an immense system of graft and corruption which may degenerate into a political cancer and eventually kill the American body politic which has nurtured it.

"An honest, careful and conscientious investigation into the evil may yet save Nicaragua from her oppressors and the United States from the loss of valuable trade, and perhaps worse, in years to come. But this investigation cannot be delayed. If it is undertaken, it must be undertaken at once. There is no time to be lost! The *honest* press of the United States will, I feel sure, do all it can to arouse public opinion and to demand an immediate investigation."

After reading the preceding letters, one is inclined to think that he understands why *Current History* has omitted asking Nicaraguan writers to contribute to its September number. It all goes to show the mistakes which even some of the best newspapers and magazines in the United States frequently commit by not being careful enough about the selection of their special correspondents abroad, and especially in Central America. More light is shed on this point (not only with regard to special correspondents on salary, but also regarding the engaging free lance writers who send articles and series of articles on Nicaragua to influential newspapers) by Mr. Torribio Tijerino, former Financial Agent of Nicaragua in New York to the New York *Herald Tribune,* published July 29, 1927:

"To the New York *Herald Tribune:*

"Mr. *Linton Wells'* cable dispatch from Managua, Nicaragua (my country), published in your issue of to-day, reveals clearly the point of view of the several American office holders in Nicaragua, paid by the Nicaraguan Government, but appointed by American bankers, who have been making handsome profits out of Nicaragua's troubles and revolts. The people for whom Mr. Wells speaks are evidently after higher salaries and larger profits. But what of the Nicaraguan people? Mr. Wells' cable dispatch contains

THE LOOTING OF NICARAGUA

several misstatements of facts, all easy to prove wrong. I will consider only the most striking ones. First: If Mr. Wells is right in stating that the United States Department of State will not allow Mr. Adolfo Diaz, now serving as President of Nicaragua, to contract any loan to be paid by the Nicaraguan people, the State Department deserves a medal. Would that it had pleased the State Department to adopt that policy before March 21, of this year, for on that date Diaz contracted with certain private banking interests in this city, *giving them priority rights over any loan contracted by Nicaragua for a period of five years.* So, as to the banking groups outbidding one another for the opportunity to remake Nicaragua into a Holland or Switzerland, it is all hokum. We Nicaraguans do not need and do not desire so specious a generosity. I can prove each and every one of my assertions.

"Why not leave us alone to work out our own salvation? That would be good international policy and sound theology. Salvation imposed upon us by the Marine Corps and the New York bankers is costing us Nicaraguans loss of life, loss of property, loss of sovereignty, loss of independence, and is costing the United States loss of moral prestige and good will throughout the Latin-American world."

In order to prove that the views of Messrs. Arguello and Tijerino are not of a chauvinistic character, I will cite also a few extracts taken from a speech Senator Burton K. Wheeler, of Montana, delivered at Ford Hall, Boston, Mass., on March 6, 1927:

". . . Let me make clear just what I mean. To all intents and purposes Mr. Kellogg and Mr. Coolidge are waging an undeclared war against the people of the little republic of Nicaragua. What is the excuse for it?

"Our State Department, throwing American honor to the dogs, recognized Adolfo Diaz as President of Nicaragua. To do this it had to violate the spirit and the letter of a treaty which it had sponsored. It had to override the spirit and the letter of a constitution which it had sponsored. It had to lend itself to all manner of legal trickery and political chicanery in the vain hope of making the worse appear the better cause in the eyes of the overwhelming majority of the people of Nicaragua, who justly despise that pet puppet of our State Department. And then, when it failed to get away with the raw deal it undertook to put over the people of Nicaragua, it began rushing warships and marines and bombing planes to the country to carry out its cowardly and dishonorable program of brutal bluff and bully.

"Who is this pet puppet of our State Department? He is an old favorite. He is a perfect rubber stamp. He is an ideal 'Yes Man.' He not only takes orders from our State Department without question, he anticipates them. Don Adolfo, sitting in the President's Palace in Managua, might easily be mistaken for the little Victrola dog listening to his master's voice.

"Listen to this abject Diaz whine: 'Whatever may be the means chosen by the State Department, they will meet with the approval of my absolute confidence.' Mr. Coolidge evidently thinks that is proper language for the puppet he has placed at the head of a sovereign State to use, for he quoted it with evident satisfaction in his message to Congress.

"In its dual capacity as loan agent and guardian angel of certain New York bankers, our State Department has been using Diaz off and on ever since it

THE LOOTING OF NICARAGUA

assisted in fomenting the revolution in Nicaragua in 1909, which resulted in the overthrow of the Zelaya Government. He is one of the two handy men. The other was Emiliano Chamorro. Of the two, Diaz is the easier tool to handle. Both are professional revolutionists, or what might better be called, in the light of the methods made use of by certain international bankers in their illegitimate methods of dealing with small Latin-American countries, *banker-bandits.*

"There is a closer relationship between the business activities of certain New York banking houses and the banditti business in these little countries than can be really appreciated by one who has never looked into their interlocking activities.

"Neither Diaz nor Chamorro has any sense of public honor whatever. They regard treason as a perfectly legitimate get-rich-quick scheme. They see no reason whatever why, if by use of force and foreign money they can get into a position to sell out their country, they should not do so. If they ever had any scruples on the subject, they are long since dead. They have sold and delivered not only the material resources but the liberty and honor of their country so often, it has become a fixed habit with them.

"It would be unfair to Judas Iscariot or Benedict Arnold to compare these men with them. For neither Judas nor Benedict was a glutton for treason. They only played the rôle of traitor once, and at least one of the two quickly revolted against his act. Neither was a 'hard-boiled' traitor. But the records of Nicaragua show that both Diaz and Chamorro are 'hard-boiled' traitors.

"Now, there is no secret about all this. It is common information, not only throughout Nicaragua and Central America but throughout the whole of Latin

America. The truth as to their bad characters has been blazoned abroad. It would be impossible, without reflecting disastrously on their intelligence, to suppose that either Mr. Kellogg or Mr. Coolidge labors under any delusion as to the moral unfitness of Diaz for the office into which they have thrust him and in which their armed support alone keeps him.

"Those of you who have read 'Oliver Twist' will recall old Fagin and his training school for juvenile burglars. Bill Sykes and other kindred spirits used the graduates of the school by putting them through windows too small for a man to enter. It was then the business of the little burglar to unlock the door so the big burglar could get in and get the stuff. This is a good illustration of the useful function performed by Diaz and his masters. He is an agile little Nicaraguan who has been thrust through the little window of the presidency several times to unlock the house of Nicaragua to certain American bankers and their faithful servant, our State Department. He is even now lending a hand in the robbery of his country of what little is left of its substance and of its sovereignty.

"It is a source of profoundest humiliation to Americans who realize what is taking place beneath the American flag in Nicaragua—and will be such to all honorable citizens when the facts become history— that the Government of our great republic is hand in glove with this political reprobate in the betrayal and the wholesale robbery of the little republic of Nicaragua.

"The chief responsibility for this crime against liberty and republicanism and good morals must rest with the executive department of our Government, into whose hands in an especial sense the honor of our country is committed! But no American citizen now living, who remains silent while this gross indecency is being perpetrated, can escape some measure of responsibility."

It would be unjust on my part to close this chapter without mentioning that the patriotic aims of Messrs. Arguello and Tijerino, as well as those of Senator Wheeler, have been also staunchly supported in every occasion by the majority of the honest American press. I will pick out, at random, the editorial of the St. Louis *Post Dispatch,* of March 15, 1927, in order to prove the veracity of this statement. It says: "If protests made by the United States restrained Messrs. Coolidge and Kellogg from imposing upon Nicaragua any such treatment as the President of that unhappy country proposed, this is the sole evidence that public opinion has been of any avail in that disgraceful affair. The country demanded that we get out of Nicaragua, but we never did; on the contrary, the Administration has continued to tighten its grip upon the country. It has gone on pouring our armed forces into Nicaragua just as if this policy of naked and unabashed imperialism had never provoked one outcry from outraged public opinion at home. It has now occupied all of the principal cities. It holds the only railroad in the country. It occupies with its artillery a height commanding the Nicaraguan capital. It has made the country a political crazy quilt with neutral zones, controls the air with planes and infests the coasts of the country with cruisers, gunboats and destroyers.

"This is the way we got out of Nicaragua.

"In the testimony of Stokely Morgan, Chief of the Latin-American Division of the State Department, before the Senate Committee of Foreign Relations, we learned what it means for our marines to control the Corinto-Managua railroad. He admitted that the Diaz forces use it to transport troops, arms and ammunition. The Sacasa forces, he said, are not permitted to use it for any of those purposes.

" 'Then you are taking sides in this fight?' asked Senator Reed of Missouri. 'We look with considerable distinction on the Diaz Government and the Sacasa so-called government,' Morgan replied.

"Meanwhile, Mr. Coolidge was assuring the United States that we were not intervening in the internal affairs of Nicaragua, and on last Saturday he announced that we do not intend to exercise a protectorate over that country. If we consult the sequence of events we discover that the Administration was flagrantly interfering in the internal affairs of Nicaragua while promising this country and Congress it would not do so. And what real distinction can be made between the condition down there now and exercising a protectorate over Nicaragua? Could a protectorate go farther than to fill the country with armed forces, set up a puppet government depending upon us for protection, take over the banks and the railroad, and deny the people of Nicaragua the right either to govern themselves or revolt? Did any protectorate ever do more than exploit a country for what it is now and mortgage its future for what it may become?

"It is in utter contempt of public opinion in the United States that the Administration continues this dreadful policy in Nicaragua. It is as if it answered every protest against its acts by dispatching more forces for the scene. Certainly there has never been a time in the history of the United States when the Government moved in such complete scorn of the people. Certainly there has never been another time

THE LOOTING OF NICARAGUA

when we cared so little what other nations might think of us.

"Our innate sense of what is fair and decent has many times been flouted, but it has never before been so ruthlessly ignored as Messrs. Coolidge and Kellogg have ignored it in their dealings with Nicaragua. They have violated every pledge of friendship made to the Latin-American peoples. They have moved counter to what almost the whole country considers to be the part of wisdom for the United States. They have aroused against us the protests not only of Latin America, but of Europe and Asia. All these brand us the world's most heartless empire.

"Let us consult the record and see with what thoroughness public opinion has been scouted in this matter.

"Diaz was inaugurated on November 14, 1926. Three days later his government was recognized by the United States. Mr. Kellogg said the State Department was gratified that a solution had been found for the Nicaraguan problem. Just one day after his announcement that this solution had been found, Diaz appealed to the American Government to protect American lives and property. On December 8th, the Navy Department announced that five American warships had been sent to the east coast of Nicaragua. On December 18th, Diaz spilled the beans all over the Caribbean by announcing that he had accepted the presidency of Nicaragua in the expectation that the United States would help him. He was quite frank in the admission that without the United States his government would fall. The Administration then virtually admitted its connivance at setting up in Nicaragua a puppet government, without any public support. It landed marines in Nicaragua, and Admiral

Latimer established the first neutral zones. Having driven the Liberal troops out of this region, he reported that he had the situation well in hand.

"On December 28th, the official spokesman asserted that the American Government was not taking sides in Nicaragua, one way or the other. Nevertheless, two more destroyers were ordered there on December 31st. By this time protests in the United States had become so vociferous that the spokesman felt it necessary to justify himself. He attempted to do so by announcing that American troops in Nicaragua were there to protect our right to build the Canal. On January 5th, the embargo on shipment of arms to Nicaragua was lifted, and it was explained by Washington dispatches that the purpose of this was to prevent the Diaz Government from being overthrown. The next day six more warships and six hundred more marines were ordered to Nicaragua.

"Four days later the tumult and shouting in the United States had become so great that Mr. Coolidge addressed Congress. He assigned various reasons for our intervention. Among others was gun-running from Mexico. He said: 'I am sure it is not the desire of the United States to intervene in the internal affairs of Nicaragua.'

"Nevertheless, on January 14th, the eighth American warship reached Nicaraguan waters and landed more marines. There was widespread indignation that we should say one thing and do another. So, on January 20th, Mr. Coolidge issued another assurance. He said, 'Least of all have we any desire to influence or dictate in any way the internal affairs of Nicaragua.' He thought matters were improving. He said, 'I have been pleased to see that influential steps for the elimination of dissatisfaction are being taken.'

THE LOOTING OF NICARAGUA

"Eleven days later, four hundred more marines were landed in Corinto. On February 15th, six airplanes and one hundred more marines were ordered to Nicaragua. Two days later one thousand six hundred more marines were ordered there. On February 18th, President Coolidge let it be known that marines were being rushed to Nicaragua because of reports that arms were being sent to the Liberals by land and sea. He again denied that the American Government was taking sides.

"On February 20th, one thousand six hundred more marines were landed at Corinto 'to give protection to the forces of the Diaz Government from the troops of the Sacasa Government.' On February 21st, it was announced that the neutralization of Nicaraguan territory was being extended. The State Department announced that nine hundred and ninety-six men of the American Naval forces had occupied three cities along the Corinto-Managua railroad. This brought the number of neutralized cities up to eight. Only two of any importance remained unoccupied by American forces.

"On February 22d, Diaz asked Washington for a new treaty with Nicaragua. The terms, as later published, would set up virtually an American protectorate over that country for one hundred years. Diaz proposed to hand Nicaragua over to the United States bodily. But on March 12th, Mr. Coolidge made it known that this was going further than our Nicaraguan policy intended.

"On February 24th, marines hoisted the American flag over the fortress commanding the capital city of Managua. Admiral Latimer reported on this same date that his men were guarding additional points along the railroad, including Corinto, La Paz, Quezalguague and Chichigalpa.

"On March 1st, it was announced that six American airplanes had arrived with their crews at Managua, and that they would be used for scouting and maintaining communications. On March 5th, one thousand six hundred marines arrived in Nicaragua on the transport *Henderson*. On March 8th, seven hundred and fifty marines and forty officers from the *Henderson* arrived in Managua.

"That is how we got out of Nicaragua.

"Nothing said in the Senate, no opinion expressed by the press, had the least effect. We had so completely occupied the country that the British cruiser *Colombo*, which on February 24th had gone to Nicaragua as a refuge for British subjects, sailed away on March 5th. Not one of the assurances of Mr. Coolidge that we would not intervene in the internal affairs of Nicaragua has been borne out in the steady sequence of events. Not one protest against taking sides, which he several times said we would not do, has in the least availed.

"Mr. Coolidge once said: 'The business of the United States is business.' The record in Nicaragua shows that under his leadership it is. He has not shown the slightest consideration for anything else. The rights of the people of Nicaragua have been as completely thrust aside as has been public opinion in the United States. It has been a complete triumph for imperialism. It has been an almost unparalleled demonstration in the philosophy of 'the public be damned.'

"That we have sown the dragon's teeth and shall, in due time, reap the whirlwind, is obvious to everybody but Mr. Coolidge and his shortsighted advisers. *That trade, even with Latin America, is declining,* abates nothing of their sinister intent. They seem to want to make Nicaragua an example. The six hundred thousand people of that country are beside the point. The point is that we need Nicaragua in our business. We need her Canal route, her mahogany and her revenues. To that end we need our own Maximilian there.

"Apparently, the American people have made a great mistake in believing that the protests of conscience have any place in the councils of the Coolidge Administration. The story of Nicaragua belies it. We may think ourselves better or more merciful than that, but in truth we are not. There are the transports, the warships, the marines, the cannon, the troop trains, the airplanes and the Stars and Stripes—all testifying to the terror of Empire. Not a man nor a boat has been withdrawn . . . !"

I am going to finish this chapter with the following short article copied from the *World,* which reproduced it from the *New Leader,* Socialist:

". . . The present plight of Nicaragua is charged with immense dangers for the peoples south of us as well as for the American masses. It constitutes the most disgraceful episode in American history. Beginning with the declaration that Washington had no intention of intervening in Nicaragua, American policy has moved from threats to shameful occupation of the country with troops and bombing planes. Our forces are openly supporting Diaz, an adventurer who, on a number of occasions in the past twenty years, has served as a vassal of American interests.

"This policy has culminated in what is practically an ultimatum to the Liberal forces. Henry L. Stimson, President Coolidge's special agent in Nicaragua, in his ultimatum, declares 'that American forces will disarm forcibly those who will not do so.' Thus the Liberals are forced to surrender in the face of American rifles and bombing planes. Eight hundred more marines are ordered to be ready.

"No despotic State in the history of mankind has ever brandished the mailed fist more openly, and this comes a few days after Coolidge made his sanctimonious address regarding the godly purposes of the United States in Latin-American countries. There is more in this policy than setting up an American dummy with our bayonets in Nicaragua. Coolidge and his apologists have already asserted the servile ethics that the American press should not criticize American foreign politics. A repetition of this advice in the next few years may easily lead to legislation muzzling the press and citizens so that any imperial upstarts at Washington may throw newspapers out of the mails and imprison editors and citizens.

"One thing we should remember. The American Government cannot be a despot abroad without becoming a despot at home. Despotism cannot stand criticism. It always commands obedience, and Coolidge has already urged this. All that remains is Federal Legislation to square with the reality of the American mailed fist in the Caribbean and Central America. Once having made us all intellectual conscripts of American imperialism the bureaucracy will have an excellent machine to hurl at trade unions and their struggles, to fill the nation with peace time spies and informers, to penalize all who dissent from an imperial will which represents bankers, speculators and others intent upon despoiling helpless peoples across the frontiers.

"This is the danger we face in the United States. American capitalism has all the dangers of Cæsarism at home and abroad, with the working people of this country being forced under the iron heel as merciless as that of any military conqueror."

It can be safely stated that Senator William E. Borah of Idaho spoke for many Americans besides himself when he addressed the Jewish Congress, meeting in Washington on Feb. 20, 1927. According to the New York *Times* report (Feb. 21) Senator Borah said in regard to Latin America:

"Our policy should not rest solely upon mahogany and oil, or depend for its execution upon warships and marines. There is an infinitely stronger power and a more compelling influence in working out the proper relationship between this country and the Latin-American countries. We ought to call home our marines from Nicaragua. I assert here to-night, without fear of contradiction, that there is no more danger to American citizens in the country occupied by Sacasa then there is in the region controlled by Diaz.

"The truth is that the great problem in international affairs at this time is one growing out of the relationship between strong nations and smaller, weak nations. China, Syria, Nicaragua and Mexico all present the same problem and reveal the same sinister policy. How shall the rights of small nations be guarded or maintained?

"Are small nations or helpless peoples to be deprived of their natural wealth, their governments set up and broken down, their own way of living denied them, all in the name of protecting life and property? Or are we to adopt such methods and such means of adjusting the controversies which will inevitably arise as will insure settlement upon the basis of justice rather than upon the basis of force?

"It ought to be regarded as a crime to defend by force and with American marines a title or a claim for property which cannot stand the inspection of an arbitrator!

"I do not believe, furthermore, when we are called upon to protect the property of our nationals that we are at liberty to disregard everything except the naked technical rights of our nationals, that we are permitted to consider nothing save the cold value of our claims. Property values are not all that are involved in such controversies or under such circumstances. We are bound in national honor and as a proper rule of decency to give due weight to the rights, the liberty, the independence and social and moral well-being of the people in whose country such property is located or which we are asked to invade. We are bound to respect their policies, their right to modify or change their policies and to inaugurate that which they believe to be in the interests of the nation as a whole. The narrow, sordid theory that we must have dollar for dollar, an eye for an eye and a tooth for a tooth, can never be made to fit into the right of every nation to determine for itself what it is wise and best for it to do.

"Substantial justice is all any nation can ask for under such circumstances. We should deal in justice in such controversies, and justice in such matters involves the rights and interests of the people with whom we deal as well as the rights and interests of our own nationals.

"Our own country would, in the long run, gather respect and confidence and reap both moral and material wealth far beyond that which can ever be gathered under a policy of exploitation and force.

"The World War did not achieve very much if we

consider alone the rules and practices which still obtain in international affairs; but make no mistake, it achieved vastly when you come to consider the views and opinions of the great mass of the people. They have come to realize that, after all, international relations should be gauged by the same standards of honor and decency which we have come to recognize as between individuals."

Chapter VIII

The Diaz-Chamorro Gang's Hold on the Conservative Party — How the Solorzano-Sacasa Coalition Government Was Formed — Reasons Why Sacasa Appointed Moncada Secretary of War — Moncada's Lurid Career — Beltran-Sandoval and the "Machete" Revolution — Sacasa's Letter Intercepted by Chamorro — Consequent Failure of the Expedition Under Irais' Command — Sacasa at Last Arrives in Nicaragua.

BEFORE going on with my story, I would like to make it perfectly clear that the aim of this book is not to defend my friends against those who may not be my friends, nor to rouse one political party against another. I am not an agitator; I am a historian. I do not pretend to be infallible, either; on the contrary, I think it possible that this book will contain some errors. However, I wish to say in my own defense that I am not making mistakes intentionally, and that I am ready to apologize beforehand to any one whom I may unjustly wrong by my statements. What I am aiming at in this book is to leave a true, impartial record—to the best of my knowledge—of the impressions which I gathered during my recent researches in Central America.

In the spring of 1927 the American press informed the public how President Coolidge's envoy, Mr. Henry Stimson, had come to an agreement with a certain General Moncada with the result that the Liberal forces would disarm. It is time now to introduce Moncada; but he must be seen in perspective, against his background. And his background is the patriotic struggles of his countrymen which he sought to turn to his own advantage.

After the death of Diego Manuel Chamorro, who was Dollar Diplomacy's fourth "dummy President," Vice-President Bartolome Martinez assumed the Presidency. He belonged to what might be rightly termed the extreme left of the Conservative party, which has always stood for law and order, even during the Diaz and Chamorro dictatorships. It is a mistake to think that because twenty-five per cent or less of the Nicaraguan Conservatives, headed by the Diaz-Chamorro gang and backed up by Wall Street, have succeeded in terrorizing Nicaragua during the past seventeen years, all Conservatives are necessarily scoundrels; far from it. There are just as many honest, orderly, law-abiding and sincerely patriotic elements in the Conservative party of Nicaragua as there are among the Liberals. Those elements have, however, been handicapped by the Diaz-Chamorro clique, which, as I said before, represents only a small percentage of the party. If it had not been for the fact that Diaz, Chamorro and Company have been always backed up by Dollar Diplomacy, they would never have succeeded in keeping all the offices, nor in monopolizing the term "conservative party" for the benefit of their small clique of *old school* politicians and gangsters. In order to prove this I have only to mention the Conservative, General Luis Mena, who rebelled during the "popular revolution" in 1912 against the Diaz-Chamorro clique. Mena was supported by both Conservatives and Liberals and even fought against thousands of American soldiers, who were rushed to Nicaragua by Dollar Diplomacy to save the really "nonexistent" régime of Adolfo Diaz from total destruction. If Mena and his confrere Zeledon, instead of resorting to regular warfare, trying to deliver battles, had initiated a guerrilla war on a big scale in the interior of the republic (similar to General Parejon's campaign during the recent revolution), the outcome of that struggle would have been very different. Dollar Diplomacy would not have been able to stand the bitter criticism which prolonged guerrilla warfare would, naturally, have stirred up all over the United States and abroad.

Don Bartolo, as President Martinez was generally known in Nicaragua, was a fairly typical representative of the bulk of the Nicaraguan Conservative party, which stood for political and economic independence. In less than a year he managed to free Nicaragua of the financial shackles which Dollar Diplomacy had imposed on that unfortunate country for thirteen consecutive years, with the aid of American armed intervention. He also succeeded, backed by the Nicaraguan Federation of Labor, in having the American Legation Guard withdrawn from Managua. And as a good patriot, he was also anxious to leave his government in the hands of a coalition government equally representing Liberals and Conservatives. I understand that the strong Conservative presidential candidate, whom he had in mind first, was supplanted, through the influence of outside elements, by another Conservative, Don Carlos Solorzano. Don Carlos Solorzano, despite his good intentions, was not a sufficiently strong and able man to hold such a responsible position. Nor was Dr. Sacasa, who, for the reasons stated in Chapter VI, was elected through Don Bartolo Martinez's *official support,* a good choice as Vice-President even though he was a Liberal.

One of the most prominent members of the rotten

THE LOOTING OF NICARAGUA

Estrada-Diaz-Chamorro clique, especially during 1910 and 1911, was José Maria Moncada. Dr. Sacasa followed the time-worn methods of old-school politicians everywhere when he appointed Moncada Secretary of War in the winter of 1926 in order to give him, as an *old timer,* the precedence over General Luis Beltran-Sandoval. Beltran-Sandoval was the real commander-in-chief of the Constitutionalist forces operating on the Atlantic Coast, because it was he who first rose in arms in Bluefields, on May 2, 1926, against the fake Chamorro Government and borrowed, through the Constitutionalist Committee, from the National Bank of Nicaragua, in that locality, $150,000 or $200,000 in order to buy the necessary materials for the revolution. It was Beltran-Sandoval who fought the victorious battle of the Laguna de Perlas and immediately afterwards marched the triumphant Constitutionalist forces across country to the Pacific Coast. To judge from his written résumé of the recent Constitutionalist revolution which was published in *La Noticia* of Managua, of June 11, 1927, and which Moncada did not dare to refute, Beltran-Sandoval *never* recognized Moncada's pretended superiority as commander-in-chief, nor did the rest of the superior officers in the Constitutionalist army; for the command was equally divided between Beltran-Sandoval and Moncada. The following statement of General Parejon, published in *La Noticia* of Managua, of June 8, 1927, testifies to that: "That morning we joined the Constitutionalist Army. From that very moment I put myself and my men at the orders of Generals Moncada and Beltran-Sandoval, the two commanders of Dr. Sacasa's Army, and, therefore, also our commanders from that very moment." Moncada therefore was never commander-in-chief of the Liberal army. And he would not have been able to make the *secret verbal* or *unsigned written agreements* with President Coolidge's special representative, Mr. Stimson (whereby he betrayed the Constitutionalist Cause), if he had not been appointed Secretary of War with *full powers,* by Dr. Sacasa. No matter how he tried to explain matters afterwards to Beltran-Sandoval, Parejon, and Sandino, the fact remains that Sacasa enabled Moncada, or helped him rather, consciously or unconsciously, *to put up that job,* apparently for fear that Beltran-Sandoval (that is, a *new man*) might get full control of the Constitutionalist army. General Augusto Sandino's proclamation, which was published in *El Comercio* of Managua, on June 8, 1927, explains that point very thoroughly. Everybody in Nicaragua knows it. On the other hand, it is really astonishing how Dr. Sacasa ever dared to appoint Moncada Secretary of War, knowing, as he did, that Moncada was a Conservative renegade who had been combating mercilessly, from 1888 until 1920, the Cause of Nicaraguan Liberalism whenever he got a chance. He may have been afraid of him. The freakish career of this man, since he entered public life to the detriment of his country, contains details of interest to the psychologist.

From 1888 until 1892 Moncada was in Granada, writing on a local paper in favor of the *Conservative Clerical* Party, with which he was affiliated. In 1893 he participated in a Conservative revolution which brought about the downfall of the President of that time whose name curiously enough was also Sacasa, Roberto Sacasa. In 1894 Moncada begged the Liberal President Zelaya to appoint him Congressman for the district of Masatepe, where he was born.

THE LOOTING OF NICARAGUA 135

But shrewd Zelaya, who knew Moncada for what he really was, refused. Thereupon Moncada went away in disgust to Costa Rica. He returned in 1897, asking the protection of Manuel Coronel Matus, who helped him to publish a pamphlet called *El Porvenir* by using the Nicaraguan National Printing Plant. Shortly after that Moncada emigrated again and lived for some time in Honduras. In 1906 he took part in the *Conservative* régime of General Manuel Bonilla, in Honduras, as his Assistant Secretary of State; and, when Nicaragua went to war with Honduras, he remained in Honduras *opposing his own native country!* Later on he went to El Salvador and then to Guatemala where he became an intimate friend of the Dictator, Estrada Cabrera. In 1909 Moncada, having returned to Nicaragua, participated in the *Conservative* revolution against Zelaya. In August of that same year he threatened the city of Granada at the head of a *Conservative* force and, immediately after that, started a newspaper in which he printed violent attacks on the defeated Liberal party! In 1910, he was holding the office of Assistant Secretary of War in the *Conservative* Cabinet of Estrada. In 1911 he became Secretary of State in that same *Conservative* Cabinet and government, which also included Adolfo Diaz. While Secretary of State in Estrada's *Conservative* Cabinet, he had, on his own initiative, *the Liberal population of Leon shot down like dogs* during a peaceful demonstration. In April 1911 he and Estrada tried to imprison the Minister of War, General Luis Mena, whom they feared. They failed and were captured and deported themselves. In 1912, while the "Revolution Popular" was being waged against Adolfo Diaz, Moncada remained in New York *receiving a salary from Adolfo Diaz* for performing such useful tasks as might be expected of a distinguished exile of his moral caliber.

In other words, his late confrere and present paymaster at that date was the same Diaz, whom he has been pretending to fight to the knife during the recent revolution. In 1920 Moncada finally forsook the Conservative party in order to join the Liberals, because he realized that his old *Estrada-Adolfo Diaz-Chamorro-Dollar Diplomacy* clique did not want to have anything more to do with him. No wonder that the Constitutionalist Army, which was entrusted to him by Sacasa (since he appointed him Secretary of War), was finally also betrayed and sacrificed by Moncada to his personal ambitions, when it had almost reached its goal at Tipitapa. For Moncada had, in reality, only been using the Liberal Cause as a means to an end in his mad endeavor to become President. He seems to have thought that if he could make a sufficient show of strength, Dollar Diplomacy would make terms with him and put him in as President of Nicaragua. In pursuit of that ambition he was ready to outdo in baseness and infamy even Adolfo Diaz—which is about as low as a man can fall!

The real reason, therefore, why the Constitutionalist or Coalition Government, integrated by the Liberal party and the majority of the Conservatives, was ruthlessly betrayed and sacrificed, is because Dr. Sacasa was not the right man to hold the responsible position of Vice-President of the Republic. As I have shown, Sacasa had been imposed on the country solely by means of the *official support* of ex-President Bartolo Martinez in 1924.

That misfortune, which has been a tremendous blow to the Liberal party of Nicaragua (because it had trusted blindly in both Sacasa and Moncada

Chinandega, Nicaragua, after its partial destruction by American bombing planes.

Nicaraguan Constitutionalist machine gun detachment.

through sheer habit of discipline), has finally opened its eyes to the fact that what Nicaragua really needs is to free itself from the rule of the politicians (both Conservatives and Liberals) of the decayed "old school" à la *Estrada-Diaz-Chamorro-Moncada-Sacasa, etc.,* who have driven Nicaragua time and again—through greed or imbecility—into the arms of Dollar Diplomacy; who have had their responsibility for shedding the blood of thousands of Nicaraguans only for the purpose of satisfying their own personal ambitions; who have passed the ball from one to another during the last seventeen years for fear that it might fall into the hands of new men like Sandino, Aleman Bolaños, Ramon Romero, Beltran-Sandoval, that is, into the hands of true patriots and standard bearers of Nicaragua's modern nationalist ideals. However, the fact that the cause of right against might has been sacrificed once more in Nicaragua, through Moncada's acts during the past revolution, does not imply in the least that the magnanimous efforts of the American People, the American press and those American statesmen who rose so magnificently in defense of the unhappy people of Nicaragua, have been in vain. On the contrary! They have achieved far more perhaps than a triumphant revolution might have achieved, for they have helped the Nicaraguans to open their eyes, to discover the root of the evil and to replace their political and military leaders, chosen heretofore only from among old-school politicians, with new leaders—men inspired with the altruistic national ideals of a modern Nicaragua.

While Dr. Sacasa remained in Washington one month after another humbly begging the favor of the Coolidge Administration, which "jollied" him along (and Sacasa well knew it!) by promising him to exercise *moral pressure* on Chamorro, something extraordinary happened. The Nicaraguan Constitutionalists, tired at last of Sacasa's "begging" policy, took the law in their own hands and, headed by General Luis Beltran-Sandoval, rose in arms on May 2, 1926, and took possession of the important city of Bluefields on the Atlantic Coast. On that memorable day, which was a Sunday, the people of Bluefields stormed the barracks and finally captured it. The Governor of that district, who had hounded down the people of Bluefields for a long time, was saved from being executed only by the prompt arrival of General M. Hoggon, who had him confined in Dr. Nelson's Sanatorium. General Luis Beltran-Sandoval, the hero of the day, was appointed Commander of the military forces, and Fernando Larios, Governor of the district. But the officer in command of the Bluff, which was a fortress situated on the point of a finger-shaped peninsula opposite the city of Bluefields, took prompt measures to retake the town. He disposed three hundred men, three machine guns and half a battery of field pieces, besides several armored craft including the steel tug *Persistence* and the *Nokomis,* which he put immediately into commission in order to deliver a counterattack.

Unhappily for him, his combination did not work. Both the *Nokomis* and the *Persistence* got stuck in the mudbanks of the bay and were riddled by the bullets of the Constitutionalists stationed on Hansack Point and in the barracks. He himself was killed during the attack. So Bluefields was lost to Chamorro for a while at least. That same day Dr. Sacasa was proclaimed Constitutional President of Nicaragua and the Constitutionalist committee borrowed a large sum

THE LOOTING OF NICARAGUA 139

from the National Bank of Nicaragua for the purpose of purchasing war material. Of this money seventeen thousand dollars was wired immediately to Dr. Sacasa in Washington. On May 6, the *U. S. S. Cleveland,* commanded by Captain John D. Wainright, arrived and declared Bluefields a neutral zone! A detachment of marines, at the orders of Captain Spencer S. Lewis, took up their headquarters in the Moravian Sunday School Hall—which had served the same purpose also in 1910.

Simultaneous with the outbreak at Bluefields a rising took place in Rama, which was also successful. The Rio Grande district was seized by the Constitutionalists without much opposition, except at La Cruz, where the Chamorro troops offered some resistance. The military leaders of the Constitutional forces in this section of the Atlantic Coast were Carlos Pasas, Daniel Mena and Heriberto Correa. Puerto Cabezas, Corn Island, Pearl Lagoon, in short, practically the whole of eastern Nicaragua, willingly recognized the reëstablishment of the Constitutionalist Government. Due to the fact that the Constitutionalist forces were wholly unprepared for war, ninety per cent of them being armed only with pistols and bushknives, this revolution was called the "Machete Revolution." Pasas, Mena and Correa immediately marched with some reënforcements to the district of Bluefields in order to save the strategic little river town of Rama, which is the key of Bluefields' famous Hinterland. Rama was being seriously threatened by Chamorro's troops, which had been rushed to the Atlantic Coast immediately after the fall of Bluefields. But the lack of proper equipment made it impossible for Beltran-Sandoval and his followers to keep up the fight indefinitely. So they disbanded their forces on May 27 and went abroad in search of support to enable them to begin again and carry on to the desired goal.

A few days after the collapse of the Machete Revolution, a tug boat, the *Barranca,* arrived from New Orleans at Bluefields, carrying twelve hundred rifles, five hundred thousand rounds of ammunition and fifty Thompson machine guns, destined for the Constitutionalists. It was manned by Horacio Zelaya and eight men. They did not know that the Constitutionalist revolution had ceased to be, for the time being, at least. However, they did not lose their heads either; for when they saw themselves surrounded by a swarm of gasoline boats loaded with Chamorro troops, who demanded their surrender, they turned on full steam and, each grabbing a machine gun, they managed to cut their way through that ring of steel and to escape to Guatemala, where they cached the armament in the neighborhood of Puerto Barrios.

Still, although the relatively insignificant bonfire of the Machete Revolution had been put out, temporarily at least, the sparks went on glowing beneath the ashes. The funds which Beltran-Sandoval and the Constitutionalist Government had borrowed in Bluefields from the National Bank of Nicaragua were wisely spent in the purchase of steamers, guns and ammunition, which enabled the Nicaraguan Constitutionalists to start the fight over again four months later, when the second attempt was made on the Pacific Coast.

Two days after the collapse of the Machete Revolution Dr. Sacasa left Washington, D. C., and, after a week's stay in Mexico City, arrived in Guatemala at the beginning of June. His first step was to commit the incredible folly of disclosing the plan of the pro-

THE LOOTING OF NICARAGUA

posed new revolution in a letter which he sent to Nicaragua without the necessary precautions. This letter fell of course into the hands of Chamorro, who had it broadcast afterwards through the Conservative press. In this letter Sacasa even mentioned the month (August) in which the new uprising was going to take place! Although there were in Guatemala at that time two really able military leaders, Teofilo Jimenez and Horacio Portocarrero, ready to take over the command of the Pacific Coast expedition, Sacasa gave the preference to Dr. Julian Irias. In Chapter V I have stated why Irias was not the proper man to have been entrusted with such an important commission. Irias began, of course, by leaving Guatemala for Salina Cruz, Mexico, too late (in the middle of August). At Salina Cruz he was to take charge of the *S. S. Concon,* later renamed the *Tropical,* loaded with about three thousand rifles, three hundred thousand rounds, and fifty machine guns of superior quality. The date announced for his arrival on the Pacific Coast of Nicaragua was August 17th; however, he did not get there till August 24th. In consequence of that announcement several thousand volunteers assembled on August 17 and 18 in the neighborhood of Masachapa, El Perico and El Tamarindo, situated along the coast, in the department of Casazo, near Leon. But due to Irias's delay and the letter of Sacasa's which had been intercepted by Chamorro, Chamorro's troops succeeded in locating and dispersing those bands of volunteers long before Irias made his appearance. Among those waiting was General Parejon, the future hero of Chinandega, who, despite the terrible blow dealt the cause by the failure of Irias to get there in time, started right away (with only five men, armed with machetes and six shooters), a guerrilla warfare which finally enabled him to gather about one thousand well-armed and well-disciplined men. With these men he succeeded in saving Moncada from total destruction a few months later at Las Mercedes. But of that anon!

Knowing, as Chamorro did, the plans of the revolution he set several traps into which Irias blundered.

On August 25th, the *Tropical* finally arrived and on the following day Irias landed sixty men, commanded by Manuel Ediles and carrying with them a considerable amount of war material, on the peninsula of Coseguina, near Fonseca Bay, where he abandoned them to their fate. This handful of heroes, or rather what was left of them after a two hours' fight against fourteen hundred of Chamorro's troops, were finally taken prisoners after their leaders had been all killed and not without having caused the Chamorro troops about five hundred casualties before they were captured. I mention this example in order to show that fighting in Central America nowadays is no "opéra bouffe," as Colonel C. B. Carter calls it in his "funny story" entitled "The Kentucky Feud in Nicaragua," published by him in a recent number of the *World's Work Magazine*. Colonel Carter's story goes to show very clearly that in ridiculing the unhappy people of Nicaragua, he is only advertising the *so-called beneficial effects of American financial and armed intervention in Nicaragua during the past seventeen years!* I am surprised at Colonel Carter's lack of knowledge of the people and the political conditions in a country which he nevertheless makes the subject of an article.

Another deplorable blunder committed by Irias was the landing, on September 1st, of another handful of men near Chaluca. This little band was also annihilated by the Chamorro forces, using such foul

THE LOOTING OF NICARAGUA

means as luring them into range by means of the white flag.

If Julian Irias had been a *modern* soldier he would never have allowed Dr. Sacasa to broadcast beforehand, through private correspondence, all the details of his projected campaign and even the month in which it was to take place; nor would he have announced his arrival off the Nicaraguan coast a week ahead of time. On the other hand, even after his failure on the Coseguina Peninsula, Irias could have turned the tide in his favor by heading south, toward the Rivas district, near the Costa Rican frontier, where General Crisanto Zapata with three or four hundred men awaited his arrival. If, instead of leaving Crisento Zapata in the lurch, Irias had disembarked and turned his armament over to Zapata, the fate of the Constitutionalist Government of Nicaragua would have been a different one; for, pressed from the south by Zapata, from the north by Parejon and from the east by Moncada and Beltran, the fake Diaz Government would have collapsed in no time and the useless slaughter of thousands of Nicaraguan patriots (as well as the unhappy conscript soldiers of the Diaz armies) would have been avoided.

After the tragic end of that expedition, which was brought about by Sacasa's stubbornness in trying to keep new men who were not in sympathy with the old school politicians from holding responsible positions in the army, Irias returned with the *Tropical,* first to the port of La Union in Fonseca Bay, and, in October, to Salina Cruz, Mexico, where his companions cached what was left of the armament. While the expedition of Julian Irias was meeting with disaster a group of Constitutionalists had embarked from Brooklyn, New York, with a cargo of war material, in the little *S. S. Foam,* on their way to Puerto Mexico on the Atlantic Coast. After picking up there, among other refugees, J. M. Moncada, they sailed on and captured, by surprise, Puerto Cabezas, Prinzapolka, La Barra de Rio Grande and other Nicaraguan ports along the Mosquito Coast. Soon after, another large consignment of war material, including some artillery, was landed on the same coast. By the end of October, the war material of the *Barranca,* which had been cached near Puerto Barrios in Guatemala, had also been landed, and the *S. S. Carmelita* had arrived with one thousand rifles, plenty of ammunition and about a dozen machine guns.

While the Constitutionalist armies on both the Pacific and Atlantic Coasts were doing prodigies in order to free their country from Diaz and the talons of Dollar Diplomacy, Dr. Sacasa remained idle for three months in Guatemala—still humbly waiting and begging for the favor of Washington. He was unwilling even to listen to the pleas of Beltran-Sandoval, who had gone, in the name of the army, to Guatemala to ask Sacasa to return to Nicaragua for the purpose of establishing a Constitutional Government at once. Only in November when the army commenced to doubt Sacasa's good faith, did he finally decide to go to Puerto Cabezas to assume the Presidency of the Republic.

Although Dr. Sacasa had never been what might be called really a popular man, yet at the news of his landing in Nicaragua everybody among the Constitutionalists rejoiced, because his presence gave their cause the legal stamp it required. With the establishment of the Constitutionalist Government on Nicaraguan soil, the Diaz régime became overnight the rebellion and the revolution, because it had no legitimate basis

THE LOOTING OF NICARAGUA

in the laws and constitution of the country. The Diaz régime—this cannot be repeated too often—had been forced on the country by Dollar Diplomacy despite the Treaty of Peace and Amity which had originated in Washington, and which had been signed in Washington on February 7, 1923, by the governments of the five Central-American republics and the Government of the United States.

Chapter IX

The Campaign of the Nicaraguan Constitutionalist Army From the Battle of Laguna de Perlas up to the Armistice at Tipitapa.

THE capture of Cabo de Gracias a Diós, Puerto Cabezas and Prinzapolka, and the occupation of the rich banana zone of Rio Grande furnished the Constitutionalists with valuable resources in the shape of provisions, some financial aid, barges and gasoline boats to transport their troops, and the use of the wireless stations at El Gallo and La Barra. Thereupon they decided to try to capture the Bluff, which, as before stated, is situated opposite Bluefields on a rocky promontory which communicates with *terra firma* by a sand bar about twenty to thirty feet wide. At high tide the sea covers the bar, turning the Bluff into a rocky island. Besides being heavily fortified the Bluff, at that time, was defended by a strong Conservative garrison.

After cutting off the Bluff by land and sea, a detachment of troops under Daniel Mena and Eliseo Duarte was dispatched to occupy the little town of Rama, situated some fifty miles up the Rama River, so as to prevent any Conservative reënforcements coming down the river from the interior. Unhappily, Mena and Duarte had to retreat from Rama after capturing it, thereby leaving the right flank and the rear of the Constitutionalist forces wholly unprotected. This unforeseen circumstance forced the Constitutionalists to precipitate their attack on the Bluff, which resulted in heavy casualties on both sides. And apparently to save the Conservative garrison, the American emissaries arranged an armistice, the garrison of the Bluff agreed readily to withdraw at once to Rama. As a result of this armistice, a peace conference was arranged in Corinto (November, 1926) which failed because the American Chargé d'Affaires, Mr. Dennis, successfully prevented the Conservative delegates from accepting, or even considering, the conditions submitted to them by the Constitutionalist commissioners. The fracas over, this conference inspired the Constitutionalists with the resolve to destroy the bulk of Adolfo Diaz's army on the Atlantic Coast, which had assembled and fortified itself in the little town of Laguna City, situated on the southwestern extreme of the Laguna de Perlas, only a short distance north of Bluefields. The trenches of Diaz's troops, according to what I heard at Puerto Cabezas, had been constructed under the supervision of American naval officers, who considered them impregnable.

The plan of the battle of Laguna de Perlas—a miniature battle when compared with the gigantic military operations during the World War—was very carefully worked out beforehand by Generals Beltran-Sandoval and Moncada; and the way it was executed speaks very highly of Beltran-Sandoval's military ability. It was not only the actual fighting, but, more especially, the terrific natural obstacles which had to be overcome in order to reach the field, which made that battle noteworthy. For about seventy-two hours the Constitutionalist forces had no sleep and hardly a bite to eat—wading at first waist-high through quagmires, holding their arms and ammunition above their heads, and afterwards, fighting, fighting all the time, without losing heart, without ever proffering the slightest complaint. I am citing this example in order to show what Latin-American volunteer soldiers are capable of when they are bent on regaining their independence. It may hint to the wise in Washington, D. C., that it would be better not to stir up Latin-American resentment to the red-hot point, for if Mexico and Central America should ever lose all hope of just dealing from the United States and make common cause, not even two or three million American soldiers would be able to subdue them in thirty years —if ever—because the natural fortresses of the Latin-American patriots are their jungles, and their most faithful allies are tropical fevers. Even in northern Mexico, where there are no jungles and hardly any mosquitoes to contend with, General Pershing had to convince himself, to his sorrow, that with or without mosquitoes and jungles the Latin Americans, *just by using guerrilla warfare alone,* are unconquerable when they make up their minds not to be conquered! The antiquated policy of "alternate threat and bluff," which Dollar Diplomacy has been using successfully until lately in Central America and the Antilles, has been recently shattered by General Sandino. He has shown the "other Sandinos" from Mexico down to Panama the right way to act when the right moment comes. I consider therefore the miniature but, nevertheless, remarkable battle of Luguna de Perlas as a splendid example of what is likely to happen if those thirty-five millions of Mexicans and Central Americans should ever get it into their heads to put up a solid front against foreign intervention.

The so-called city of Laguna de Perlas, or Laguna City, is in reality only a fair-sized hamlet, situated on a small peninsula in the southwesterly corner of the lagoon. It is margined on the east, north and partly also on the west by the olive-green waters of that

THE LOOTING OF NICARAGUA 149

large estuary, while on its south side it is flanked by a big dusty plain which reaches almost to Bluefields. On this plain the battle of Laguna de Perlas was really fought. To the west and south, which were its exposed flanks, Laguna City was protected by a semicircle of strategical positions, with a thoroughly effective network of modern entrenchments. At the extreme right flank of this semicircle and on the northernmost extreme of the peninsula, was situated the fortified camp of Ratipura, held by a force of picked Conservative troops; while on the extreme left flank of this fringe of fortifications there reached far out into the plain the buttresses of the Bodega bridgehead, represented by a group of heavily fortified buildings controlling the Laguna entrance of the Bluefields-Laguna road. Directly behind and a little to the right of the Bodega rose the main stronghold of the town, called Hallover and Hallover Bottom, which controlled the entrance of another road leading from Bluefields also to Laguna City by way of Cucra and the Cucaragil bridge (across Esik Creek). The Cucaragil bridge, a couple of miles west of Hallover, was a strategical position of first magnitude and had been chosen by the Constitutionalists as the defensive base of their future military operations against Laguna City. The reason why most of the places in that part of the country bear English names is because Bluefields and Laguna used to be the seat of the Mosquito Indian reservation government in the days when that territory was still a British protectorate. Besides the ring of fortifications about Laguna City, the Diaz forces occupied a very good fortified position at the entrance of the Lagoon, called Bar Point, which the Constitutionalist auxiliary gunboat *La Carmelita* had been shelling for several days in order to make the enemy believe that the attack of the Constitutionalist army against Laguna City was going to be effected by means of a landing expedition. The real plan was different, however. According to this plan the Constitutionalist forces, stationed at Tasbapownie (i.e., on the northernmost, narrowest point of the peninsula, which forms the Pearl Lagoon) were to be transported on barges, towed by gasoline boats, to the mouth of Esik Creek, and thence they were to march between the right bank of Brown Bank Creek and a low ridge, which runs parallel to it, as far as the Cucaragil bridge, which faced the enemy's center and controlled, as I have said, one of the main roads from Bluefields to Laguna City. After having spent about a month in the Indian village of Tasbapownie the order of departure was given and the different units of the Constitutionalist Army embarked on barges towed by gasoline boats. Preceded by the vanguard, under the command of Daniel Mena, they crossed the lagoon, and after landing at the mouth of Esik Creek, plunged courageously into the frightful swamplands of the Brown Bank Creek jungle section, which, so far as I know, no human being has ever crossed before. It was truly a heroic march through those treacherous everglades—wading to their waists, sometimes to their breasts, carrying their rifles, machine guns, ammunition and provisions high above their heads, while millions of mosquitoes and other hideous vermin tortured them incessantly, and snakes and alligators endangered their lives. Finally, at dawn of December 23rd (1926), the little Constitutionalist army, starved and tired to death, lay down for a few hours' rest near Cucaragil bridge, the first real rest it had had during the three dreadful days which it had taken it to cross those dismal,

THE LOOTING OF NICARAGUA

dreary swamps. After cleaning their weapons of the thick layers of mud which covered them, and providing themselves with the necessary ammunition and something to eat, the different brigades formed into flying columns and, headed by their respective leaders, departed silently and disappeared in the dusty plain, to take up the positions assigned to them by their Commander, General Beltran-Sandoval. Colonels Alejandro Plata (Honduran) and Juan Escamilla (Mexican) with four hundred men and a platoon of machine guns were ordered to take La Bodega by storm. Colonel Daniel Mena, at the head of a similar force, was to advance against Hallover, while Colonel Gutierrez and Major Gilberto Morris (both died fighting at the head of their troops) were ordered to take Raitapura, which was situated at the northern extreme of the Laguna City peninsula, by surprise. Beltran-Sandoval, himself, remained with the rear guard protecting the bridge of Cucaragil, so as to block the way for any reënforcements coming from Bluefields to the relief of General Rivers Delgadillo, the commander of the Conservative army entrenched in Laguna City, while José Maria Moncada, with a couple of hundred men and the armored motor schooners, *La Carmelita* and *Leon del Mar*, was detailed to patrol and defend, if necessary, the entrance of the lagoon. Juan Campos with the armored schooner *Anita*, on which he had embarked some light cannon and a few machine guns, was to distract, with his fire, the attention of the garrison of Raitapura while Abel Gutierrez's flying column was getting ready for the assault. On the Chancho Island, José Coronado was posted with some machine guns and a ninety millimeter field piece to keep up a slow, continuous fire on Laguna City itself, while the different Constitutionalist columns were performing the attack.

At four A.M., of December 24th, the fight began all along the line. At nine A.M. the fortress of Bodega was taken by Plata and Escamilla after a fierce fight. Shortly afterwards Raitapura was also taken by the forces of Abel Gutierrez, who fell, as I said before, fighting at the head of his men. At three P.M. a detachment of three hundred Conservative troops which was advancing to the relief of Rivers Delgadillo, from the direction of Bluefields, was repulsed with heavy loss by Beltran-Sandoval at the bridge of Cucaragil. At seven P.M., after another fierce struggle, in which six-shooters and machetes finally played the leading part, and which ended with a dramatic duel to the knife on the battlefield between Alejandro Plata and the commander of the Conservative troops (who fell), Hallover and Hallover Bottom also were captured by the Constitutionalists. Only Laguna City now remained in the hands of the enemy. Some time about two A.M., of December 25th, the Conservative commander, Juan Moraga, headed a counter-attack to retake Hallover, but was promptly repulsed. At six A.M. arrived the news that Laguna City had been evacuated, Rivers Delgadillo having fled during the night with a few followers. And at seven A.M. Beltran-Sandoval and Alejandro Plata entered and took possession of the town. Among the numerous war material captured were about a dozen machine guns, seven hundred rifles, sixty thousand rounds of machine-gun ammunition and forty thousand cartridges, besides one field piece, an enormous quantity of provisions, and approximately three hundred prisoners who joined the Constitutionalist army voluntarily and accompanied it faithfully until the end of the war.

THE LOOTING OF NICARAGUA 153

Due to lack of time and the proper tools, the corpses of the dead, both Conservatives and Constitutionalists, were cremated, while the wounded of both sides were forwarded in care of the American Marine Forces for treatment in the hospitals of Bluefields. Among these was also a wounded American volunteer, who had been fighting on the side of the Conservatives. Unhappily all the Constitutionalist wounded were taken prisoners and locked up by the Diaz Government officials after they had been released from the hospitals.

The behavior of the Constitutionalists during the recent war has been humane and considerate in every respect when compared with that of some of the Diaz forces.

The plan of the battle of Laguna de Perlas, which had been carefully thought out and prepared by Beltran-Sandoval and Moncada, had worked out admirably. The discipline of the troops had been perfect. For some of the American officers, who had witnessed the performance, the battle of Laguna de Perlas must have been a bitter disappointment, but on the other hand, for those who are used to looking a bit into the future, it was a standard lesson—in fact, a revelation; for it went to prove that Latin America is rapidly waking up even in matters relating to the art of war.

Now, in order to prove that the commander-in-chief of the Constitutionalist forces during that fight was not Moncada, as some people have been led to believe, but Beltran-Sandoval, I will reproduce the following extracts taken from Beltran's résumé of the recent campaign, which was published in Managua after the armistice.

". . . I (says Beltran) was just getting ready to

take up the pursuit of Rivers Delgadillo—who had fled from Laguna City without even firing a shot, although he had still over seven hundred men, thirteen machine guns and a considerable amount of provisions and ammunition left—when a messenger arrived from La Cruz announcing that the Conservative commander Baquerano was advancing on that locality on the double quick; also, that the American Marines, who had declared La Barra del Rio Grande a neutral zone while the battle of Laguna de Perlas was going on, had seized forcibly and thrown into the Rio Grande about two million rounds of rifle, machine-gun and artillery ammunition belonging to us, so as to leave us without the necessary war material to continue the campaign. Those were anxious moments indeed, which required nerve and immediate action. Happily I did not lose my head. Forgetting the Americans for a while, I concentrated all my attention for the moment on Baquerano. It was indispensable to defeat his advancing forces at no matter what price. The rest could be attended to afterwards. I had consequently four hundred men mobilized at once, provided with four machine guns and plenty of ammunition and provisions. This flying column I placed under the command of Alejandro Plata, who departed on December 26th at seven A.M., forming our vanguard. Realizing the great danger which threatened our forces and overcoming incredible obstacles during his ascent of the river Curinguas, while following the flooded old jungle trail of Rama, Plata reached La Cruz on December 28th. From there he hurried to Batitan where he met and put to flight Baquerano after a sharp encounter. The whole Atlantic Coast, except Bluefields and La Barra, was in our hands. Immediately after that I embarked our expeditionary forces in *La Carmelita, La Estrella,* the *Jansen* and a flotilla of barges which they took in tow, and, following on Alejandro Plata's tracks, I arrived with the army at La Cruz on January 1st; from there I proceeded to San Pedro del Norte. There I reorganized our troops. During the days which followed, while advancing in the direction of Matiguas, we crossed virgin forests perhaps never before trodden by a human foot. We were marching most of the time through seemingly endless jungle swamps. We were crossing the heart of the jungle section of Central Nicaragua. Realizing beforehand what we had ahead of us, we were carrying only little provisions with us, but plenty of ammunition. I had our main convoy of supplies and ammunition carried in big dugout canoes [called 'pipantes' and mostly manned by Mosquito Indians] up the Rio Grande and the river Tuma as far as Willike, where it was loaded on packmules and freight oxen, which carried it across the Rio Blanco forest section to Matiguas."

The little town of Matiguas lies in the very center of Nicaragua and represents the divide, so to say, between the Departamentos of the Atlantic Coast, or Mosquitia, and those of the Interior, or the Pacific Coast. Matiguas is therefore a very important strategic point. From there two roads lead to Managua, the capital city of Nicaragua. One starts in a southwesterly direction, by way of Tierra Azul, Las Mercedes and Teustepe to Tipitapa, where it crosses the Penaloya channel which connects the lakes of Managua and Nicaragua only a few miles away from the capital. This road had the drawback, for the Constitutionalists, that it leads through the Departamento of Chontales which was inhabited almost exclusively by Conservatives and was therefore hostile to them. Besides, there was every probability that at the time of their arrival at the Tipitapa bridge, which they would have to pass forcibly, Admiral Latimer would declare Tipitapa a neutral zone in order to stop their advance on Managua and deprive them in that way of the fruits of their victorious campaign. No experienced soldier would ever have dared to follow that road, which led to an impasse, unless he wanted to be bottled up on purpose. The other road, which leads also from Matiguas to Managua, was the Matagalpa, Esteli, Leon highway, or Camino Real, which had the advantage of being perhaps a little shorter and which led almost entirely through the Liberal districts and Departamentos of Matagalpa, Jinotega, Segovia, Chinandega and Leon, where Generals Sandino and Parejon were conducting military operations, independently, with one thousand or two thousand men. By adopting the Matagalpa road, the Constitutionalist forces would have disposed also of considerable material resources, for those Departamentos are rich in mines, agricultural produce, etc. By adopting that road they could have controlled also the Nicaraguan section of Fonseca Bey, which would have put them in contact with the outside world, and, by descending on Leon, they could have cut off Managua from the American naval base at Corinto by intercepting the railroad. At the same time they could have distracted the attention of a large body of Adolfo Diaz's army by threatening, with a flying column, to break through the Conservative lines at Tipitapa in order to attack Managua from the rear.

Despite the efforts of Beltran-Sandoval to the contrary, Moncada decided to adopt the Tierra Azul-to-Tipitapa road, either because as a newspaper man posing as a soldier he did not know any better, or because he premeditated already at that time the betrayal of the Constitutionalist cause by tricking its valiant little army, on its arrival at Tipitapa, into surrendering its arms in the hope that Dollar Diplomacy might appoint him, as a reward, President of Nicaragua during the forthcoming elections. Another reason which may have influe.ced Moncada to follow the Tierra Azul-to-Tipitapa road was perhaps his desire to shun as much as possible the presence of Generals Sandino and Parejon, because he realized that those were men whom he could not command but whom he had to consult. In the case of Sandino, particularly, fear had probably also a whole lot to do with it, for Sandino had apparently not forgotten yet that Moncada had done everything in his power at Laguna de Perlas to keep him down. Moncada seems to have scented from the very start that Sandino was a *new man* and a real one, who would not stand for any trickery. It is a well-known fact that owing to Moncada's refusal to furnish him the necessary weapons, and in order to arm *some* of his men, at least, Sandino had been compelled, after the battle of Laguna de Perlas, to fish out of the sea about forty rifles which the Conservative soldiers had thrown away during their retreat. Provided only with those rusty guns and another dozen rifles which he managed to gather in Puerto Cabezas, Sandino ascended the Rio Coco as far as he could in canoes, and, heading for the south, afterwards made himself at home in the Departamento of Jinotega, where, by following guerrilla tactics, he finally managed to gather a group of over one thousand men, with whom he occupied and has held the central part of Nicaragua ever since, despite all the efforts of the traitor Moncada to discredit him, and of Dollar Diplomacy to dislodge him by means of the

American Marines. For such reasons as these, Moncada, as soon as he got to Matiguas, rejected the shorter and far more advantageous Matagalpa-Esteli-Leon route in order to follow that of Tipitapa, which was bound to lead the Constitutionalist army to its destruction in the end. But before I go on describing the campaign of the eastern expeditionary forces in the Interior, I will mention also a few details of General Francisco Parejon's victorious campaign on the west coast, which has a particular value because it goes to demonstrate how easily and how effectively a guerrilla warfare on a large scale can be conducted in Nicaragua, even in that most densely populated part of its territory, which is not given over to swamps and forests.

General Parejon belongs to the Labor Party of Nicaragua. At the time of the Chamorro coup d'état, in 1925, which caused the ruin of President Solorzano's administration, he was tranquilly working on his little ranch near Posoltega, in the State of Leon, without ever thinking that a year later he was going to be classed among the cleverest fighters that Nicaragua ever had. Such is destiny! After Irias's unsuccessful expedition to the Pacific Coast, and seeing no other way of getting guns and ammunition, Parejon decided to start a little guerrilla war of his own. He took to the bush with five or six men, armed only with machetes and six-shooters, and whom he told that he would dig up for them rifles from behind the rocks. And so he did. For by hiding behind rocks and shooting straight, he wound up by totally destroying General Noguera Gomez's expeditionary forces at Las Grietas. He captured during that occasion three hundred rifles, six machine guns, seventy-five thousand rounds of ammunition, some money and a considerable amount of provisions. This little stake put him firmly on his feet. And when he was getting ready to inflict on Noguera Gomez another decisive defeat, which would have provided him with thirty-six additional machine guns and forty cart loads of provisions and ammunition, his men unhappily got the "big head" on account of their constant successes, and, despite Parejon's efforts to prevent it, they literally forced him to undertake an attack on the fortified city of Chinandega, which, he knew, he would never have been able to hold in the long run, even if he captured it. On February 6th, when everything was ready for the attack, Parejon's plan miscarried because a telegraph operator, who had been captured three days previously but had managed to escape, notified General Viquez, the commander of the Conservative troops stationed in Chinandega. Viquez took all the necessary steps to repulse Parejon's attack and asked Adolfo Diaz in Managua to send him reënforcements. However, after two days of attacks and counter-attacks, during which he captured the town—except the cathedral, in which Viquez had entrenched himself—Parejon succeeded in breaking through the Conservative reenforcements which were already threatening his rear guard, and in making a clean getaway with his convoy of ammunitions and almost all his men, for his losses had amounted only to twenty dead and sixty-three wounded. The fight at Chinandega would never have caused so much attention and, let us say also, so much indignation both in North and Latin America, if it had not been for the fact that several American fliers took an active part in it, wantonly destroying large areas of the town with their incendiary bombs (for all bombs are incendiary) and killing—just for sport's sake—among other numerous members of the defenseless civilian population of Chinandega also *scores of women and children*. Referring to the barbarous behavior of the American fliers, says Parejon in his short, soldierly report: "During the attack of General Noguera Gomez, on February 8th, the airplanes arrived, throwing bombs on El Calvario and El Caimito. They caused considerable damage in El Calvario and also killed two of my men. Other bombs fell on the surrounding ground, causing several conflagrations."

In his story "Gypsy Birds," published in the New York *Herald Tribune Magazine* of July 31st, Mr. Linton Wells endeavors to "hush up" that hideous crime with considerable cynicism, by trying to make it look "funny." In this story Mr. Linton Wells even prides himself on having participated (as a passenger) in that little *joy ride,* during which those two "gypsy birds," as he calls them (Messrs. Mason and Brooks), slaughtered in a most wanton and cowardly way numerous defenseless Nicaraguan women and children—just for the fun of it, and perhaps too because Dollar Diplomacy had hired them to do so! For does not Mr. Wells say textually: "I was asked (by Mason and Brooks) if I would like to go along. *A little 'joy ride' as Mason expressed it!* I had no business in the world in mixing in these affairs, but a Sunday afternoon in Managua is no different from a Sunday afternoon elsewhere, etc." Now, is that not plain enough? What is the "big idea" of Mr. Linton Wells, I wonder, in trying to "kid" the American public with such childish talk as: "Don't get the wrong impression—Mason and Brooks were not 'hired assassins,' slaughtering people just for the sake of the inadequate salary the government paid them. They made it clear when they took the job that any attacks

THE LOOTING OF NICARAGUA

that they might be called upon to make on the Liberals would consist only in dropping bombs on, or machine gunning, certain areas *simply for moral effect."* And then again: "For another five minutes we played tag with our friend below. *Will Brooks had wandered off toward another section of the town and was apparently having a good time annoying the Liberals, without hurting anybody* . . ." After reading that balderdash, I cannot help asking again—What is the big idea? Has Mr. Linton Wells perhaps taken the American public for a bunch of fools? What about the pictures of *his* and Mason's and Brooks's victims published in this book, and which everybody in Nicaragua knows to be genuine? Let him look at those torn-off limbs and dare state that those wounds were inflicted by rifles or machine-gun bullets! Or does Mr. Linton Wells perhaps intend to imply that General Francisco Parejon lied when he said in his report, published in *La Noticia* of Managua of July 8, 1927, that the bombs of the airplanes, manned by Americans, killed some of his men and started conflagrations around Calvario and El Caimito? If so, why does not Mr. Linton Wells begin by denying first certain statements which appear in Mr. Torribio Tijerino's letter to the New York *Herald Tribune,* of July 29, 1927.[1] In this letter Mr. Tijerino accuses Mr. Linton Wells publicly, through the press, of having made *misstatements of facts* in his cable dispatches which, in other words, practically amounts to calling him a liar and hired collaborator of Dollar Diplomacy.

It is really regrettable that such a serious paper as the New York *Herald Tribune* has, apparently, also *fallen in line,* to judge by the way it continues patronizing this sort of collaborated story which carries all

[1] See Chapter VII, page 114.

the earmarks of Dollar Diplomacy propaganda. Eventually this may wind up by drawing upon the *Herald Tribune* the suspicion of belonging also to that group of papers which, deliberately or not (no matter!), keep on working in perfect harmony with Dollar Diplomacy in order to "hush up" things in Nicaragua, Cuba, Haiti, Santo Domingo, Panama, etc.

There is, for instance, the *Journal of Commerce,* which, according to the New York representative of *El Universal de Mexico,* stated in its editorial of February 4th (1927), the following: "Things in Nicaragua are progressing satisfactorily. The marines seem to have the military situation well in hand. According to recent Washington reports we intend to keep that control. *In the meantime we have thrown off the mask of apparent neutrality which we had been using so far, and openly recognized Diaz, as we really had done from the very beginning!* Despite all that, the interest of public opinion (on this subject) seems to be waning rapidly, and in another few weeks the incidents which occurred during the past few weeks will probably be forgotten by the majority of the American people, much the same as they have been in the habit of forgetting all previous incidents around the Caribbean Sea." [2]

And there is that other rooter for Dollar Diplomacy, *Liberty,* to which Senator Burton K. Wheeler refers in his speech, delivered by him at Ford Hall, Boston, Mass., on March 6th, 1927, in the following way:

"Fortunately for our sanity, in the midst of this moral murkiness, at the very moment when it seemed confusion was becoming worse confounded, something

[2] Translated by me from the Spanish.

THE LOOTING OF NICARAGUA

happened. There was a revealing flash of literary lightning. Not from the State Department. Not from the White House. But from the editorial department of the administration weekly that has swallowed the whole of the Kellogg-Coolidge Latin-American policy—except the uncertain, apologetic language in which that policy has been explained to the American public.

"Madame Roland once cried, 'O liberty, what crimes have been committed in thy name!' Conspicuous among the petty crimes committed in the name of liberty is the paper called *Liberty*—or *five-cent Liberty*—I am not quite sure which. The latter seems more appropriate. If the former is the correct way, it is a significant instance of the subtle way in which the propaganda of greed is taking the meaning out of the English language. I understand this flashy American Tory weekly was fathered and is fostered by the shrieking circus-calliope of modern American Toryism, the *Chicago Tribune*. The editor of this five-cent *Liberty* has rushed in with his literary lightning—or flashlight—to the rescue of the Kellogg-Coolidge policy, where administration angels feared to tread. To him the actions of the administration speak louder than its words. He interprets its words by its deeds. He boldly proclaims that the acts are all right. It is only the halting or apologetic words that are wrong. They are responsible for the confusion.

"With a wave of his editorial wand he sweeps off the landscape what he calls 'our little Americans, our Borahs and Wheelers, our professors, sentimentalists, and self-appointed wailers for the rights of small nations.' Next, he admits with a fine frenzy that the Kellogg-Coolidge policy is exactly what he says those opposed to it have called it: Piracy, highway robbery, vicious and depraved, morally! But, he shouts, it is progress! That is all he wants to know. He is perfectly certain he knows that. He washes his hands, and holds himself ready to wash the hands and the feet of the Secretary of State, of the President, of all the mud and the blood it may be necessary to wade through in following this path of progress. The whole responsibility lies at the door of what he calls 'Destiny.' He is terribly infatuated with 'Destiny' spelled with a capital 'D.' You see the big 'D' gets a big rise out of you if you happen to be built that way. He is so infatuated with the word that instead of seeking moral guidance from some real character like Lincoln or Parker or Lowell, he puts a stage character—poor distracted Hamlet, of all people—in the seat of authority, and then misquotes him to meet his needs as follows:

'There is a Destiny that shapes our ends,
Rough-hew them how we will.'

"Hamlet said 'divinity,' not 'Destiny'—and he did not use the big 'D' either. But the bold editor was a hundred per cent for 'Destiny,' so he read the riot act to Shakespeare and kicked 'divinity' right out of the line.

"Glancing back over American history, discounting every generous impulse and glorying in our every grab, and seeing as in a Balaamlike vision a 'Bigger Yet America,' this spokesman for the Spokesman of the White House and *Liberty* prophesies: 'Destiny was at work behind the selfishness of immoral politicians. Destiny is still busy, and seventy-five years from now the inhabitants of Nicaragua, Mexico, et al., will be singing "The Star-Spangled Banner" and scoffing at the idea that any one would return to the old government.' This noble outburst by 'Five-cent *Liberty*' was followed the next week by a double-page feature article under the caption 'Southward the bird of empire wings his way.' "

According to the moral standards of *Liberty* and its kind, even the *Herald Tribune* ought to agree with me that Mr. Linton Wells is a most "progressive" member of the one hundred per cent American make-the-Eagle-screech fraternity. Happily for Latin America and the United States themselves there are yet the New York *World, The Nation, The New Republic,* the *Boston Transcript,* the *St. Louis Post Dispatch,* the *Christian Science Monitor* and many other conscientious and independent American daily papers and weekly and monthly magazines and reviews left to prove that Dollar Diplomacy does not really represent more than an infinitesimal fraction of the sane, honest and good-hearted American people.

Another word about Mr. Linton Wells, for his pen is a busy one. Before writing to tell the American public that he and Messrs. Mason and Brooks, who were doing aviation stunts for Diaz, weren't dropping bombs to *hurt* any one, Mr. Linton Wells should have seen William Brooks's own stories published in the New York *Times* on March 5, April 10, and May 29, 1927. In the March 5th dispatch Brooks says that his machine was being hit by sharpshooters as he passed over a village three miles from Chinandega; and, he continues:

"I had about decided to be nice to the village and keep my bombs for a better day, but this made me angry. It wouldn't do any harm to let them have one, I thought, and so I pulled the trip rod. That homemade bomb made more dust than a 100-pound missile would in a wetter country. *The whole landscape seemed to rise.* When the dust settled I saw Liberal troopers running in every direction . . . when I dived on them they ran and clung to trees. By this time I had circled back over Chinandega, only three miles away, and the sharpshooters started to work again. . . . After I had figured out where the sharpshooters were hidden I heaved a bomb at them. The traffic jam which followed that bomb was probably the worst ever known in Chinandega. . . . Men, *women and children* dashed up and down the streets through the squares and back again. They seemed to be crazy they ran so fast and aimlessly."

Am I unjust to "Major Wm. S. Brooks, Nicaraguan Military Air Service," and too keenly alive in my sympathies for the women and children of Nicaraguan villages, when I say that Major Brooks's jaunty reports seem to me too incredibly gross, callous and cold-blooded smart-aleck stuff to be penned by an American officer?

In his dispatch of April 10, in which he likens Nicaraguan battles to "foot races," Major Brooks gives some interesting facts about the ranks of Diaz's army and as to how they are recruited under the protecting aura of Uncle Sam:

"Most of our regiments in that section now *have women in them.* They are picked up by the recruiting squads just as the men are. 'You loyal? All right then, come and serve your country!' That is the rigmarole which puts men, boys and women under colored hat bands and makes them eligible for Government liquor and bullets."

One wonders why the gross humor about "liquor," when Major Brooks himself says elsewhere that these pathetic women, who have been dragged out on the battlefields to die or be maimed for Dollar Diplomacy and its puppet President, are "not immoral" but are good wives and mothers. One wonders too why this dispatch roused no public word nor action from American women in their various powerful organizations. Is the slaughter of women in the interests of sordid business and sinister politics of no moment to them, because these poor helpless victims are only Nicaraguan women?

Chapter X

General Beltran-Sandoval's Report — Sacasa's Government, as the Constitutional Régime, Fully Acknowledged by Latin America — North American Outlaws in Nicaragua Not Arrested by the Marines — Who Asked for American Protection? — Letters From Prominent Foreigners, Both British and American, Testifying to the Conduct of Sacasa's Troops — Marines Cracking Safes and Forcibly Entering Homes — Dollar Diplomacy and the Peonage System.

AFTER his unsuccessful attempt to capture Chinandega by surprise, General Parejon went for a few days to El Salvador in order to get his bearings. There he was joined by Carlos Castro Wassmer, the noted patriot. And after his return, he started with about one thousand men for Esteli, with the intention of taking it. But Adan Velez, who was holding that place with four hundred men and numerous machine guns, evacuated it before he got there. In Esteli and Jinotega, both Lopez Irias and Augusto Sandino joined Parejon with another thousand men, and a week later they headed south, in the direction of Las Mercedes, where the combined forces of Moncada and Beltran-Sandoval were reported to be in a rather difficult situation, in fact, practically surrounded by the Conservative generals Viquez, Noguera Gomez and Rivers Delgadillo.

The following extracts of Beltran-Sandoval's official report give an approximate idea of how the little Constitutionalist army fared after its arrival in Matiguas, on February 7, 1927:

"Some time about the end of January I heard that Baquerano had taken possession of the little town of

THE LOOTING OF NICARAGUA 169

Muy-Muy with about one thousand men, provided with numerous machine guns. So I decided to attack him, which I did on February 9th, supported by Generals Escamilla and Alejandro Plata. After chasing Baquerano from there we returned to Matiguas, where we were joined by a large group of volunteers, hailing from Matagalpa. Thus reënforced, we decided to cross the Rio Grande and to entrench ourselves in the neighborhood of Tierra Azul. I took up, there, strong positions on the Cerro de Caballo, while Moncada remained in Matiguas (covering our rear). No sooner had we settled down when I heard that the enemy was trying again to take possession of Muy-Muy. So I occupied it once more, while Moncada took charge of our fortified camp at Cerro de Caballo. Supported by Colonels Mena and Alfred Miller (a Russian, from the Baltic provinces, who had volunteered in Mexico) I finally located the Conservative commander, Salvador Reyes, entrenched with about one thousand men and fifteen to twenty machine guns on the heights of El Chomipe and San Jacinto. We had only three hundred and fifty men and five machine guns. At five A.M. our attack commenced, and at seven P.M. the show was over. After a continued struggle of fifteen hours, during which twenty to twenty-five machine guns had been playing havoc, General Reyes decided to withdraw on the double quick, leaving behind everything, even his saddle horse and all of his personal belongings. After the fight was over, we returned to Tierra Azul where the enemy had been massing troops in considerable numbers. General Noguera Gomez even dared to send me a letter advising me to surrender! In the meantime I heard that a Conservative force, commanded by Rivers Delgadillo, was advancing again on Muy-Muy. So I took said place for the third time, where the Diaz forces shelled us for a while, although unsuccessfully. Knowing, however, the real intentions of the enemy, which were to hold us there while the rest of their army attacked us at Tierra Azul, I immediately returned to Palo Alto, which we reached about three A.M. At six A.M. the combined forces of the enemy stormed our positions, time and again, with great courage, but finally had to fall back after sustaining heavy losses. Immediately after that victory, we evacuated Palo Alto and left for Boaco. Unhappily we were ambushed on the road and had to take up new positions in Las Mercedes, where we fought for two consecutive days, until our ammunition nearly ran out; when, through a happy chance, Escamilla arrived with the convoy of munitions, which saved the day. This happened on Easter Sunday. Two days later the rear guard of Adolfo Diaz's army was attacked by the combined forces of Generals Parejon and Sandino; which caused the enemy to set fire to its depot of munitions before making a hasty retreat. On the following day we joined hands with the forces of Parejon, Sandino, Castro Wassmer, Lopez Irias, etc., and, after reorganizing our army, I ordered Escamilla to take up positions with his cavalry between Teustepe and El Chiflon, where Castro Wassmer and J. Caldera were ordered to support him as effectively as possible. Thanks to the timely arrival of Castro Wassmer the frantic attacks of Escamilla on Teustepe, and of J. Caldera on El Chiflon, resulted in a complete victory for us. In the meantime the rest of our four thousand men had caught up with us, thus enabling us to complete the iron ring with which we finally surrounded Adolfo Diaz's army near Teustepe. Almost immediately after that, Castro Wassmer, Escamilla and Lopez Irias defeated and cornered the few remaining Conservative forces left around La Cruz. Unhappily, at that very moment, when a complete victory had almost crowned the efforts of our brave little Constitutionalist Army, the first American commissioners arrived and with them also the armistice . . . !"

During the week or ten days which I spent in Puerto Cabezas I had occasion to converse very freely with Dr. Sacasa and was astonished to notice his rather superficial way of judging the international side of the Constitutionalist problem which confronted him. He seemed to be very bitter at the rest of the Latin American, and specially South American, republics because they had not recognized his government; without ever stopping to think that such a step on the part of those countries was absolutely unnecessary because they had already, one and all, recognized the Solorzano-Sacasa administration after its election in 1924. To have formally recognized the Constitutionalist government over again would have been absurd. By trying to force them, therefore, by means of bombastic circular proclamations, to recognize his administration over again, just because he had succeeded Don Carlos Solorzano in the Presidency, Dr. Sacasa was showing not only considerable lack of wisdom but also that he was absolutely ignorant of the fundamental principles of international law. It was very kind of the Mexican Government, indeed, to recognize the legally reëstablished Solorzano-Sacasa administration, over again, after Sacasa had assumed the presidency in default of the elected President, Don Carlos Solorzano; however, it was not really necessary. Dr. Sacasa ought to have known that! Besides, how did Dr. Sacasa expect the governments of Costa Rica, Honduras and El Salvador to show him a similar kindness, as Mexico, by recognizing over again the Constitutionalist Government, notwithstanding the fact that he had officially recognized the validity of the Bryan-Chamorro Treaty which the Central American Court of Justice, created in 1907 under the joint auspices of Mexico and the United States, had repudiated and declared void and nil because it illegally deprived Costa Rica, El Salvador and Honduras of certain water rights which these three republics undoubtedly possess in San Juan River and Fonseca Bay? The fact that the Conservative governments of Honduras and El Salvador *were practically forced by Dollar Diplomacy to recognize the fake Diaz régime* does not imply by any means that they and the Honduran and Salvadoran peoples, whom they represented, had, by doing so, recognized also the validity of the Bryan-Chamorro Treaty which Diaz had made with the United States without even consulting them as to their joint rights on those waterways! Referring to the manifest invalidity of said treaty, which Dr. Sacasa had officially recognized (as a bait, apparently, to obtain the recognition of the government of the United States) Mr. Thomas P. Moffatt, former United States Envoy to Nicaragua, said in a speech, which he delivered on July 25th, 1927:

"We negotiated the Nicaraguan Canal treaty in 1914 without the free consent of a sovereign people. Under the circumstances surrounding its recognition, if impartially viewed, the rights secured under its terms were tainted and far from clean. Our government, at that time divested of all deceit and evasion, to all intents and purposes entered into a contract practically with itself when it bargained with its maintained-in-office agent, Diaz." It is obvious that by promising to recognize the validity of the Bryan-Chamorro Treaty Dr. Sacasa officially and deliberately was trying to legalize, even at the expense of Nicaragua's sister republics in Central America, one of the most scandalous and felonious acts ever committed by the fake Diaz administration against the Constitution of Nicaragua. Therefore, I think it is plain enough that Dr. Sacasa was showing very little judgment, to say the least, when he kept complaining time and again that the rest of the Latin-American republics had left the Constitutionalist Government in the lurch, because they had omitted to recognize it all over again. Is it not obvious under such circumstances that an old, professional politician like José Maria Moncada should have taken all possible advantage of Sacasa's almost childish naïveté in order to feather his own nest later on at the expense of the unsuspecting Constitutionalist cause and its valiant little army? Am I not right in saying, and saying it over and over again, that what Nicaragua needs is *new blood, new men*—that, by supporting and forcing into that unhappy country's government fossils of the rotten old school régime, Dollar Diplomacy has been fanning the embers of dissatisfaction beneath the ashes of an apparent peace into a new nationalistic conflagration? Is not even Panama, which Dollar Diplomacy considered already dead to the world, giving to-day new, unexpected signs of true nationalistic agitation; even to the extreme of expressing its determination to submit the new, proposed treaty with the United States to the consideration of the League of Nations? Why does the United States Government persist in keeping its eyes shut? Why does it persist in its blindness to the fact that President Wilson's League of Nations has become a two-edged sword? Or has it really no belief in the metaphysical inevitability of the moral law which its members invoke to lay corner-stones, greet the B'nai Brith, address Rotarians, open Museums and admonish college graduates?

During my permanence in Puerto Cabezas an American bandit who was said to be a native of Texas, and who had been accused of several murders, both in Honduras and northern Nicaragua, had been spotted in the railroad camp of Sikaikwas, of the Cuyamel Fruit Co. At the request of the American local manager in that camp a detachment of American marines was dispatched from Puerto Cabezas to capture him. But the marines somehow or other must have thought the matter over on the road for they soon returned without having had even a look at the man. Thereupon and in order to protect the defenseless Nicaraguan population as well as the American employees of the railroad in Sikaikwas, three Nicaraguan policemen, armed only with six-shooters (because Admiral Latimer had ordered them to be deprived of their rifles) rushed to Sikaikwas and, after a lively skirmish, got their man; thus giving, both to the Nicaraguans as well as the American railroad employees in that camp, the protection which the detachment of American marines had failed to give them—who knows why? Another example which goes also to prove that it was not the Americans resident in Nicaragua really who were in need of protection against the Nicaraguans, but the Nicaraguans themselves who were badly in need of protection against the Americans residing in that country and the American marines, is that of another American, who was living some fifteen or twenty miles from Puerto Cabezas in a hamlet called Waba-Brown. This honorable member of the American colony in Nicaragua was waited upon by a native woman whom he used to maltreat in a scandalous way, until, one day, she walked into the office of Captain Antonio Duarte, the local Constitutionalist Chief of Police, asking for protection. On hearing that, the American, who was a violent man, rushed after her into the police station, threatening with a six-shooter Antonio Duarte and his men. He also notified the American Naval Commander in Puerto Cabezas to send a detachment of marines *because his life was in danger,* as he put it! Whereupon, shortly afterward, despite the fact that Waba-Brown was situated fifteen or twenty miles inland and, therefore, outside the two-mile limit of the neutral zone of Puerto Cabezas, a strong heavily armed detachment of marines, sent apparently by special order of Admiral Latimer, arrived at Waba-Brown and, after turning the girl back to her employer, confiscated all the arms and ammunition of the Chief of Police and his men! And, although the girl's tormentor next morning profusely apologized to Duarte, confessing that it was all his fault, and telegraphed at once to Puerto Cabezas explaining everything, Admiral Latimer refused to return their arms to Duarte and his men, leaving them and, therefore, also the defenseless population of Waba-Brown at the mercy of outlaws of the most violent type, who were taking advantage of the state of war existing in Nicaragua in order to kill and rob its inhabitants whenever they got a chance. These are only two of the many cases which I could cite in order to prove that if, in those days, protection was needed in Nicaragua, it was not protection of the Americans against the Nicaraguans, but protection for the defenseless Nicaraguan population against the arbitrariness and outright lawlessness of some of the American residents and the American marines in Nicaragua.

Another example which goes to justify the deep resentment of the Nicaraguan population against anything related to the American Government, is that of a certain American mine manager who had been employed to oversee some workings near Matagalpa, who went even to the extreme of *trampling under foot, publicly!* the Nicaraguan flag. Notwithstanding this act, Dollar Diplomacy exacted from its puppet president, Adolfo Diaz, the man be appointed by the Nicaraguan Government inspector of the construction works of the Matagalpa-to-Managua automobile road, at a monthly salary of $500, which he undoubtedly has continued drawing ever since. No wonder that Sandino has taken to the hills and that many other patriots, like Gral and Salgado, are following his example!

Now, in order to prove by means of written statements also, that the much advertised need of protection for American residents and their interests in Nicaragua has been only one of the many farces invented by Dollar Diplomacy in its efforts to justify the sending of American warships and marines to that country, I will reproduce a letter, sent by Mr. Gordon Bryan, Superintendent of the Cuyamel Fruit Co. of El Gallo, to the *Constitutionalist* military commander at La Cruz, Col. Messer. This letter says:

"El Gallo Pit., 25 December, 1926.
"Col. F. G. Messer, La Cruz.

"*Dear Sir:* In fairness to you I wish to state that during the entire time you have been in command of this river there has been no cause of complaint on my part. The movement of the power barges, of the

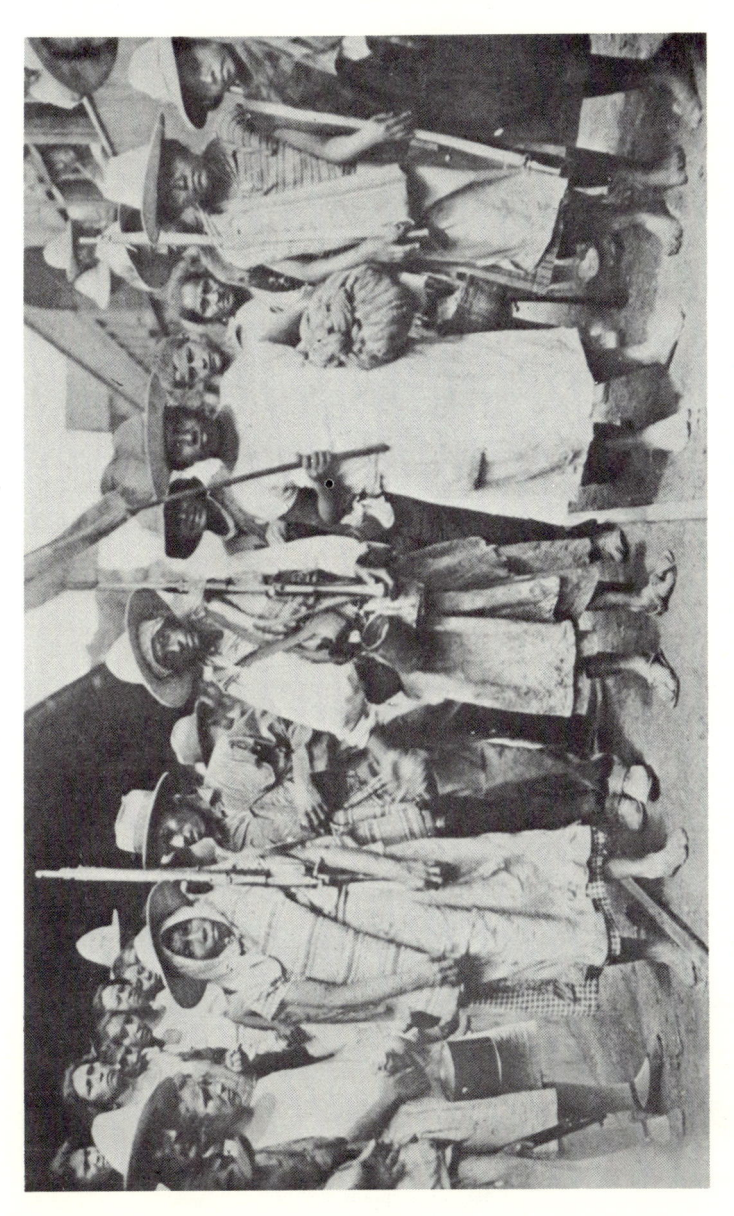

Nicaraguan woman conscripts in Adolfo Diaz's Conservative Army.

Victims of the American fliers at Chinandega, Nicaragua.
(Effect of airplane bombs.)

Victim of the American fliers at Chinandega, Nicaragua.
(Effect of airplane bombs.)

river tugs and traffic in general, has not been impeded. There has been no grafting or any semblance of it, by suggestion or otherwise. All friction has been avoided. We have had no difficulties with your troops, who have not committed any abuse, and crime of any kind has been no more than in peace time. Any revolution necessarily upsets matters but, I am pleased to say, we have had no cause to complain of any actions on your part.
"Very truly yours,
"GORDON BRYAN,
"Superintendent of the Cuyamel Fruit Co."

I should judge that the foregoing written testimony of the representative of practically the biggest group of American investors operating in Nicaragua ought to be sufficient to prove the veracity of my statements regarding the pretended necessity of American warships and marines to protect the lives and interests of the four hundred American citizens resident in Nicaragua!

On the other hand, with the view of proving also that the pretended necessity of protecting the lives and interests of the British subjects in that country has been likewise only a "put up job," I will reproduce the following letters of *three representative members of the British colony in Nicaragua,* which are self-explanatory.

"La Barra de Rio Grande, March 3, 1927.
"SR. MINISTRO DE HACIENDA, DR. ARTURO ORTEGA,
"Puerto Cabezas.

"Having received a letter from you, dated February 28th, ulto., I take great pleasure in answering it. I beg to say that . . . from the latter part of the

month of August, 1926, until the latter part of December of the same year, I have seen from one thousand to one thousand five hundred men at different times, and all the time not less than five hundred to six hundred soldiers of the Liberal party of Dr. Sacasa, and in my opinion you could not desire better behavior from such men up to the present time, or day of their departure. I beg to remain with respect,
"Yours very truly,
"J. H. HARDY."

"Rio Grande Bar, 2d March, 1927.
"EL MINISTRO DE HACIENDA Y CREDITO PUBLICO
"*Sir:* In reply to your favor of February 28th inquiring of me as to the behavior of the Liberal troops stationed here, I beg to report that nothing better was to be desired in the behavior of officers and men in said troops. They were quiet, orderly and well behaved. I am in a position to state this authoritatively as I was authorized by General Moncada to attend them medically. I attended over three hundred of them and in no case found any reason for complaint, as to their behavior. On the contrary, I have nothing but praise for them. I am, Sir, your very obedient servant,
"L. G. MACPHERSON."

"Rio Grande Bar, March 3d, 1927.
"DON ARTURO ORTEGA,
"Ministro de Hacienda y Credito Publico.
"*Dear Sir:* I am in receipt of your letter of February 28th, and in answer must impartially say that *as an Englishman* and resident practitioner I have been here during the entire stay of the army of the Constitutional Government of Dr. Sacasa, and that the behavior and general deportment of the Liberal troops

and government were all that could be desired, and both individuals and property were unmolested and respected. I beg to subscribe myself,
"Very truly yours,
"R. K. PALMER."

The foregoing letters ought to be a sufficient proof that no protection of the lives of British subjects in Nicaragua, or of their interests, was really needed, and that if such protection was demanded by Mr. Patterson, British Consul General at Managua, it must have been due in all probability to that gentleman's lack of knowledge of *actual conditions in Nicaragua*. The fact that His Majesty's cruiser *Colombo*, which was dispatched in March, 1927, to Nicaragua, to give shelter to any British subjects in want of protection, left again almost at once without any one having sought refuge on it, goes to show also very plainly that the much advertised persecution of British subjects was only a farce and probably also only a "put up job" to furnish Dollar Diplomacy a pretext for soliciting armed American intervention in Nicaragua.

On the other hand, and in order to prove that in La Barra and Rio Grande, as in Waba-Brown, Sikaikwas, etc., it was not the Americans who needed protection against the Nicaraguans but both *the Nicaraguans and the British subjects* who sorely required protection against the arbitrariness and violences of the American landing forces. I will briefly mention the two following instances which were related to me, at my arrival at La Barra de Rio Grande, by Mr. Ralph Sinclair (British subject), son of the wealthy British merchant, Mr. Wm. Sinclair, in the presence of Col. Newhall and Mr. Arthur Felton Hogson:

(1) That immediately after the landing at La Barra (on December 23d, or 24th, 1926) of the detachment of American marines at the orders of Lieut. K. B. Chappel, of the United States cruiser *Rochester*, some of its members blew open, or forced open by means of an iron bar, the safe in the office of the Orr Fruit Co., to search for arms and ammunition, as they put it! And (2) that immediately after that, and also under the same pretext, they forcibly entered not only the private residence of Mr. Wm Sinclair (British subject) but also the bedroom of Mrs. Sinclair. They were finally ousted by Mr. and Mrs. Sinclair, while Mr. Sinclair kept reminding them, at the top of his voice, that during all the time that one thousand seven hundred Liberal soldiers had been stationed in La Barra order and respect for foreign lives and property had been religiously observed; and that the "Spaniards" (meaning the Nicaraguans) never had violated the sanctity of the home! The Englishman's home is his castle, as the old English proverb goes, and Mr. Sinclair was a very angry man. No wonder that the behavior of some of the American marines abroad has earned them, in Latin America, the nickname,—"the barbarians from the north!" I wonder if Mr. Patterson, British Consul General at Managua, ever reported this case to the Foreign Office in London!

While Col. Newhall, Mr. Ralph Sinclair, Mr. Arthur Felton Hogson and myself were standing on the wharf of La Barra, Mr. Hogson, pointing at the olive-green waters of the Rio Grande, explained to me in detail how Admiral Latimer, without regard whatsoever for international law and taking mean advantage of the fact that the Liberal army was busily engaged fighting Adolfo Diaz at Laguna de Perlas, had ordered the United States cruiser *Rochester* to steal up on La Barra, like a thief in the night, and to declare it a neutral zone, while Lieut. K. B. Chappel, without loss of time—probably for fear that the Liberal forces might return unexpectedly—commenced, by order of Admiral Latimer, to seize and destroy the ammunition depot of the Constitutionalist army in La Barra, consisting of eight hundred rifles, one thousand eight hundred and seventy-three boxes of ammunition (each with one thousand rounds) and a considerable amount of artillery ammunition, which Lieut. K. B. Chappel and his detachment dumped immediately into the waters of the Rio Grande, not three hundred yards away from where we were now standing, after having ripped open, with axes, the tin lining of the boxes so as to prevent the Constitutionalists from fishing them out again and using them later on. Mr. S. Vega Lopez, a merchant from La Cruz, told me, when I got there, a few days later, in the presence of Dr. J. P. Mollgaerd, graduate of the University of Copenhagen, and Mr. Lalinde, a well-known Colombian mahogany contractor, that not only in Puerto Cabezas and Rama, but even in the neutral zone of Bluefields itself Admiral Latimer's landing forces never moved a finger, but on the contrary, had been quietly looking on while their allies, the Conservative rabble, looted to their hearts' content the establishments of defenseless merchants; for instance those of Carlos Martinez, Leclair, Ramon Rostran and others.

It would seem to be high time for the American people to demand from Congress a *thorough investigation,* not only of Admiral Latimer's and his subaltern officer's behavior during the recent revolution in Nicaragua, but also of that of the different American landing forces in Haiti, Santo Domingo, Panama,

Honduras and practically also the whole of Central America.

Unless the scandal is stopped within a reasonable time, Latin America will probably be forced to throw in her lot—wisely or not—with the League of Nations or no matter whom, even at the risk of having to prove to ex-Secretary of State, Mr. Hughes, that he was badly mistaken when, during an address which he delivered in Minneapolis on August 30, 1923, he haughtily exclaimed: "As the policy embodied in the Monroe Doctrine is distinctly the policy of the United States, the government of the United States reserves to itself its definition, interpretation and application!"

The little town of Puerto Cabezas did not—with the exception of half-a-dozen buildings—really exist until the government of Dr. Sacasa was established there, in December, 1926. Up to that time it practically consisted of the mill and the lumber yards of the Bragman's Bluff Lumber Co., which had been exploiting for many years some very rich and extensive pine tree concessions in that neighborhood; much to its liking, for up to December, 1926, there had been practically nobody to check up on it. A short time previously, that is, during the short-lived Emiliano Chamorro Government, the company had bought from Don Emiliano for the amount of fifty thousand dollars the stretch of land on which the new town site had been located, with the right of expelling the settlers at will whenever it chose to do so. This high-handed method, so characteristic of the Dollar Diplomats (it should not be forgotten that the Bragman's Bluff Lumber Co., the La Luz and Los Angeles Mfg. Co. in Bluefields and Pis-Pis, and the Cuyamel Fruit Co. in Rio Grande, Rio Escondido, etc., have been for many years, and continue being, the standard bearers of

Dollar Diplomacy in Eastern Nicaragua) did not meet with the success expected owing to the Constitutionalist Government, which, after establishing itself firmly in Puerto Cabezas, overruled and annulled the Chamorro concession and authorized the Indian "sindico," Noe Colon, to continue selling town lots to settlers. With the result that, by the time I left, Puerto Cabezas had grown to be quite a little mushroom town with about thirty or forty new buildings and storehouses under construction. Thus the Constitutionalist Government, although disarmed and constantly handicapped by the presence of the marines, had yet been able to help the Nicaraguan people by frustrating one of the pet schemes of Dollar Diplomacy on the Atantic Coast of Nicaragua.

At that time, and despite the state of war which was reigning in that country, the Cuyamel Fruit Co. continued extending its railroad beyond the western limits of its banana plantation, in the direction of the rich mining district of Pis-Pis in which are located a number of large gold mines; as, for instance, the La Luz and Los Angeles Mine, the Panama, Neptuno, Bonanza, La Estrella, La Constancia, Siempre Viva, etc. All these mines are rich and have mills counting all the way from ten to thirty stamps. Their main drawback was lack of transportation. The Cuyamel Fruit Co., which was naturally interested in the development of those mines, because by tapping that rich ore zone the profits of its railroad would increase accordingly, was not enthusiastic about the prospect of a "long-term" revolution, for most of its laborers had quit work to join the contending parties. The same thing happened in the mines at Pis-Pis, most of which had closed down even before the revolution had got started because their laborers refused to be paid in "scrip." The only one among them which continued working, although with half of its former crew only, was the La Luz and Los Angeles Mine; for, although it paid only "hunger wages," it at least paid in spot cash. It ought to be remembered that the "scrip" system is in reality the old Mexican "peonage" system which Dollar Diplomacy has been trying to establish, under a different name, wherever it has set foot in Central America and the Antilles. Its way of applying it has been always the same. The Dollar Diplomats would commence by paying splendid wages at first—which they would go on reducing gradually, until they had reached the limit of "hunger wages." Once that far, they practically forced their laborer to draw half their salaries in merchandise, furnishe to them by the company stores, and the other half 1 "scrip," or I. O. U's. As soon as these laborers wer well in debt to the company stores, they would be forced to take seventy-five per cent of their salaries in merchandise, while the remaining twenty-five per cent was paid in "scrip," which the companies refused to cash unless they had been discounted, at a loss of perhaps fifty per cent, apparently by special agents of those companies. The *real reason* why the Dollar Diplomats established on the Atlantic Coast of Nicaragua have always *rather welcomed* the fact that the Wall Street Fiscal Agents of the National Bank of Nicaragua and of the Nicaraguan Railroad Co. have failed, during seventeen years, to live up to their agreement to extend the Nicaraguan railroad clear across from the Pacific to the Atlantic Coast, is obvious, for if that extension of the railroad had been built, the price of foodstuffs and other articles of first necessity which these companies had been, and continue, importing from the United States with the purpose of selling them to their laborers on account of their wages at a big profit, would forcibly have dropped at least fifty per cent, thus enabling the workers to save up at least half of their scanty salaries. For example: If a laborer employed by those companies who has got to pay to-day out of his, let us say one dollar per day salary, seventy-five cents for merchandise (foodstuffs and other articles of first necessity, imported from the United States and which the company stores sell to him at a considerable profit), could buy that same merchandise imported from the agricultural and industrial sections of western Nicaragua, for half its price, he would save thirty-five cents on his living expenses plus the remaining twenty-five cents of his daily wages. He would thus be able to save sixty cents a day out of his dollar wages for a rainy day. That would make him independent to a certain extent of the "scrip" or "peonage" system of those companies. We see, therefore, why the Dollar Diplomats, operating on the Atlantic Coast of Nicaragua, have always welcomed the failure of the Wall Street Fiscal Agents of the Nicaraguan Railroad to construct a branch line across country from the Pacific to the Atlantic Coast! The *real reason* why the Dollar Diplomats in Nicaragua have been working hand in hand for seventeen years so as to prevent the extension of that railroad from coast to coast, has been evidently for the purpose of keeping the Nicaraguan peon in eternal bondage, much the same as they tried to do in Mexico previous to and after the fall of Porfirio Diaz.

One of Nicaragua's natural resources which Dollar Diplomacy continues exploiting without practically any benefit for that country is that of its forest products; such as mahogany, cedar and other precious wood.

The mahogany concessionaries, who are ninety per cent foreigners, have been, during the past seventeen years, ruthlessly destroying the national mahogany and cedar tree forest reservations, regardless of the requirements of the law as to length, width, etc. As they do not have to pay the nominal duty of five dollars per one thousand square feet *except for those logs which they actually deliver on board the ships* in the regulation export harbors of Gracias a Diós, Prinzapolka, La Barra, Bluefields, Grey Town, etc., practically sixty per cent of the trees which they annually chop down in the forests, *indiscriminately and without ever thinking of reforesting the exploited areas,* generally go to waste. They cut them down only on speculation. If the rainy season should turn out good, that means, if the rivers should rise sufficiently for them to drift down the greater part of their yearly crop, they are bound to make a "killing." Whereas if the rivers should not carry enough water, they always would be able to float down enough logs to cover their expenses and leave them a handsome profit besides; no matter if eighty or ninety per cent of the remaining logs be left to rot in the forests or on the dry river beds. The forestry inspectors, who are sent down every year from Managua to check up on the concessionaries, are generally their personal friends, or bosom friends of the Dollar Diplomacy presidents. For a comfortable bribe they are willing to close not only one eye, but both; and, if they had three or four, also those. In the days of President Zelaya, before Dollar Diplomacy methods were introduced in Nicaragua by ex-Secretary Knox, the laws regulating the exploitation of the forest reserves were strictly obeyed, so much so that even the powerful Emery Co., for not having complied with them on a certain occasion, had its concession annulled by the Nicaraguan Government. All these facts have, of course, been carefully withheld by the Dollar Diplomacy press agents from the knowledge of the American public for reasons which everybody can easily understand. These various subjects remind me of a certain four-column story which was published in the Sunday edition of the New York *Times* of August 21, 1927. The party who wrote it was a Whiting Williams, who, by the way, refers to "an American who was." I imply that this must be some disappointed foreign merchant or concession hunter who probably went to Managua in the expectation of collecting some claims for alleged damages suffered during the revolution. This story, which seems to cry to heaven also (like most stories of that well-known type) "did I not tell you? what is the use of wasting sympathies on those people? those Nicaraguans are nothing but a gang of savages!" is, so far as its military part is concerned, about the most extraordinary joke I ever read.

Mr. Williams goes to the extreme of claiming, in a most nonchalant way and on the strength of Diaz-Chamorro partisan hearsay only, that General Luis Beltran-Sandoval, the commander of the Constitutionalist Army during the battle of Laguna de Perlas, had ordered, after the battle was over, that all the Conservative officers who had been taken prisoners be executed. And also that the Constitutionalist forces, which stormed Chinandega on February last, were composed of one thousand five hundred men, when even the children in Nicaragua know that General Parejon did not at that time have more than five hundred volunteers, and that, of those, two hundred were unable to participate in the attack on the town because they had been left in charge of the convoy of munitions and of the protection of the rear of the attacking forces. I am convinced that if the Sunday editor of the New York *Times* had taken the trouble of inquiring first at the War Department at Washington, D. C., about the veracity of those statements, he would surely have desisted from publishing that "funny" four-column story. However, I must confess on the other hand, that outside of its pseudo-military details that story is all right, because it gives a magnificent testimony and a proof unsurpassed of the incredible, criminal negligence with which Dollar Diplomacy allowed its four dummy presidents, Estrada, Adolfo Diaz, and the two Chamorros, to turn Nicaragua into a financial wreck and practically also into a living cemetery. Mr. Williams' description of the means to which the Dollar Diplomacy hirelings were allowed to resort *during the seventeen years of American financial and armed intervention in Nicaragua,* in order to recruit their armies and to enrich themselves and their masters in Wall Street is a magnificent example of how easily sometimes the weapons which Dollar Diplomacy is in the habit of pressing into the hands of its press agents or "professional knockers" become boomerangs. Some of the several bitter truths, which I have referred to already in this chapter and which this Mr. Williams has committed the blunder of admitting, apparently without realizing it himself, are contained in the following statements copied from his story:

". . . Nevertheless we send yearly up to the capital hundreds of thousands of dollars from our custom house here (in Bluefields) but get back hardly so much as a penny for repairing our disgraceful streets. Besides, most of the local officials, from the Governor down to Postmaster, are sent over by the leaders and told to go as far as they like. One governor recently, on a monthly salary of two hundred and fifty dollars took out in four months a total of twenty thousand dollars."

And again: "This discontent comes close not only to every Bluefielder but to every one on Nicaragua's Atlantic Coast. In fact, it gets expression at least three times a day, *because the country's roadlessness forces most of the local beans and rice—Central American for bread and butter—to be imported instead of brought across the country; and such importation means always high duties and, therefore, high cost of living!* Altogether it is quite certain that men would need to do much less fighting in Nicaragua if the various parts of the country could be brought into better contact and if men could everywhere be helped to earn a decent living *without being forced into the army or persecuted out of business by their political enemies. Nothing would serve this end better than more railroads, and specially one across the country to the Atlantic Coast!*"

Am I not right when I say that Dollar Diplomacy must have had its *special reasons* for holding back Nicaragua from all logical progress during those years, since 1909, when ex-Secretary of State, Mr. Philander Knox, turned it loose—like a rabid dog—on the unhappy people of Nicaragua?

Am I not right when I claim that American financial and armed intervention has brought on Nicaragua only ruin, desolation and death—setting it back at least fifty years?

Chapter XI

I Leave Puerto Cabezas for Managua — By Motorboat, Barge and Canoe Up the Rio Grande — A Pair of German Military Trousers Rouses Suspicion — A Wrecked Safe — How Laborers Who Demand More Pay Are Answered in the Banana Country — Ancient Indian Inscriptions on the River Rocks — Opportunities for Legitimate Business in Nicaragua.

ON April 4, 1927, I took my departure for Managua, across country from the Atlantic to the Pacific Coast. The "salvo conducto" or passport extended to me by the local Constitutionalist authorities at Puerto Cabezas reads as follows:

"El suscrito Comandante de la Policia de Puerto Cabezas da pasaporte al corresponsal de la prensa europea y americana Sr. Nogales Mendez, que en esta fecha se dirige a La Barra de Rio Grande a bordo de la embarcacion 'Anderson.' Seruega a las authoridades de transito no impedirle su marcha. Dado en Puerto Cabezas, a cuatro dias de Abril de mil novecientos veintisiete. (f) José Maria Zacarias G., Comandante de Policia. 4 April 1927. Approved W. E. Terry, Ensign U. S. N."

Which means translated into English:

"This passport has been extended by the undersigned Chief of Police of Puerto Cabezas to the European and American press correspondent Mr. Nogales-Mendez, who leaves to-day for La Barra de Rio Grande on the 'Anderson.' No obstacles shall be put in his way. (s) José Maria Zacarias G., Chief of

THE LOOTING OF NICARAGUA

Police of Puerto Cabezas, April 4, 1927. Approved W. E. Terry, Ensign, U. S. N."

After I had said good-by to Dr. Sacasa and his entourage as well as to Commander Bischoff and the rest of the officers of the American Landing Forces, Mr. Fuchs drove me in his machine at about five P.M. to the wharf, and I climbed on board the motor-schooner *Anderson*.

Next morning I woke up while we were laying to off the dangerous bar of the Rio Grande. I had been so fast asleep that I had never noticed how we had stopped at least for an hour at Prinzapolka in order to take on some passengers and mail. While I was trying to rub the sleep out of my eyes I came near being washed overboard by one of the heavy breakers which constantly threatened to capsize our schooner. Happily our captain turned out to be an old sea dog who finally managed to slip in behind the lee of the bar, which practically closes the mouth of the Rio Grande, turning it into a large estuary which is surrounded by a ring of everglades and marshy lagoons, inhabited only by alligators, snakes, egrets, pelicans, blue cranes and other wild fowl. On the southern shore of the bay were several power barges loading bananas in front of the Cuyamel Fruit Co.'s buildings and warehouses. Opposite, on the northern side of the bay, the little town of La Barra showed up in the shape of a long row of wooden shacks, storehouses, etc., which was called "Main Street"; I do not know why, because I did not notice any other street in La Barra. All the houses were built on stilts, including the thoroughfare of "Main Street" itself, which was really only a big sidewalk of rotten planks. At the wharf, Corporal H. M. Anthony, of the United States cruiser *Cleveland* (an awfully nice young chap from New York, by the way) examined my passport, not without a certain air of suspicion—caused probably by the gray German officer's regulation riding breeches which I was wearing. From there I was escorted by Mr. Felton Hogson to the residence of Col. Francisco Espinosa, the military commander of the place, where I hung up my hammock and made myself at home. After breakfast Corporal Anthony made his appearance and invited me in the name of Ensign Mann, commander of the detachment of American marines stationed in La Barra, to report to his office, which I did at once. It seems that Ensign Mann too had got kind of suspicious of me on account of those blessed German military riding breeches of mine. However, after looking over my passport with all due attention, he must have convinced himself that I was O. K., for he commenced thawing by inches; so much so that when I left next day for La Cruz, he gave me as a souvenir a big package of Lucky Strike cigarettes which came in very handy during the seven weeks which I was going to spend, almost immediately after my departure, cut off from the rest of the world in the jungle districts of Central Nicaragua.

Among the several interesting stories which Col. Espinosa told me was one referring to Admiral Latimer's way of taking mean advantage of the good faith of the people of Nicaragua. It seems that immediately after Lieutenants Chappel and Buchanan of the United States Cruiser *Rochester* had landed in La Barra to loot the depot of ammunitions of the Constitutionalist army, they had detailed a group of marines to go to a place called Sandy Bay, some five or six miles up the coast from La Barra, with explicit orders to destroy the arms of a dozen or so Constitu-

The Author (center) at his arrival at Matagalpa, Nicaragua.

Some of the victims of the massacre of El Guayabo, La Cruz, Nicaragua. (Laborers of the Cuyamel Fruit Co., slaughtered in cold blood because they requested a raise in their salaries.)

tionalist volunteers who had been stationed there by order of General Beltran-Sandoval for the purpose of maintaining order in the surrounding villages. In this case, as in the case of Waba-Brown and others which I could mention, Admiral Latimer committed an unpardonable breach of international law, for Sandy Bay like Waba-Brown, lay outside of the two-mile limit of the neutral zone of La Barra. That afternoon I went to have a look at the safe of the Orr Fruit Co., which, according to Mr. Sinclair, Jr., and other informants, had been blown or forced open with an iron bar by some of the American landing forces at the time of their arrival at La Barra. I found the office empty. It was being used at the time by the marines as a sort of laundry establishment, because it was situated on the shore of the river. It was surrounded by big piles of mahogany logs, worth thousands of dollars, which had been washed ashore. The concessionaries had left them there to rot on the burning sands, rather than go to the expense of having them rolled back into the river and stored away in a safe place. In front of the office a sentry was pacing up and down. And while he kept telling me about a tiger cat which he had noticed sneaking about that neighborhood a few nights before, I entered the office and saw the empty safe with its door half open and its lock showing distinctly that it had been tampered with. When I started back to town I saw a dozen or two Indian canoes, loaded with market produce, tied to some bushes near the wharf. Their crews were busily engaged in trying to dispose of their goods to a crowd of city folk. They were pure blooded Suma-Mosquito Indians, without the slightest sign of Negro blood. I could not help stopping for a while to examine them, for they represented one of those mysterious branches of the Indian race which, after having been for centuries a cultured nation, had gone back so fast to primitive nomad life that they do not even remember to-day their ancient religion or folk lore. According to what I can find out about their origin the Mosquito Indians proceed from a fusion of the Carib and the Trujillo Indian tribes which drifted down the river from the Pacific Coast after having enjoyed for over a thousand years, perhaps, a very advanced civilization of their own. They obtained their fusion of Carib blood probably after their arrival at the Atlantic littoral, which the roving tribes of the Carib nation used to inhabit long before the Spaniards conquered Nicaragua. The numerous highly artistic picture writings which I noticed on the basalt walls on both sides of the upper Rio Grande, between El Gallo and San Pedro, bear a resemblance to the antique Maya and Nahua school, and especially to that of the ancient so-called empire of the Xibalba, or "the serpents," which left indelible signs of its highly advanced culture not only in Chiapas and Cuba but practically also all over Central America as far down as Panama. Unfortunately for the Central American vassal States of the Xibalba empire this was ultimately destroyed (about the VI century of our era) by the Nahua nations and subsequently by that of Anahuac, or the Toltec empire, which finally brought about—probably through its extreme cruelty—the total separation and isolation of Central America from its ancient center of civilization on the Peninsula of Yucatan. The efforts of the Chichimacas—who destroyed, in their turn, the Toltec empire—to regain control over Central America must have been in all probability the real cause of the exodus of the larger part of the highly civilized nations and tribes of Western Nicaragua toward the Atlantic Coast, where they were conquered and assimilated by the wild Carib tribes. After their later conquest by the Spaniards, those of their tribes which had settled on the Atlantic littoral, were also greatly influenced by a strong fusion of Negro blood.

The Suma tribes, which roam the jungle sections of Central Nicaragua, represent in my estimation the prototype of the Mosquito Indians before these were absorbed by the wild Carib nations. Their blending with sturdy, savage alien peoples is plainly shown by the fact that the average height of the Mosquito Indian is five feet nine inches, whereas that of the Suma, only five feet seven inches. The origin of the marvelous picture writings, belonging to the old Maya-Nahua school, which embellish the massive, lustrous, basalt walls of the upper Rio Grande, belong, probably, to the epoch when the Suma tribes, which settled along the Atlantic Coast, had not yet been conquered and blended with the sturdy, savage Carib tribes. The Mosquito Indians are as a rule very hospitable. They are also great hunters and expert fishermen. Their favorite dish, consisting of a mush made of boiled bananas, is called by them "vaviel." They are constantly bathing, yet they are never clean. Their dwellings are thatched huts made of canes or reeds. Some of them are big enough to shelter several families. The women generally do all the work while the men hunt, fish and provide for their families very conscientiously. But they are a gross people and are afflicted with diseases which they generally neglect because of their medicine-men or "sukias," who seem anxious to prolong them rather than to cure or prevent them. The women bathe and paint their faces several times a day. They are also very fond of wearing bead ornaments and jewelry. They present a rather attractive sight, especially when they row out into the ocean in their narrow dug-out canoes, with gaudily painted faces, accompanying the strokes of the paddles with long-drawn-out, sadly sounding songs like this:

"Vaya, yang vaya yang vaya Boocra, vaya yang vasina vaya, vanki bila miraim, vaya, aisabe bisura aula yang, vaitna ate . . . !" Which means, translated into English: "I am going, I am on my way, I am going with my lover up the river! Good-by, you women who speak the Vaki language! I am on my way, good-by! I will soon be back with my lover . . . !"

The day after my arrival I took passage up the river on the Power Barge Number Two, Captain William Bevy, and about four P.M. she put her prow to the west and, after tooting her head off for several minutes, finally commenced moving lazily. In time we disappeared out of sight of the town and plowed on between the walls of dark evergreens which line the river on both sides for a stretch of about thirty miles, where they gradually begin to give way to occasional banana growths. After another six or ten miles, both banks of the Rio Grande show only the swaying fronds of millions of banana trees for perhaps seventy miles, past La Cruz and El Gallo as far as Palpunta. Ninety per cent of this highly cultivated banana zone is either owned or controlled by the Cuyamel Fruit Company, which also owns enormous banana plantations along the lower course of the Rio Recondido and in the hinterland of Puerto Cabezas. The only other foreign company established in the Rio Grande zone is the Banana Rio

THE LOOTING OF NICARAGUA

Grande Company, a French concern, which is situated opposite La Cruz.

Our Barge Number Two was a powerful shallow draft boat which had been commandeered and used by the Constitutionalist forces as an auxiliary cruiser during their attack on The Bluff in December 1926. She had been riddled by machine gun fire during that attack. Her funnel looked like a sieve. A shell had ripped open some of the cabins on her upper deck. Power Barge Number Two was certainly a veteran, covered with scars all over, and so were Captain Bevy and his two pilots who, rather than give her up, had stuck to her to the bitter end. I met on board, among other interesting parties, Mr. Frank Lucas, a merchant from La Cruz and brother-in-law of the ill-fated Major Gilberto Morris who fell while storming Raitarapura, during the battle of Laguna de Perlas. Two other passengers whom I met were a Syrian and a Hindu, both merchants and established in La Cruz. I indulged in interesting reminiscences with them for a couple of hours about the beauty of their native lands—the magnificent Mosque of Omar in Jerusalem, for instance, and the marvelous Taj Mahal—while our veteran barge, snorting and puffing like an old faithful cab horse, kept plowing bravely through the sixteen-fathom-deep main channel of the Rio Grande, considerably handicapped by two heavily loaded lighters which were attached to her sides and an endless string of native dug-out canoes which she had taken in tow. These belonged to some of our steerage passengers who, on approaching their destination, cut them loose, without waiting even for the barge to halt, and paddled silently through the balmy night in quest of their thatched huts hid away, God knows where, among the mysterious swamplands or beneath the slumbering vegetation which hangs motionless over the still shores. Here the banks are covered with tall Scotch grass and crowned by trumpet trees, swampwood and giant *ceibas* and *guayabos,* from whose lofty branches hang, like swinging cradles, the nests of the *oropendulos,* a tropical variety of the oriole or Oriolidæ family (ploceus textor), which are famous for their lustrous black and golden plumage.

In this dramatic setting of a perfect tropical night the only signs of life to be noticed were perhaps the shadowy outlines of a wandering night hawk, gliding on listless wings over the softly rippling waters.

Just before daybreak or thereabouts I was awakened by the prolonged howl of a band of Indians, on shore, who were probably greeting us. And a quarter of an hour later, from somewhere behind the lapis-blue sky line, tints of rose, creeping slowly into nothingness, announced the dawn.

By sunrise everybody on board was awake. The atmosphere thickened with the heat of the sun, while the olive-green waters of the Rio Grande resumed their metallic glints with an occasional splash of gold. Along the shores of the awakening jungle turtles scrambled heavily through the tall grass and plunged headlong into the river; alligator snouts and their cruel cold eyes—so repellent by day, and at night glowing like greenish diamonds—rose cautiously above the surface of the softly running waters; humming birds darted from flower to flower, trembling in the air like living jewels; black and yellow plumed orioles flew excitedly around their bag-like nests, hanging from the tops of graceful bamboo trees or from the dry branches of a giant guayabo, on which a flock of parrots or a band of monkeys was joyously saluting the day.

In the meantime the heat wave continued increasing until about noon, when deep silence settled once more over the river and the jungle, interrupted only by the lopping of the barge and the incessant chant of countless cicadas.

At noon, more or less, some of the passengers pointed out to me a *guayabo* on the left river bank, which rose solitary above a sea of swaying banana trees. They called it "the *guayabo* of the Banana of Rio Grande Company." According to their story some time in September, 1925, a group of forty to fifty laborers, employed by the banana companies, were paddling up the river in their canoes with the intention of asking their superintendents for a raise in their salaries. It seems that on knowing this, a party by the name of Estanislao Gusinai notified the companies at once of their approach, whereupon these informed Felon Lacayo, the Chamorrist commander at La Cruz. As a consequence Lacayo telephoned to Antonio F. Gomez, who was stationed with a detachment of soldiers at El Gallo (*à la disposition* of the Cuyamel Fruit Company?) to proceed down river at once to exterminate the approaching laborers. Following superior orders of—whom? that is the question! Gomez ambushed his men behind that very guayabo and opened, at about one hundred yards, such a murderous fire on those unsuspecting and unarmed laborers that only very few of them managed to escape the gun fire by jumping overboard and swimming down the river, followed by the volleys of Gomez' men. Alligators are thick here, and it is doubtful if any of those poor peons who escaped the rifle fire ever reached shore safely. This story was fully confirmed to me, at my arrival at La Cruz, where I also acquired a picture of the corpses of three of the victims, while they were being fished out of the river. It is published in this book. I have not the slightest intention of accusing the Cuyamel Fruit Company of this crime, but I think that it ought, in its own interest, to have the matter cleared up as soon as possible unless it wants the people of Nicaragua to continue believing that the Cuyamel Fruit Company was really responsible.

That same day at about three P.M. our barge arrived at La Cruz. The little town reminded me of Juneau, Alaska, because the buildings of its main street, facing the river, were also partly built on stilts. Although the river bank rises at La Cruz to about thirty or forty feet above low watermark, the Rio Grande frequently floods that city and would have washed it away long ago if it were not because it is built on a rocky ledge which crosses the river at that particular spot. At La Cruz I had the pleasure of meeting Dr. J. P. Mollgaerd, a Danish physician belonging to a group of Danish immigrants who had arrived during the Diego Manual Chamorro régime with the intention of colonizing a section of Central Nicaragua but who did not meet with the expected success. After having spent all their money in useless efforts to secure suitable properties, and having lost some of their members from fevers and the bullets and machetes of the native settlers, who objected to being despoiled forcibly of their homesteads, the colonists had to return to Denmark practically penniless, and with several of them sick from tropical fevers. Dr. Mollgaerd told me that another Danish physician, a Dr. Koeford, and a young Danish medical student of the Copenhagen University, Miss Myken

Borring, who belonged to the Constitutionalist army's medical corps, had passed La Cruz together with that army, attending, voluntarily of course, its sick and wounded soldiers, even as they had been doing since the days of the attack on The Bluff of Bluefields and the battle of Laguna de Perlas. Colonel J. L. Miranda, who had been already waiting for me at the landing-place, conveyed me to Headquarters, where I met Colonel Cajina Mora, the military commander of the place. He was exceedingly attentive to me, as were also his son, who was acting as his secretary, and Mr. Angel Plazola, the Constitutionalist Financial Agent at La Cruz. There I managed to get a big "pipante," or dug-out canoe, four or five rifles "con-con" with plenty of ammunition (mostly explosive bullets) and provisions and medicines to last me for two or three weeks, as well as a mixed crew of six Indians and Nicaraguans. Several of the crew were deserters from the Conservative army. Colonel Newball, who had decided to accompany me as far as San Pedro, put them to work at once, so that on the following day we hitched our canoe to a gasoline launch which had been ordered to tow us up stream as far as she could. After waving our sombreros for the last time to Colonel Cajina Mora, Dr. Mollgaerd, Mr. Lalinde, Colonel Miranda and a group of curious ones who had assembled on the steep river bank to see us off, Newball and I lighted cigarettes and started discussing the political and military situation in the country ahead, which I was going to cross all by myself. According to current rumors the Conservatives in that neighborhood and especially the Conservative settlers in the jungle district of Central Nicaragua, for which I was headed, were supposed to be on the brink of an uprising in order to cut off the Constitutionalist army fighting in the interior from their base on the Atlantic Coast. My situation therefore promised to become lively, even hazardous. Although Colonel Newball did not exactly admit it, I realized that that was the real reason why he had volunteered to accompany me only as far as San Pedro. Despite the fact that civil strife continued raging in Nicaragua stronger than ever, nobody seemed to interfere in the least with the Cuyamel Fruit Company's interests. Cuyamel power barges, towing strings of lighters loaded with bananas, kept drifting down the Rio Grande without the slightest interruption and the Constitutionalist authorities had never even dreamed of pressing the laborers on the plantations into military service. The Constitutionalist Army was composed entirely of volunteers. Ninety per cent of the Diaz forces, on the contrary, were conscripts; even women were dragged from their homes and children to fight and be shot down to keep Diaz in power. A few hours after our departure we reached El Gallo. Here are the main offices of the Cuyamel Fruit Company. A little way beyond El Gallo the waters of the Rio Grande cease to be navigable not only for power barges but even for small gasoline boats and launches, because at La Cruz and El Gallo the bedrock formation of the Rio Grande begins. For the one-hundred-mile stretch, more or less, from its mouth at La Barra to La Cruz, the Grande flows over an alluvium or mud bottom. But from La Cruz to El Gallo up-stream, its waters foam shallowly over the successive layers of the countless petrified lava streams overlapping one another, which the volcanic cones (some of them still active) of the Cordillera Central de Nicaragua have poured down through the ages in the direction of the Atlantic Ocean. This fact accounts for the numberless rapids and cataracts which render the upper course of Rio Grande and its tributaries unnavigable, except by dug-out canoes. Practically the same thing applies to other Nicaraguan rivers running into the Caribbean Sea, which have also only a relatively insignificant stretch of navigable water along their lower courses. Half an hour after we had left El Gallo we had to dismiss the gasoline launch and take to our paddles and poles in order to navigate the first of the seemingly endless rapids which I had to pass during the seven weeks of my trip to Matagalpa. Beyond the mouth of the Cano Sisiquas, a small tributary, my attention was caught by a cluster of cocoanut trees which seemed to be bending protectively over a basalt wall, half hidden from sight by a thicket of bamboos and bijaos, or wild plantains. On nearer inspection I noticed on the polished face of the basalt ledge which rose perpendicularly out of the water one of the numerous picture writings which embellish some of the rocky embankments of the upper river. Several of these pictures represent jaguars, wild pigs, migratory fowl, as well as plume-crowned warriors and snakes; some apparently represent images of devils and others show the sun's disk, from which I imply that they must have some astronomical meaning. I noticed that most of these pictures were separated from one another by distances which, if covered on foot, would be roughly speaking equivalent to a day's journey each. This makes me think that they may have served at one time as mile-stones to mark the relay stations of perhaps some ancient system of transmitting messages by means of runners. I hope that Professor J. W. Schoenberg, to whom I furnished, in Managua, all the necessary data, may succeed later in visiting and studying them, for they may lead to important discoveries about the origin of the ancient culture of the Suma-Carib race. I am sorry that the photographs which I took of these rock engravings, and of the mysterious, legendary Monte Musun, were lost, together with an article of mine for the *Lokal Anzeiger* in Berlin, which I sent in the early part of May to Puerto Cabezas with an Indian messenger, who never arrived because, as I heard later, he had been killed by a jaguar in the neighborhood of San Pedro.

When the paddles of our crew commenced plowing once more the limpid waters of the Rio Grande, I could not help turning my head time and again to have a last look at the engraved faces of those ancient warriors, covered by the shadows of the overwhelming jungle, whose petrified eyes had been staring for God knows how many hundred, maybe even thousands of years, mysteriously into eternity. Several hours later, when the bloodshot clouds on the evening sky began to fade and the incurious shadows of the slumbering jungle spread silently over the river banks, the prow of our pipante rose suddenly and sank deep into the muddy shore at the foot of the plantation buildings of a plantation called Doris, where Mr. Carlos Vogel offered us shelter for the night. Next morning we passed another picture writing in the vicinity of El Progreso, and shortly before sunset we scrambled up the steep Palpunta hill on which is situated the banana plantation of Colonel Julio Monterey, the Constitutionalist commander of that section of the Rio Grande, who had an excellent supper prepared for us. He gave me some interesting information about the Cuyamel Fruit Company and its doings in that neighborhood. He was a civil engineer by profession and, although he had been treated, personally, very well by that company, he could not help feeling very bitter at it for what he felt was the ruthless way in which the Cuyamel Fruit Company had been trying to get absolute control of the upper Rio Grande banana zone, which centers about Palpunta and reaches all the way from El Gallo to the Surrutara rapids. He claimed that the Cuyamel, by taking advantage of the fact that some of the smaller independent planters were depending on it entirely (for lack of competitive companies) as a market, had tried to freeze them out by rejecting part of their crops. According to Colonel Monterey most of those independent planters, as far down as El Gallo, were hoping that something would be done in order to check the monopolizing system which the Cuyamel was employing for the purpose of getting absolute control of the enormously productive upper Rio Grande banana zone. As an example he cited the Orr Fruit Company to which, although its capital was only very limited, all those independent planters of the Upper Rio Grande zone had sold their crops even at a loss, in order to show the Cuyamel Fruit Company that it was *not wanted* in that part of the country any longer. Unfortunately the Orr Fruit Company was forced to sell out—to a sister company of the Cuyamel, if I am not mistaken—which left those poor planters once more at the mercy of the Cuyamel and its Superintendent in Bluefields, Mr. S. H. Baker. No wonder that the Nicaraguans are getting sick and tired of the Cuyamel Fruit Company. From what I have seen of it myself the upper Rio Grande banana zone is extremely fertile, perhaps more so than the lower zone. Its only drawback is lack of communication with the navigable waters of the Rio Grande west of El Gallo. Palpunta is situated about one hundred and forty miles upstream from La Barra and hardly one day's journey from El Gallo. By building a narrow gauge road of about twenty miles, the crops of the Palpunta and other independent plantations in the upper Rio Grande zone could be easily transported and shipped down the river on power barges and lighters towed by gasoline tug-boats. I think that it would pay for some independent banana company to send down a man to investigate and, if possible, to have a talk with Colonel Monterey. There is a chance for some level-headed American business man to make a million or two over night and to show the Nicaraguans that there are lots of people left in the United States who do not depend nor care to depend on Dollar Diplomacy, but on the contrary, are perfectly willing to make fortunes for themselves as well as for the people of Nicaragua by honest business methods.

Next morning I went to inspect the picture writings at the foot of the Palpunta hill. Then after shaking hands heartily with Colonel Monterey, who had given us of his best, we headed upstream once more with the intention of reaching San Pedro as soon as possible, because the situation along the river was getting critical indeed, owing to the unpardonable mistake of Moncada in abandoning Matiguas to its fate, without leaving there even a garrison of a hundred men to maintain communications with Puerto Cabezas. No wonder that the Conservative settlers in the jungle districts of Rio Blanco, Willike and Kepi were getting restless and ready to join the Conservative forces in case they should make an inroad into the Rio Grande district by way of Matiguas. This strange behavior on the part of José Maria Moncada had made the people along the Atlantic littoral suspect that he had done it on purpose to free himself from the supervision of Dr. Sacasa's cabinet in Puerto Cabezas, which he had been forced to consult and to keep informed of what he was doing.

On April 9th we continued paddling and poling our way upstream under most difficult circumstances for, beyond Palpunta, the river forms, in places, torrential currents which wind their tortuous course through big brownish lava beds, flanked by high, perpendicular walls. Here the canoe-man's slightest mistake means death. To judge by the signs of erosion caused by the action of continuously falling waters, I came to the conclusion that this chaos of rocks was due to earthquakes which had shattered the edges of some ancient lava flow. On both sides of this miniature canyon we noticed three new picture writings one of which, the first on our right, was extremely beautiful. How I regret having lost those photographs! At noon we passed the Surrutara rapids, which mark the western limit of the upper Rio Grande banana zone. There the plantations cease. From Surrutara on as far as San Pedro only occasional patches of sugar cane and plantains, surrounding the thatched bamboo huts of a few dozen settlers or half civilized Suma Indian squatters, or a logger's camp here and there, skirt the fringe of the dense untracked forest which lies, like a solid belt, on practically the whole of Central Nicaragua, from Honduras down to Costa Rica. *This immensely rich and almost wholly unexplored section of Nicaragua which represents more or less forty per cent of the whole country, could easily be tapped and opened up to agriculture, etc., by means of a railroad from the Pacific to the Atlantic Coast or by criss-crossing it with heavy truck or automobile roads!* There is another chance for legitimate American capital to make big profits for itself and Nicaragua as well.

After I had got my second wind, so to say, and despite the fact that many a loaded rifle in the hands of deserters, turned into desperadoes through necessity, had been leveled on us time and again from the shadows of the jungle thickets along the river banks, I commenced to enjoy our little trip. I like hunting, and now I had an occasional shot at big game. It was interesting, too, to harpoon at night, with the help of my flashlight, all sorts of fish, from a *zabalo* to a shark. Strange as it may seem, sharks can be found, occasionally, even during the dry season, as far up as the upper Tuma River, confined to the limits of the deep pools wherein they remain stranded after the waters of the rainy season, which rise sometimes forty to fifty feet (covering the rapids and cataracts), have subsided. The weather was wonderful. That day an Indian, whom I baptized Inapaquita just for fun, joined us voluntarily, probably out of fear of the many armed deserters, who kept flowing back to the Atlantic Coast because they realized that, by following the Tierra Azul-to-Tipitapa road, Moncada was leading the Constitutionalist army only to certain destruction. Those fellows were not stupid by any means. They too, as almost everybody whom we met on the river, advised me very earnestly, whenever we met, to desist from my trip across country for, as they said, death was lurking behind almost every tree and in every march in the central jungle district, either in the shape of professional bandits or wild beasts or disease. Shortly after noon we noticed in the distance a dark brownish rock screen blocking our way. It looked flat and square like a gigantic altar. Those were the Olea-Olea Falls, of ill repute, which forced us for the tenth time during our three days' journey to unload our canoe in order to drag it by means of ropes, or half carry it waist deep or with the water up to our necks, over and across the roaring minor cataracts along the steep rocky shores of the rapids. This performance, which I went through about fifty or sixty times before I managed to get to Matiguas, seven weeks later, reminded me of *portages* in the interior of Alaska, only with the difference that there we could carry our light canoes on our backs, whereas the water-soaked heavy pipantes had to be dragged across at the expense of considerable loss of time and tremendous physical effort beneath the scorching rays of the tropical sun. However, we managed it somehow and landed finally on a rocky flat on which we unloaded our canoe and got busy preparing our frugal supper, consisting chiefly of two or three ducks which we had shot on the way. During that night we were awakened several times by sporadic detonations caused by the explosion of the highly bituminous rocks on which we had lighted our campfires.

On April 10th we changed our pipante for the fourth time, at a nearby logging camp, in order to pass the Trus-Trus Rapids, which are supposed to be one of the shallowest places on the river, and at five P.M. we finally arrived at San Pedro del Norte, where the river Tuma empties into the Rio Grande.

Chapter XII

San Pedro; a Concrete Example of the Ruin Which Dollar Diplomacy Has Wrought in the Interior — A Spanish-American Frontiersman — By Canoe Up the Tuma and Willike Rivers — Seven Weeks in the Heart of the Jungle — How I Became a Marked Man — Dodging Bandits and Deserters — The Clever Ruse of the Bandit, Rodriguez, to Get My Rifles — Indian Medicine — Hunting Pigs, Tapirs and Jaguars — A Black Tiger — The Glamor of the Jungle — Matagalpa at Last.

AS soon as I stepped ashore, at San Pedro, a squatty, middle-aged man by the name of Mercedes Reyes hurried down from his lofty perch on a hill—which means his tin-covered bungalow—in order to greet us. He was carrying a six-shooter strapped to each hip and, without giving me even a chance to present my credentials, introduced himself as the local representative of the Constitutionalist Government. According to what he told me his situation was really dangerous, not only on account of the threatened uprising of the Conservative settlers in that neighborhood, but also because of the reign of terror which some of the deserters of Adolfo Diaz's army had started around San Pedro. Almost every day a new crime was reported. That particular day, for instance, a group of seven had surrounded a ranch about two miles down the river and, after hanging its owner and riddling his body with bullets, had mercilessly chopped down, with their machetes, his wife and three daughters. They had been giving San Pedro a wide berth so far, probably because they did not believe that Reyes was practically alone. With the exception of two wounded soldiers all his men had left him to join the Constitutionalist army when it had passed through on its way to Matiguas. Realizing that if that rabble ever got possession of San Pedro not only Reyes but practically every rancher in that locality would be butchered, I sent a letter at once to Colonel Cajina Mora, at La Cruz. On receiving it, three days later, he immediately dispatched a detachment of troops with explicit orders to disarm the deserters and reëstablish normal conditions in that community. I readily understood, from what Reyes told me, that I would be only wasting my time if I tried to obtain the necessary pack and saddle horses for my projected trip to Matiguas by way of the San Pedro-Matiguas trail; so I decided to continue my journey by water, going up the Tuma River, if possible, as far as the foothills of the Matagalpa mountains, in the neighborhood of El Cacao, which were supposed to be held by some forces belonging to the extreme right wing of the Constitutionalist Army. In case that the river higher up should be found too shallow we—that is, I and my men, for they had decided to accompany me —could always continue our trip overland by chopping our way across the jungles. And why should we not? I had two splendid pipantes manned by three Indians and four Nicaraguans, all of whom were old woodsmen, as well as plenty of provisions and ammunition. Even if, for some reason or other, we should not succeed in reaching Matagalpa in that direction, we could always retrace our steps and try our luck by way of Willike and the Rio Blanco.

After my conversation with Mercedes Reyes I ordered my men to unload and pull our canoes ashore, where they set up camp and started getting everything ready for an early departure next day. Reyes, who was an old back-woodsman and ex-Indian trader, had distinguished himself several months before by defending San Pedro at the head of only seventy men against a strong flying column of Conservatives commanded by one of Baquerano's lieutenants called Pedro Pablo. While he was showing me the trenches which he had been using during that defense I could not help looking in amazement at one, which was lined with solid blocks of white, polished marble.

"Where did you get those?" I asked him.

"Do you mean those marble slabs? Why! They used to form part of the marble floor of my house when San Pedro, instead of a heap of ruins, as it is to-day, was still a busy little town, like Kepi and Willike, during the big rubber boom, some twenty-five years ago. Unhappily President Zelaya was forced to resign at that time by the American Government and Kepi, San Pedro and Willike were gradually swallowed up by the jungle. Look at the house in which I am living now—that tin-covered canary-bird cage! Why! We would not have thought of using a thing like that even as a chicken coop during the days of the Zelaya administration! Ah! then Nicaragua was not a cemetery as it is to-day, ruled by a swarm of buzzards, but a free and prosperous country, where the law was *the law!* and everybody had a chance to make an honest living if he wanted to!"

After seeing with my own eyes a few weeks later what was left of the once also prosperous little jungle towns of Kepi and Willike, I saw that Mercedes Reyes was not exaggerating. The régime of ruin thrust on Nicaragua by Philander Knox had here not only stopped progress but had aided the dark jungle in swallowing up what were once the habitations of human beings.

As there was no place on the beach to hang our mosquito nets Newball and I had our hammocks hung up in an old abandoned hut near the trenches. After supper I sat down, as usual in front of one of our campfires, smoking and listening to the macabre "seigua" or spook stories which my men loved to tell, for the Nicaraguans are exceedingly superstitious. A little bit of a fellow, whom they called "el zorrito" ("the fox"), and who had participated in the defense of San Pedro, suddenly pointed at the hut, on the brow of the hill, in which Newball and I intended to spend the night, and exclaimed:

"Do you see that hut? Well, it happened right next to it, in a trench. Talk about impudence! While we were keeping an eye on the enemy, who were not more than two hundred yards away from us, I noticed a big shadow gliding noiselessly over the ground in our direction. Thinking that it might be a Conservative soldier trying to spy on us, I had already raised my rifle, when the shadow suddenly rose way up in the air and landed with a hair-raising growl on top of the man next to me. It was a jaguar, and a man-killer at that! Realizing in the wink of an eye that my long army rifle was of no use to me at so close quarters, I grabbed my machete and let him have it."

After listening to "el zorrito's" story both Newball and I thought that it would be wiser perhaps not to tempt the gods, so we took our hammocks out of the hut and sneaked back into camp.

Early next morning, after thanking Newball for his kindness and after shaking hands with Mercedes Reyes, whom I liked as a good example of the true frontier type, we pushed our canoes off and paddled in the direction of the mouth of the Tuma River which is flanked, along its lower course, by steep, canyon-like walls topped with two stripes of dense jungle vegetation. In the larger canoe, manned by my four Nicaraguans, we had placed our bedding, rifles, cooking utensils and ammunition; while in the smaller one, manned by my three Suma Indians, we were carrying our provisions and medicines. I climbed into this myself not only in order to keep an eye on the provisions but because Nicarao, the oldest of the three Indians, who was steering it, was a very intelligent chap and had told me already quite a few interesting stories from the lore of his people. He was also a good hunter. Every time he spotted an exceptionally big alligator, or land game in the jungle thickets, he would point it out to me at once, thus saving me the trouble of being constantly on the lookout myself. One of the things which I was glad of was that I would not have to look a newspaper in the face again for a long time and that there would be nobody, absolutely nobody—except the alligators, perchance—talking politics to me until we got to Matagalpa or Matiguas. I was cutting myself loose altogether from the rest of the world for at least two or three weeks; and, remembering other jungles in which I had had the pleasure of losing myself in former years, I faced the prospect of these new explorations with joy.

During the seven weeks that it took me to cross the jungle districts of Central Nicaragua, I convinced myself that in spite of our sophisticated day of subways and skyscrapers, real romance flourishes undiminished on the golden shores of the old Spanish Main and among its virgin forests, which slumber as peacefully as ever beneath the deep, blue splendor of the tropical sky.

THE LOOTING OF NICARAGUA

After paddling for many hours over the glittering waters of the Tuma River we rested for a while at the foot of the mile long Isague Rapids, which it took us about all afternoon to cross. At sunset we finally headed for the shore, tired and hungry, and set up our camp as near as possible to the water's edge for we were already in the dreaded "no man's zone," which even the Indians used to shun. Half-a-dozen buzzards, perched on the bare limbs of a nearby tree, gave us warning. The "compadre" had made a kill there and would be coming back after dark. So we had to be careful. Less than an hour after our landing the tropical night had fallen and a pale moon was struggling upward through clouds. Soon several constellations commenced to blaze on the southern heavens. The atmosphere was charged with the fragrance of exotic flowers. After supper I went to join Nicarao. I had posted him as a sentry on the top of a nearby ridge. With myriad changing luminous lines, the "cocuyos" (large fire-flies or lightning bugs) were crisscrossing the yawning darkness about us. Every now and then we heard from the distance the voices of the night prowlers of the jungle howling into the black cavernous silence. The river was glowing mysteriously in the distance below us, and so were the bloodshot clouds of smoke of our campfires, around which our men lay, rifle in hand, wrapped in their blankets, or crouched on their haunches, smoking or humming the mournful songs of their native mountains in the interior, the homeland which they had forsaken to plunge into the jungles and swamplands of the Mosquito Coast. Finally the moon rays broke through a towering mass of silver-fringed clouds and fell full on the still form of Nicarao, who was squatting in front of me on a felled tree, with his loaded rifle leaning against it and his arms dangling loosely over his knees. Rigid, motionless, he was listening tensely to every noise from the narrow jungle trail which skirted the river bank; for there death was likely to be waiting in the soft gloom. Every now and then he would snatch up his rifle and his eyes would travel swiftly over the sights; without pressing the trigger, however, for, every time that he raised his weapon, the pair of glowing eyes which had been staring at him from beneath the bushes, only for a fraction of a second perhaps, would have disappeared as by magic, to gleam again presently from some other direction. That "compadre," or "Satan's godfather," as the hunters in those jungles call the jaguar, was surely an old-timer!

To judge by his dignified way of speaking and the deference which his companions showed him, Nicarao must have been one of the chiefs of his tribe, or perhaps its medicine man. It was a perfect night and a perfect scene for strange tales. After lighting a cigarette, he commenced looking back into the misty past of his race, telling me stories and legends of the sort I had been longing to hear. Stories of ruined cities buried beneath the dust of ages in the depths of the voracious jungle; of the sibilant hiss of the feathered rattlesnake, turned into a god; of the rolling grasslands toward the west; of those silent plumed warriors, who continue staring with petrified eyes into space along the rocky shores of the Rio Grande; of ivory-hued goddesses, who glorified, in the night of time, the Olympus of the Maya-Nahua mythology; of all the singing things which whisper at night and murmur in the eddies of the cool, green jungle streams; and of the sacred Quetzal bird, of iridescent plumage, which crowns the holy mountain toward Septentrion, whence his ancestors hailed.

The following day we started on. It was just another of the many days which I was to spend in those cruel yet beautiful forests of Nicaragua before I managed to cut my way through to Matagalpa.

The chief cause of my delay in the jungle was salt. At San Pedro, Mercedes Reyes had requested me to take along with me about two hundred pounds of salt for the rear guard of the Constitutionalist forces. The army had run out of salt, the settlers scattered here and there along the banks of the Tuma and Willike rivers had had none for weeks, bandits, Indians and deserters likewise. In all the jungle district between San Pedro and Matagalpa there was no salt but mine; which was not mine to eat but merely to worry about. Now, the saline crystal is ordinarily a silent commodity. But, by some means unknown to me, this consignment of salt had succeeded in announcing its advent in that territory where everybody needed it. And immediately everybody made up his mind to get it. Apart from those who were determined to get it because they needed it, the Conservatives at Matiguas heard about it and sent out men to look for me and to prevent me from delivering to the Constitutionalists the salt—which rumor had now increased from two hundred pounds to several canoe-loads! I was a marked man for another reason also. I possessed practically the only pipantes on the river, and, in the dense jungle country, the rivers are the only thoroughfares. There were deserters from both armies, and other men, who wanted to get out of that territory in a hurry, but had no canoes. I had salt, I had canoes, not to mention my equally desired good rifles and supply of ammunition.

I became the focal point of interest. The embarrassing attentions of these people in posting invisible reception committees for me at strategic points along the river forced me repeatedly to double on my tracks and kept me some five weeks longer in the jungle than it would ordinarily have taken me to reach Matagalpa. We had several skirmishes with these "committees," but no casualties on our side. My troubles would lessen, I thought, if I rid myself of that salt. So one night I sent it off, on a settler's ox, in the care of two of my men with orders to bury it in a certain place; for all I know it may be there yet.

While determined to hold on to my canoes, guns and shoes, I could not help feeling a sympathy for those deserters and bandits who were after them, for most of the poor fellows were in rags and needed all that I had. They kept up a hot pursuit and constantly forced us to change our camp. Their favorite ruse was to try to sneak up on us at night, but our dogs were alert and always gave us warning in time to prepare for the visit. The cleverest attempt was made by a bandit named Rodriguez who, in a short time, had made his name feared among the settlers. One night when we were camped in an abandoned hut, our dogs set up a fierce barking. We sprang up at once with our rifles. From the dense blackness outside we heard a voice calling to us not to shoot.

"I am alone, señores. I have lost my way. Give me shelter for the night."

I slipped out and stood behind a tree. The man came on alone and presently I turned my flashlight on him. He was a sturdy-looking ruffian, armed only with six-shooter and machete, which were strapped to his waist. He still held in his hand the *cocuyo* (the large and brilliant jungle fire-fly) which he had

THE LOOTING OF NICARAGUA

been using to light his steps. It made a curious impression on me, the sight of this swarthy, bearded, tattered bandit coming out of the jungle darkness, which looks like uncountable thicknesses of black velvet, and finding a way for his feet where there is no path, among snakes and wild beasts, by stooping and holding a cocuyo close to the ground. We brought him in, gave him some coffee, and a cowhide—the usual bed—on which to sleep. The slight rattling of that dry cowhide later on awoke me. Rodriguez was sliding slowly towards my rifle, which was leaning on the wall beside my hammock. I yawned aloud and sat up, my six-shooter in my hand. Rodriguez by that time was slumbering as innocently as a mouse. Before dawn he gave up the hope of surprising us and slipped out and joined his men who had been stationed in the thicket waiting for the signal from him that he had got a rifle and was ready for them to help him in getting the rest of our outfit. Men armed as we were with rifles and explosive bullets (for big game) were literally too many guns for bandits armed only with six-shooters. After sending a few disappointed shots in our direction, Rodriguez and his friends made off.

To avoid not only such gentry as Rodriguez but also the detachments of Conservatives which had been sent to cut me off at Willike, I was obliged to make a permanent camp halfway down the Willike River in the very heart of the jungle at a lonesome spot which none could reach except by canoe because no trails led to it.

As we were making our way in our two pipantes over the shallow rapids to this campsite, we had a lively experience. We were suddenly, and overwhelmingly, surprised by the roaring descent of a wall of water, I should judge about fourteen feet high. It was caused doubtless by a cloudburst in the mountains. Fortunately the larger pipante bearing our ammunition was close to shore, and the men saved everything. But mine, containing our provisions and medicines, received the full shock. The first thing I knew I was clinging to a rock with water boiling around and over me, which—so kind is fate sometimes—a moment later swirled my pipante practically on top of me. My canoemen were good swimmers and fast thinkers, as jungle watermen have to be, and they had got safely ashore. I followed them there with the pipante which the tossing flood had returned to me. We had now to depend entirely on our rifles and harpoons for food, and I confess that a diet of fresh and smoked flesh without salt is not to my liking. To make matters worse for me I contracted swamp fever of which nausea, delirium and very high temperature are the common features. One day when it seemed even to me that my men were correct in saying I could not recover, we came to an Indian hut. I lay on the floor too feeble even to speak. The Indian woman sent her man to cut a gourd or fungus-like growth from a tree nearby. She prepared from this a frightful concoction of an evil greenish hue, and with a worse odor, and poured it down my throat. Kill or cure! The decision was in favor of cure.

To add to our difficulties as men now obliged to live by hunting, the rainy season commenced several weeks ahead of time. The chief staple in our larder was wild pig. We did not bother with the "sahinos," or peccaries, because they usually trotted about only in pairs. The pigs of the jungle go in large droves, however, like the good civilized porkers on a Texas farm. Their strong musky odor would lead us unerringly to their feeding grounds. After tying our canoes to a tree we would steal upon the drove under cover of the wind, kill as many as we needed for a few days and smoke the meat, Indian fashion, by covering it with green plantain leaves and letting it lie overnight on a platform about three feet high above a low smoky fire. On one or two occasions the pigs saw us approaching and resented our intrusion. Angry pigs are not to be trifled with. They made us take speedily to the trees where they kept us marooned for half an hour or more hammering away at the trunks with their tusks till the chips flew. The jaguar's method of hunting them is to wait in a tree for the stragglers after the main drove has passed. Then he pounces on one and immediately leaps back to his low branch with it. There he waits until the furious pigs below have given up trying to dislodge him and have gone on. When the coast is clear he comes down and eats at his leisure. We varied our pork diet with the meat of both large and dwarf deer, which we hunted by drifting down in our canoes along the banks just before sunrise when the deer were browsing in the open, before the heat of the sun sent them into the shade of the forest.

Sometimes, at night, we hunted tapir, more for sport than for food, for its meat has rather a strong flavor. I remember we set out one day at the close of a rainy afternoon, while the sun, setting out of our sight, was throwing the long shadows of the forest across the rapidly flowing Willike. In the dusk we ran our pipante's prow into the muddy shore under the long grass thickets. To right and left of us on the surface of the stream the eyes of alligators gleamed with greenish, amethyst, and orange flashes, brilliant as diamonds. These two fierce jungle creatures, the alligator and the jaguar, repay something of their havoc surely by the indescribable beauty of their eyes at night. The jungle silence—so intense it is that one seems actually to *hear* silence rather than the little whispers of breeze or insect life which shudder across it—was broken for us by the shouting chorus of a tribe of bullfrogs. Snakes on the hunt too, as we were, would also hear the frogs; so one of my men went ahead along the trail we had cut the day before to scare off any tabobas who might be using it as a convenient highway. The taboba, by the way, is the most feared snake in Nicaragua. It is about the thickness of a man's wrist and averages two yards in length. In color, it is light brown, spotted with black. Its poison is considered mortal. Tabobas are plentiful in this jungle. Sunset and dusk are their favorite hunting seasons by both land and water. At these times, if canoeing, we kept a sharp lookout because tabobas, looking as innocent as huge drifting leaves or bits of wood, float, coiled and ready to strike, on the surface of the rivers and, if they collide with a canoe and leap to strike, they may be over the prow, or stern, and into the low pipante with you before you know it.

The tapir, like most large animals, makes his own road to the water where he goes to drink at night. We did not use the one we had discovered, for fear of giving him a scent of us and scaring him off. We cut a short trail to tap his and waited at this fork.

When we reached the spot where we expected to ambush the tapir we took up positions behind trees with rifles ready for immediate action. One hour, and another, passed without sign of our quarry. Even a hunter's patience is not sorely tried by waiting in a scene so beautiful as this. All around us the cocuyos were flashing broken incandescent patterns in the darkness, and the moon riding the heavens far above the interlacing fronds, dropped her tropical white-silver rays through the mesh of the tree tops to sprinkle the jungle floor with pools of light which seemed, because of the density of the surrounding shadow, to be suspended over the ground rather than to lie upon it. In time we heard the crashing sound of a heavy body coming towards us through the thickets. The tapir had come close up without suspecting our presence, when one of my men turned my flashlight full on him, and I shot him. The tapir is not dangerous to hunters as a rule. The female is ferocious when she has young to care for, as with most wild animals. Our tapir showed the scars of an old battle with *el tigre,* the jaguar. The extremely tough hide of his back had been sliced like strips of bacon by a jaguar's powerful claws. The jaguar is seldom successful in getting the tapir unless he springs on him from the undergrowth, seizes him by the snout and rips his throat. If he leaps on him from above, fastening his claws into that thick epidermis, the tapir runs like mad, making for the toughest bit of jungle he knows and through which he crashes like a cannon ball. Unless the jaguar has the sense to let go, he may be beaten to a jelly. Our tapir had evidently given some tiger the joy ride of his life.

The "slickest" citizen of the jungle is the jaguar, the large, tawny, black-rosetted tiger of the tropics. You will see his tracks almost everywhere you go in our jungles, but him you seldom see. "El Tigre walks alone," as the jungle saying goes. Nobody sees nor hears him, but he sees and hears everything. If you catch a glimpse of him, you will not have time to raise your gun. He is gone like a streak of lightning. Hereabouts, the jaguar is not generally dangerous to man except in the stray case of the man-eater. The jungle gives him plenty of food, and so do the poor settlers, whose cattle he so often steals. Still, he is seldom averse to investigating a sleeping camp, as we found on several occasions. We shot two or three jaguars along the Willike; one from the top of a tree. El tigre at his best is a big powerful beast, able to drag a full-grown cow over the grass as if it were a wet rag. Like the jaguar, the "leon" or puma of the well-stocked jungle will seldom stalk a man. Both animals are really dangerous, though, up in the mountains where game is scarce. The "black tiger" on the contrary is always ferocious or so the natives claim.

When my men first spoke to me of the black tiger, I paid little attention. I had heard of this beast before, in Panama, and I had then set him down as a myth, like the much-talked-of but never seen "striped" tiger of Colombian and Venezuelan jungle lore, which may date from the heraldic device of some ancient and cruel Conquistador; for certainly the Indians of those jungles have never seen nor heard of the Bengal tiger. Now again I heard of the black tiger, and did not believe in him. One evening when we were paddling swiftly home, Nicarao called to me.

"There he is, señor! the black tiger!"

Wheeling instantly, I fired and downed him. He turned out to be a big fellow and of the color of black coffee—black with a brownish sheen. I thought I could distinguish rings or spots more darkly dappling the brown-black of his ground color, but the light was so bad that I could not be sure. I consider the venomous snakes of the jungle far more dangerous than its four-footed creatures, and, of course, the always hungry alligators add nothing to the safety of any man who upsets his canoe.

Death intertwined with colossal majesty, and with both rich and delicate loveliness, is characteristic of the vast jungles of the tropics. And no man who feels the lure of the jungle's indescribable and magical splendor can answer with a faint and timid heart. Soaking rains, mosquitoes, bandits and other human pests, fevers, could not spoil for me the joys of that experience along the Tuma and Willike rivers. By day my pipante glided on the softly shining stream which was like flowing emerald under the latticed roof formed by the interwoven top branches of forest giants. Hanging from the huge boughs and winding about the trunks, looping from tree to tree, and dipping, here and there, their lovely colors in the stream, were blossoming parasitic plants in endless profusion. The air was slumbrous, dreamful, with their scent. Occasional sunbeams cut through the leafy canopy like sabers of light. Enormous blue butterflies on metallic wings fluttered through the speckled veil of shadow and sun. Multicolored birds pierced it like painted arrows. Gay parrots eyed us, and sometimes shrieked, perhaps at us, from the high branches of the guayabo. Sometimes we saw a kingfisher, or a lone blue heron, resting on a mass of black rocks over which the water tumbled; or startled from among the blossoming vines a flock of snowy egrets. Not infrequently we saw a monkey, of a fair size, with grave countenance and dignified air crossing the stream at an enormous height by swinging his lithe hairy body from one long looping vine-stem to another. After him came the ladies of his household, each carrying her little black-bead-eyed and gayly baby chattering on her curved back.

At the day's end, as we sat over our supper and watched the purple-black night descend, my Indians would tell me old legends of the mysterious Monte Musun, looming up before us, which none save perhaps some Indian demi-god of the long past has ever scaled. I will never forget my first view of Monte Musun. Standing solitary in the center of the jungle, it towered against the blood-red sunset sky like a titanic black pyramid. The red faded and the sky, darkening and beginning to show stars, seemed to lower about that great peak like a veil of gold dust.

"On the crest, señor"—it is Nicarao who speaks—"there is a crystal lake. And, in it, swims forever a golden alligator."

At night I lay wakeful in my hammock for hours enjoying the enwrapping velvety darkness of the jungle; a darkness that seemed only more intense for the lights that sought to pierce it. Stars blazed above me. Below, where the river rushed darkly, the diamond eyes of alligators shone from the water and from the opposite bank where several of the great reptiles had pulled themselves up on shore for a while. For a moment or so two gleaming, opaque, yellow, glass balls told me that a puma was looking our camp over from the nearest thicket. Or, more often, the glass balls had not that look of opacity but were translucent, as if fire burned behind incredibly thin flakes of crystal. Then a movement of the sentry would send the jaguar off, too, as silently as he had come. In every direction the cocuyos embroidered their sparkling crystal beads on the thick blackness. And the moon, rising, turned the dark river far below into rushing silver flame.

In the end, we had to abandon the rivers, where too many bandits and Conservative detachments waited to waylay us, and to traverse the partly unexplored defile of Matiguas where for the first few days

THE LOOTING OF NICARAGUA

we hacked out our path, much of the time step by step, with our machetes. A few days later a tattered, mud-covered and fever-stricken rider jumped off a bridleless mustang in front of the United States marine headquarters at Matagalpa. I was a sight; and it was no wonder that the young lieutenant looked at my passport and at me with sternly scrutinizing glances. Finally he said:

"I know this name. But you cannot be the Nogales who wrote a book called 'Four Years Beneath the Crescent'?"

"Oh, yes, I am," I replied.

"Why," he exclaimed, "I read that book in the library of the Naval Academy in Annapolis!" We shook hands, friends at once. And presently I went off in search of a bath and a shave and a suit that was whole.

Chapter XIII

The Golden Alligator Remains Unseen of Man — A Friendly Deserter Warns Me in Time of Impending Capture by Conservatives — Some Proclamations by General Moncada and Admiral Latimer — Sandino Answers a Captain of Marines — Moncada Betrays the Army Under His Command — Mr. Stimson Represents President Coolidge — Moncada Bargains With Stimson Behind Closed Doors.

WHILE I was in the jungle I made a resolute but futile attempt to climb Monte Musun. I wanted to see that golden alligator swimming forever in his crystal lake. Places enwrapped in story or legend, where men of ancient times have focused their holiest faith or their fairest fancies, have for me an irresistible attraction. In the Orient, and especially in Palestine, this passion of mine for storied places almost ended my career more than once. As for instance, when I plunged downward suddenly into the neglected, bat-haunted hole which is the Tomb of Lazarus; where I would be yet but for my orderly, a trusty Albanian savage, who had become accustomed to my erratic tastes and who found me at last and pulled me out. I managed to climb, not high to be sure, but high enough to discover that Monte Musun's stone flank on that side might as well be glass as far as offering foothold to an amateur mountaineer was concerned. No doubt the spirits of the old Indian demi-gods circling about it laughed when Monte Musun shook off the rash intruder like a fly, at last. Probably only the fact that I landed on some bushes instead of the ground saved my neck; the effect of the shaking up endured for days.

Soon after my unsuccessful encounter with Monte Musun I came within an inch of falling into the hands of a troop of Conservative cavalry, which was chasing Captain Juan Funes, late of the Constitutionalist Army, and his forty mounted followers. This worthy, who finally managed to escape to San Pedro with a string of horses, which he was supposed to have stolen in the neighborhood of Bul-Bul, Sais or Bijagual, before he deserted, was, luckily, thoughtful enough to let me know, just in the nick of time, by a messenger, the dangerous position I was in. He told me also that General Escamilla was coming down by way of Rio Negro to the Rio Blanco-Matiguas mountain trail, to take over the rest of the convoy of munitions which was in charge of a major of ill repute by the name of Ruben Jiron, who had done all he could to make the Constitutionalist cause hateful to the settlers, both Conservatives and Liberals, of the upper Willike jungle section. Funes's letter, in which he gave me that information, as well as the wild rumors spread by the deserters, who kept flocking toward the Atlantic Coast, were about the only information in regard to current events which I managed to gather while I was roaming those jungles, ducking right and left, and always on the lookout for the first chance to make a getaway in the direction of Matiguas. Only when I got there, that is, to Matiguas, on May 27th, did I receive all the information I wanted. This was furnished to me by Colonel Jacinto Gadea, the new Constitutionalist commander of the place. It was not encouraging at all, but on the contrary, rather discouraging, for it verified the doubts which I always had entertained in regard to Moncada's ability as a soldier and his sincerity as a patriot. Among the various printed data which I got from Gadea was

Moncada's hypocritical "proclama," or proclamation, dated in Managua on May 5, 1927, in which he tried to justify his treason to the Constitutionalist cause; and to the army, after he had forced it into a cul-de-sac,—but of that, later! Another printed proclamation handed to me by Gadea was that of Admiral Latimer, dated May 10, 1927, in Managua, in which he says: "The Government of the United States, having accepted the request of the Government of Nicaragua to supervise the election in the latter country in 1928, believed a general disarmament of the country necessary for the proper and successful conduct of such election and has directed me to accept the custody of the arms and ammunition of those willing to place them in my custody, including the arms and ammunition of the forces of the government, and to disarm forcibly those who do not peaceably deliver their arms, etc."

I wonder why the Government of the United States did not have itself "requested" to do all this by the dummy Diaz administration immediately after it had recognized Diaz as the legal President of Nicaragua on November 17, 1926? Why did it wait for six months, until Diaz's army was surrounded and in danger of getting exterminated at Teustepe? Why did it wait until thousands of Nicaraguans had lost their lives during that bloody civil strife, before it declared that *it had been requested by its puppet Diaz administration* to supervise the elections of 1928? Secretary Kellogg acted in this case rather childishly, to say the least. The following printed statement of Dr. T. S. Vaca, representative of the former Constitutionalist Government of Nicaragua in Washington, goes to substantiate my remarks.

"Propaganda and misrepresantation, profiting at

present by the exclusive use of news agencies, is at work endeavoring to create the impression that an *agreement* was reached by the contending parties in Nicaragua through the efforts of Special Envoy Stimson. It might be said, with the same propriety, that a man facing a double-barreled gun and a demand *agrees* to it! And so it was. The Delegates sent to Managua by the Constitutionalist Government at the invitation of Mr. Stimson not only protested against the dictation by the latter of terms of peace conditioned upon the continuance of the usurper Adolfo Diaz in power, but flatly refused to enter into any understanding on that basis. Immediately Mr. Stimson threatened them by word and by written communication with the use of the naval forces of the United States to forcibly disarm the Constitutionalist troops. The State Department was compelled to show its hand in this manner because the Diaz régime was unable to stand any longer on its own legs, and the Constitutionalist armies were already threatening the approaches to the Capital. By a cunning combination of cajolery and threats deftly employed, a semblance of peace has been hung over the Nicaraguan affair by the Stimson Mission in order to keep the public's eye away from it while the little Central American nation is being roped and made ready for the New York market pending a much advertised *popular* election for 1928. The irony of the promises must be very poignant for those who *elected* Solorzano and Sacasa in 1924, only to see them outlawed by the State Department at the same time that a powerful mantle of protection was thrown around the Diaz régime made in Wall Street! An election in Nicaragua supervised by the power that upholds the rule of Diaz at the cost of thousands of Nicaraguans dead, against the rights of those whom the people elected, is evidently a misnomer and can have but one outcome! The report of extreme cruelty in the Nicaraguan strife released from Washington, may or may not be truthful; on one point, however, there can be no dispute: It is calculated solely to extol the policy of imposing peace as if it were not known that for the last few months, or longer, the policy of enforcing war has been openly followed. The fight was made possible only by the intrigue and coöperation of New York interests, and it would have ended long ago if the tottering Diaz régime had not been propped up by the State Department and plentifully supplied with arms and ammunition to continue this inhuman warfare that is now denounced by Mr. Stimson and held out as the best excuse for enforcing peace! Shall we welcome Dr. Jekyll as we think of Mr. Hyde?"

The third document of the Moncada-Latimer brand which was handed to me by Gadea was a written proclamation translated into Spanish and signed in a primary schoolboy handwriting by a *corporal* William Lindsay of the U. S. M. C. at Matagalpa, in which this worthy, representing the United States Government and that of Nicaragua, ordered the neighbors of Matiguas and the surrounding country to surrender their arms unless they wanted to be imprisoned and treated like outlaws! No wonder that General Sandino, referring to a similar insolent intimidation published by Captain G. D. Hatfield in the form of a circular letter, in which he declared Sandino and his followers to be highwaymen, answered Hatfield in another circular letter which stirred the people of Nicaragua to the bones. It read:

"Who are you, anyway? How dare you threaten with death, and otherwise, the legitimate sons of my

THE LOOTING OF NICARAGUA

country? Do you think that you are in the heart of Africa? Don't believe that I am afraid of you! If you are any kind of a man come out and fight it out with me single-handed on neutral ground, whenever you want. I will be waiting for you. I am sure you would not dare to repeat those insults while facing me as man to man!" And Sandino followed this up with action. Seeing that Hatfield did not show up to answer his challenge, Sandino went to look for him at Ocotal. But finding that even then Hatfield refused to come out to fight with him single-handed, Sandino attacked him, hoping to come face to face with him during the battle. And he would have remained there until he met his man if he had been possessed of the necessary incendiary machine gun ammunition to down the bombing planes.

Practically the same thing happened during the American armed intervention in Nicaragua in 1912, of which the present intervention is a faithful repetition. During that occasion General Zeledon, if I am not mistaken, or some other Liberal leader of high standing, challenged also, although fruitlessly, the American Commander, as a soldier and as a gentleman, to fight it out single-handed with him wherever and whenever he chose. Shortly after that Zeledon fell fighting at the head of his troops at Masaya, on October 12, 1912—as Moncada ought to have done at Tipitapa, instead of crawling like a beaten dog on hands and feet before Stimson, whining: "I would never advise any of my men to dare to fight against the American troops." And this, although he knew perfectly well that Latimer's marines had been sent to Nicaragua only to help Dollar Diplomacy to keep on bleeding it to death. Previously Moncada had bragged all the way down, before Stimson invited him to have a *private talk* with him, "that if he should find any American troops trying to block his way he would fight them to the bitter end!" What a farce! However, what else could be expected from a crooked politician and a Conservative renegade of the type of Moncada who has succeeded in outdoing in baseness and abjectness even Adolfo Diaz? Did he not, according to a story published in *El Comercio* of Managua, in July, declare at the top of his voice, during a banquet given by General Logan Feland, "that Nicaragua needed not only a permanent fiscalization of its finances, but also a permanent active intervention, as the destinies of Nicaragua remained closely linked and required being constantly guided by the wings of the American Eagle?" In view of that wonderful burst of oratory I suggest that if the Dollar Diplomats should perchance be looking for a suitable presidential candidate to replace their pet and special favorite, Adolfo Diaz, during next year's elections, they should not forget Moncada. They could not find a better man for that job in Nicaragua even if they looked around for one for a hundred years with the famous lantern of Diogenes!—though we remember that the lantern was not used in the beginning to seek for traitors. During my two days' stay in Matiguas as well as during my trip to Matagalpa by way of the Tierra Azul and Muy Muy trail I had ample opportunity to convince myself not only of the tactical and strategical mistakes committed by Moncada, more particularly during his unsuccessful advance on Boaco from Palo Alto, which led him instead to Las Mercedes; but also of the undeniable fact that he intentionally chose the Tierra Azul-to-Leon Road, for fear of coming in contact with Sandino whom he had unjustly and mischievously wronged at

THE LOOTING OF NICARAGUA

Laguna de Perlas. He knew that Sandino could never forgive him his cowardly conduct and, besides, that if Sandino and Beltron-Sandoval should coöperate as they undoubtedly would have done, for both were valiant and independent spirited soldiers, the fictitious control which Moncada had been exercising all along in the Constitutionalist army—because nobody could check him on account of Sacasa having appointed him Secretary of War—would have come very swiftly to an end. Beltran-Sandoval says in his official report, published in *La Noticia* of Managua, that when he and Moncada arrived with their army at Matiguas, they found the Conservative commander Baquerano heavily entrenched in Muy Muy, which is the first of the several strong positions which protect the Matiguas-to-Matagalpa road. The fact that the Conservative commander-in-chief never had thought of taking possession of Tierra Azul and Palo Alto but instead had fortified himself in Muy Muy goes to show that the Conservatives themselves considered the town and district of Matagalpa as their most vulnerable point. If Moncada, instead of occuping Palo Alto with a view of advancing by way of the Tierra Azul-to-Tipitapa road had used the rest of the Constitutionalist army to support Beltran-Sandoval after his successes at Muy Muy and El Chompipe, they could have easily taken Matagalpa before it was declared a neutral zone. Then joining hands with Sandino's and Parejon's two thousand men, who were in possession of practically the whole of the northern provinces of Matagalpa, Jinotega, Segovia, Chinandega and Leon, the Constitutionalist army could have literally walked into Leon and advanced from there to Managua before the American landing forces could have the necessary time to organize themselves properly and to occupy the railroad for the benefit of the Diaz forces only.

To illustrate the spirit which prevailed at that time among the Constitutionalist forces operating along the Pacific Coast, I will reproduce a few extracts of a letter which Col. Vicente Lovos, one of Parejon's lieutenants, sent on February 25, 1927, to Captain G. Kattengell, U. S. M. C.:

"In answer to your letter of February 22d, last, informing me that you have disembarked for the purpose of protecting with your forces the Corinto to Managua Railroad, etc., I wish to state that your intention of protecting said railroad from its legitimate owners surprises us very much indeed. You seem to ignore the fact that the road belongs exclusively to our government which has bought back every share which the American bankers used to own in this railroad company, and, therefore, that there is no reason why the railroad should be classed among the 'foreign interests' which you have been ordered to protect. Besides, you ought to know very well that we Nicaraguans have never interfered in any way, either with the lives or the properties of foreigners residing in our country. Referring to your resolution not to allow any fighting to take place in certain zones, we wish to inform you that we do not recognize within the boundaries of the sovereign, independent republic of Nicaragua other authority than that of our legitimate government represented by Dr. Juan Bautista Sacasa; and that—according as circumstances may demand—we are most assuredly going to do as we please wherever and whenever we choose."

If Moncada had made his appearance, as he should, at Matagalpa and, after joining hands with Sandino and Parejon, had kept marching in the direction of the Pacific Coast, President Coolidge's special representative, Mr. Henry L. Stimson, could have saved himself the trouble of going to Nicaragua in order to butt into things which did not concern either him or the American Government at all. In a letter from the Constitutionalist soldier, Col. Lovo, the writer stated that the pretended necessity of protecting the lives and interests of Americans and foreigners residing in Nicaragua was being used by the United States Government only as a pretext to land troops, etc.; a measure which the United States was not in the habit of taking in countries which were not small and weak like Nicaragua!

After the battle of Palo Alto, which was undoubtedly a big triumph for the Constitutionalist army, Moncada could have exclaimed like Pyrrhus—"another such victory and we are lost!" for the careful maneuvering for which he was credited by the Central American press in order to attract the bulk of the Conservative Army toward Palo Alto, had not been intended for that purpose at all but with the view of checking Beltran-Sandoval's triumphal march on Matagalpa after his victories at Muy Muy, San Pedro, El Chompipe, San Geronimo, Santo Domingo and San Ramon. Moncada realized that if Beltran-Sandoval and his brilliant lieutenants Plata, Mena, Miller and Escamilla (the latter actually managed to cross Matagalpa on the gallop at the head of his cavalry) succeeded in getting hold of Matagalpa, Sandino would join them right away. Thus his carefully premeditated plan to lead the Constitutionalist Army by way of Tierra Azul and Boaco to Tipitapa—in order to barter it away there to Stimson in exchange for his official support during the forthcoming elections—would have been foiled. Therefore, after the battle of Palo Alto Moncada was very anxious to get his men away from the direction of Matagalpa, so anxious indeed that he almost sacrificed his convoy of ammunition in his hurry. This is a fact which Moncada's secretary, Mr. Heberto Correa, omitted to mention in a certainly very meager and superficial *résumé* of that campaign which Moncada ordered him to write out for me. But when I asked Correa about that incident he admitted that such had actually been the case, for he had been himself at that time in charge of the convoy of ammunition. It seems that after the battle was over and when Correa had already ordered the ammunition boxes, etc., to be strapped on the pack animals—this was about eleven A.M.—he received a message from Moncada ordering him not to move from there until four P.M. when he would send him a scout to conduct him to where he wanted him to go. Such an order, which would have been under ordinary circumstances an unpardonable mistake, was madness itself in that case or treachery. For Moncada knew very well that the minute he abandoned his positions at Palo Alto in order to move elsewhere the Conservative Army was going to cling to his heels like a pack of wolves, making it impossible for his convoy to catch up with him afterwards; which really happened. No sooner had the rear guard of Moncada's troops vanished in the distance, than Correa's convoy was cut off almost immediately by the Conservatives. Luckily Escamilla happened to arrive at that moment from his Rio Negro expedition with his cavalry and, realizing that everything would be lost if the convoy fell into the hands of the enemy, he conducted it by roundabout ways until, after seventeen days of continuous battling against the Conservative forces which were pressing him and constantly trying to block his way, he finally succeeded, just in the nick of time, in joining Moncada at Las Mercedes, when the Constitutionalist army had spent almost its last cartridge. This incident, among the many which I could cite, but which Moncada was very careful not to have mentioned in Correa's report, goes to prove that Moncada was in reality only an amateur soldier—a newspaperman, and a poor one at that, posing as a military genius! If Escamilla had not happened to join him with the convoy of ammunition just in the nick of time, followed a few days later by Parejon, Sandino, Castro Wassmer and Lopez Irias with two thousand men, Moncada and the brave little Constitutionalist army, which was by that time already surrounded by the Conservative generals Viquez, Noguera Gomez, Rivers Delgadillo, would probably have succumbed to hunger, death and capture in less than a month.

Shortly after the Constitutionalist army had left Las Mercedes, Major N. B. Humphry, Lieutenant E. J. Moran and Lieutenant I. N. Tresbil made their appearance, accompanied by fifty marines. Their efforts to make the Constitutionalists come to terms with the fake Diaz régime did not meet with the expected success. So they returned to Managua and Mr. Henry L. Stimson, special representative of President Coolidge, got busy. He invited Dr. Sacasa to send three delegates to Managua to confer with him. Consequently Doctors Leonardo Arguello, Rodolfo Espinosa and Cordero Reyes left Puerto Cabezas on the United States Destroyer *Preston* on April 27th, and arrived at Corinto on April 29th. According to a printed circular published by those delegates in Managua on May 6th, they were shocked when Mr. Stimson made clear to them that there was no chance to come to any kind of settlement unless it were based on the continuance in power of Adolfo Diaz. Their answer to Mr. Stimson was that they would rather have their right hands cut off than sign such a base and traitorous pledge. As Moncada, on the invitation of Mr. Stimson, had also taken part in the final, unsuccessful conference between Stimson and the delegates, Señores Arguello, Espinosa and Cordero Reyes forced him to sign with them a letter to Stimson, dated in Managua, on May 5, 1927. In this letter they made clear to Stimson their surprise at having been invited to Managua to be imposed on rather than to be consulted, and declined all responsibility for the outcome. Doctor Cordero Reyes told me afterwards in Guatemala that, at that time, Mr. Stimson, who was supposed to be a diplomat, had told him, talking about the Tacna-Arica imbroglio, that the United States had made a mess of it there because Chile had had the control; but that in Nicaragua, where the American Government had the whip hand, so to say, they would show them how! According to that extraordinary statement made by President Coolidge's special representative, Mr. Henry L. Stimson proved himself a member of the Dollar Diplomacy school. He was not much of a diplomat according to the standards of civilized nations. Although Moncada had apparently also protested (by co-signing the letter of the delegates to Mr. Stimson objecting to any settlement based on the continuance in power of Adolfo Diaz), he was not loth to wink a beckoning eye, at the same time, at Stimson and Latimer, by exclaiming dramatically in their presence, at Tipitapa and publicly also several times at Managua: "I could not be so cruel as to advise anybody to forcibly oppose the American troops!" Naturally Latimer and Stimson, who were used to

General Augusto Sandino, Commander of the Nicaraguan Constitutionalist Army.

American Sailors awaiting attack of General Sandino's forces, Nicaragua.

treat with old crooks of the Moncada school in the Diaz puppet government, lay low until the honorable delegates had departed for Puerto Cabezas. Then it was that Moncada had at last the opportunity of his life, for which he had been longing for so many months! Then he had a nice, quiet little tête-à-tête with Mr. Stimson, with absolutely nobody else around to look through the keyhole; and in that quiet interview he bartered away, like a modern Judas, the plucky little Constitutionalist Army which had trusted him out of pure habit of military discipline, only because Dr. Sacasa had appointed him Secretary of War! Referring to this incident General Sandino said during a recent interview of his, published in the Managua press: "I consider Moncada not only as a traitor but also as a deserter who passed over to the enemy. Nobody ever authorized him to leave the Constitutionalist ranks in order to enter into any secret treaties in the name of the Constitutionalist army with the enemy and, more particularly, with the invaders of our country. His high position demanded of him to die like a man rather than tamely to permit the humiliation of our country. Moncada has made himself responsible for a crime which calls for vengeance."

After his private conference with Mr. Stimson during which he made, with Stimson, the shameful secret agreement in regard to the disarmament and the dissolution of the victorious Constitutionalist Army—which was then holding Diaz's forces completely surrounded at Teustepe and at the point of unconditional surrender—he returned to the Constitutionalist headquarters at Teustepe. There he proceeded at once to the execution of his premeditated treason in the expectation that Stimson would reward him for his faithful services by getting him appointed, next year,

President of Nicaragua by the grace of Dollar Diplomacy. He claimed that Mr. Stimson had promised him in the name of the American Government that, if the Constitutionalists surrendered their arms he would guarantee them, among other valuable considerations, the absolute political and economical control of the six provinces (out of the twelve or thirteen which comprise Nicaragua) which the Constitutionalist Government was controlling at that time. None of these verbal promises, made by President Coolidge's special representative, have been kept even halfway, so far. Minister Eberhard has attended to that! Besides, the fact that Moncada has not dared to press Stimson on the subject as yet although the Constitutionalists, whom he willfully betrayed, have demanded it from him time and again, releases the cat from the bag so far as Moncada's personal disinterestedness is concerned at least. As Moncada realized that if he put the question of surrender point-blank up to the Constitutionalist Army commanders they would have only laughed at him, he decided to demoralize the army before he took up the matter with them. Consequently he ordered, without the knowledge or the consent of the War Council, that the convoy of ammunition and the troops stationed at Las Banderas and Teustepe be concentrated at Boaco, thus enabling the Conservative army, which had been held surrounded up to that time by those troops, to slip away and join the American forces which were waiting for them at Tipitapa. After that flagrant treason which caused the total demoralization of the Constitutionalist Army, Moncada summoned and tried to convince the Council of War of the necessity of accepting Stimson's conditions, to save what could be saved yet out of that wreck which he had brought about himself intentionally and without the knowledge of the army. Several of the minor leaders, such as Margarito Espinosa, for instance, turned about, without saying a word and walked home with their men, carrying along with them their machine guns, ammunition and rifles, which they refused to sell at ten dollars apiece to the American commissioners representing the Diaz régime, as they had been ordered to do by Moncada. Most of those who did actually sell their rifles delivered only the old, used-up and defective guns which they had captured from the Conservatives. The good ones they took home with them and hid them away somewhere to be ready for the next revolution en masse if the American Government should continue to assist Dollar Diplomacy in bleeding Nicaragua to death by refusing to withdraw its marines *altogether* from that country. Among the superior officers of the Constitutionalist Army the only one who called Moncada's bluff during the War Council at Boaco was General Augusto Sandino who, on hearing Moncada express the necessity of surrendering their arms, asked his men in front of Moncada and the rest of the assembled officers if they wanted to surrender, whereupon they all shouted indignantly: "Never!" If Sandino had not used some diplomacy at that time in order to slip back unmolested with his troops to his native mountains in the Jinotega district, Moncada would surely have had him disarmed forcibly. After his cynical and hypocritical CONSUMATUM EST performance, which was well staged but did not succeed because Sandino, Salgado and some other leaders managed to sound the alarm in time, Moncada has been trying to obtain the official support of the United States Government during the next elections. No matter what the price in manhood and honor, Moncada will pay it! During his public speeches, manifestoes, etc., he has divested himself like a prostitute of every vestige of shame or of self-respect. Of course, it is always a question how far such men as Moncada and Diaz—every nation and type of civilization produces them—are to be blamed for what they do. They are moral freaks. The man on whom all the responsibility falls for the agonies which Moncada has caused to the people of Nicaragua through his treason is in reality Dr. Juan Bautista Sacasa who, knowing all the time what Moncada really was, appointed him first his personal delegate and later his Secretary of War with no other purpose than to prevent *new men* from getting into power and doing away with the rotten system of the old, crooked Estrada, Diaz, Chamorro, Moncada school.

After spending a couple of days at Matiguas, as the guest of Mr. Abel Flores, I left for Matagalpa escorted by a mounted bodyguard which Col. Gadea had been kind enough to furnish me. From the Tierra Azul-to-Muy Muy road I had an opportunity of studying the lay of the country around Palo Alto, where the battle of that name had taken place. In Muy Muy, which I found practically empty, the plaza or marketplace was still covered with human bones and skulls, intermingled with the putrefied carcasses of numerous pigs. After their return the Constitutionalists had shot the pigs because they had found them devouring the corpses of their dead soldiers and those of the Diaz force, whom they had not had the time to bury or to incinerate after Baquerano's retreat. Every day new murders and robberies were reported; old feuds were being fought out. While I was having lunch at the home of Mr. José Maria Medrano—whom the Conservatives had ruined by burning and otherwise destroying his extensive coffee plantations, because, although a Conservative himself, he had sided with the Constitutionalist cause—a member of my escort rushed in and told me that some one had stolen his saddle mule which he had left tied to the house porch.

At the San Pedro and El Chompipe battle fields, which I passed on the following day, the ground on both sides of the trail was literally strewn with the skulls and bones of the dead whom neither of the contending forces had had the time to bury during their deadly running fight. Of the several pictures which I took of them only two turned out to be any good because a thin rain was falling. Clouds of buzzards kept hovering over the stricken countryside. While I was wandering with my camera through the bush—where men had so recently swarmed in the darkness, with bloodshot eyes, spreading death and destruction—dozens of black-winged "zopilotes," those hideous carrion eaters and scavengers of the jungle, would fly up every now and then with much noise and flapping of wings. They cursed angrily at me all the time, in their hoarse, guttural buzzard lingo, for having interrupted them during their macabre meal—some half dried up, stinking skeleton perchance whose blood-smeared, grinning skull seemed to be shouting yet through its bare, yellow, decaying teeth: "Viva Dollar Diplomacy!" In every direction piles of empty shells marked the places where machine guns had been hammering away and sputtering angrily, in the mist, at the bombing planes, which continued roaring or sinking to a pulsating drone as they drew their deadly circles over the mournfully swaying forest giants, enveloped at times in a thick screen of smoke or lit up fantastically, at intervals, by the blinding flash of the exploding projectiles. From the tin roof of an abandoned farmhouse, on which they were roosting comfortably, a string of vultures looked at me suspiciously. They were seemingly enjoying the fragrance of a couple of decaying corpses which lay prone on their faces on the mud floor of the sitting room; while around the building the dried up carcasses of several pack oxen lay in the same position in which death had surprised them in the shape of stray bullets—with their limbs stretched out rigidly and wide gaping mouths, over which swarms of green flies were buzzing and humming.

In Matagalpa I spent a few days as the guest of Consul Wm. Hueper and the rest of the German colony, composed of Messrs. Bornemann, Carl Eger, Rudolf Haase and others. They also had suffered considerably through the exactions of Adolfo Diaz's forces and of the Conservative civil authorities during the revolution, but they were game and took their medicine like real men. They too seemed to be very much upset by the current rumors to the effect that Mr. Frantz Bunge, the German Consul in Managua (a former foreman of one of the Bahlke plantations and a typical product of the black-red-yellow post-World War social revolution), had solicited, together with the British and Italian Consuls, the American armed intervention in Nicaragua. Despite the fact that Congressman Dr. Ramon Romero assured me, both verbally and in writing, that such had been the case, I continue to give Mr. Frantz Bunge the benefit of the doubt for, if he really should have done such a thing as that he would only have lessened still more Latin America's already much shattered faith in the old pre-war honor of the German "Grosshandel" (big import and export firms), which has suffered, among

THE LOOTING OF NICARAGUA

us already, a mortal blow through the criminal paper mark swindle which some of those business houses perpetrated cold-bloodedly on the unsuspecting masses of our republics, who had trusted them. One of the proofs submitted to me by Congressman Romero was an extract taken and copied from the protocol of the Nicaraguan Congress, which I intend to submit to the German Foreign Office next winter. In a letter of Dr. Romero, addressed to me from Managua, on August 16, 1927, he corroborates his assertion in the following way: "Dije a Ud. y le afirmo ahora que los consules de Italia y Alemania pidieron la intervencion." Which means, in English—"I told you before and I now say it again, that the Italian and German Consuls solicited the intervention." I think that if Mussolini gave a severe reprimand to the Italian Consul at Managua for meddling in things which, as Mussolini claimed, did not concern *him* but only the Italian Foreign Office, and if our Holy father in Rome told the Papal Count and Catholic Archbishop of Nicaragua, Monseigneur José Antonio Liscano, in a rather sour way, not to mix in politics, because that worthy prelate had ordered his shepherds and lambs to pray for the triumph of the Diaz-Chamorro clique! —it is about time also for Mr. Stresemann to do some investigating in his turn about what *his* shepherds and lambs have been doing, and continue doing, in Central America and, more specially in Nicaragua—unless he wants the Latin American press to do the investigating for him. As an impartial observer and a historian it would be unjust if I were to expose American Dollar Diplomacy only, without trying to expose in turn all those who have made it possible for Dollar Diplomacy to play its game.

During my stay in Matagalpa I had the opportunity

of meeting almost all the officers of the third Battalion of the Fifth Regiment of the United States Marine Corps stationed there, who were getting ready by that time to start a drive on General Sandino because he had threatened to shoot Moncada at sight if he dared show up anywhere near his hunting grounds in the Jinotega mountains. Moncada had arrived at Matagalpa, proud as a peacock of his escort of armed American marines, for the purpose of persuading Sandino to surrender his arms.

At that time I was also informed as to the way in which the Dollar Diplomats had managed to have Matagalpa declared a neutral zone. Fearing that Beltran-Sandoval would occupy it after the battle of El Chompipe, the American Vice Consul in their locality, Mr. De Savigny, Sr., was found one morning in front of his house almost beaten to death. Immediately his son, Mr. De Savigny, Jr., boiling over with rage had rushed to the local barracks and demanded to be confronted with the officer of the day, who had made the rounds that night—but somehow or other that officer had disappeared. Everybody in Matagalpa understood at once that Dr. De Savigny, Sr., had been the victim of the try-it-on-the-dog, for-raisons-d'état system—but there were no proofs and, as Mr. De Savigny apparently did not remember (?) and so forth, the matter was hushed up. However, as soon as the news was flashed to Managua and thence to Washington, the State Department immediately declared that, whereas the American Vice Consul at Matagalpa had been attacked, that city must be declared at once a neutral zone and occupied immediately by United States Marines. The Dollar Diplomats are certainly no good but you must give them credit for one thing; you will never catch them napping! Another favorite system the Dollar Diplomats' press agents utilized to stir the good-natured American people consists in playing up women as presumptive victims. There were two American ladies in Matagalpa who had been reported in the American papers to have been tortured or God knows what else—to their great amusement, for it was news to them! People in the United States do not realize what "easy marks" they are. They will fall every time for any sensational story which the press agents of Dollar Diplomacy may spread through the yellow papers in order to make the Nicaraguans appear a nation of savages and enemies of the United States. In reality there are few countries in the world where the Americans who know how to behave and respect the laws are so much liked as in Nicaragua.

Chapter XIV

From Matagalpa to Managua — How Long Hate Can Last — Report of the Pan-American Federation of Labor — H. Blanco Fombona Gives a Series of Shameful Facts About the American Occupation in Santo Domingo.

ON June 4th, having received my passport from the American authorities,[1] I left Matagalpa for Managua in Consul Hueper's machine. It was about time, for the weather was already beginning to get bad, which means that a couple of rainy days would have been more than sufficient to put the mud road to Managua completely out of commission, so far as automobiles were concerned. The reason why the rainy season was only then commencing in the interior could be perfectly explained by the difference between the vegetation east and west of Monte Musun, which was really remarkable. For no sooner had we left that mountain behind us, in the neighborhood of Bijagual, a few miles east of Matiguas, than the virgin forests of the Atlantic Coast gradually gave place to a dry, dusty jungle, full of thorny underbrush, that is, the typical wooded steppe which forms the interior section of Nicaragua as far west as the eastern shores of Managua and Nicaragua lakes. The strip of ex-

---

[1] Headquarters Third Battalion, Fifth Regiment, Second Brigade U. S. Marine Corps, Matagalpa, Nicaragua.

1 June, 1927.

To whom it may concern:
This is to certify that the bearer is—Rafael de Nogales—a citizen of Venezuela, traveling from Matagalpa to Managua. He shall not be interfered with nor molested in any way.

(s) MAJOR M. E. SHEARER, U. S. M. C.
5th. Regt. etc.

Dist: Rafael de Nogales; file.

THE LOOTING OF NICARAGUA

ceedingly rich agricultural soil which stretches between those lakes and the Pacific Ocean, from the Coseguina peninsula on Fonseca Bay down to the Departamento of Rivas, on the Costa Rican frontier, is covered again, like the forest sections of the Atlantic Coast, with the exuberant vegetation typical of the wet tropical jungle lands. It is along this belt, west of the lakes, that the Nicaraguan railroad, measuring about one hundred and twenty-five miles in length, connects the harbor of Corinto with Chinandega, Leon, Managua and Granada, which are, so to say, the only good-sized towns of Nicaragua outside of Matagalpa, which controls the second biggest coffee zone of the interior. From Matagalpa, which is situated in the same mountain section which comprises, to the north, the wealthy agricultural and mining zones of the Departamentos of Segovia and Jinotega, the road descends gradually for about eighty or ninety miles, until it reaches Tipitapa, which is situated between lakes Managua and Nicaragua and, therefore, also in the center of the big depression or agricultural basin which environs those lakes. The sixty or seventy miles between the foot of the Matagalpa range and Tipitapa is not composed of rolling grasslands, as some people claim, but of a choppy terrain crossed by partly bare long ridges, such as the San Jacinto mountain. From one end to the other it is a dry, thorny bush steppe which in the neighborhood of La Madera becomes a deep, bush-covered and almost untraversable mud desert during the rainy season. South of the Matagalpa-Matiguas road lies the Departamento of Chontales which the Constitutionalist Army crossed during its victorious march from Matiguas and Tierra Azul to Tipitapa.

Half way down the road, in a small town called

Dario, a detachment of American marines stopped our machine to examine our passports. And a couple of hours later my attention was called toward the south, where a rather inhospitable-looking, dry and partly barren ridge stood out solitary against the sky. We were going at about thirty-five miles an hour over a mud road, strewn with rocks and full of cracks and holes, caused by the constant traffic of the heavy, native, two-wheeled ox carts. Notwithstanding that he was inviting almost certain death, our driver kept pointing out to me with his left hand that blessed ridge, while his eyes shone like burning black diamonds and his twisting lips, causing his handsome face to assume an almost satanic smile, repeated again and again: "Señor, it was on that ridge of San Jacinto, that our Indians caught, about seventy years ago, that cursed gringo buccaneer Walker and his band of outlaws, whom they dragged at the end of their lariats over this very road to Managua." His speech was a revelation to me; for it went to show that, if the grandchildren of those who fought against Walker at that time keep on hating his very memory, the future generation of Nicaraguans will probably never forget the incredible and unpardonable crimes which have been committed in their unhappy country from 1909 up to the present time. The American armed intervention in Nicaragua since then can justly be put down as a crime. Here are the proofs of it in black and white, copied from the Report of Proceedings of the Fourth Congress of the Pan American Federation of Labor:

"This intervention (that of 1912) had a totally different aspect than the one effected in 1910. In 1910 the American Government protected the revolutionary movement against the Constitutional Government (of President Madriz) on the pretext that the latter was an unpopular government. But in 1912 American protection was given to the Diaz Government, a government which was decidedly unpopular and repudiated by the whole country, thus contradicting the popular will which was made manifest in every way. And it was in 1912, more than at any other time, that the intervention of the American Government was most felt and was effected in a most emphatic manner. American troops actually waged battle against the people of Nicaragua; the American troops were powerfully armed, with all sorts and descriptions of war instruments, while the Nicaraguans were almost unarmed, and had not offended in any way either the government of the United States or its people. The proofs of the above follow: On September 26, 1912, Mr. Diego Manuel Chamorro, Minister of Foreign Relations, addressed a circular letter to the Central American governments in which he said as follows: 'I have the honor to inform your excellencies that on the 24th instant General Mena surrendered in Granada with more or less seven hundred of his forces *to the Commander of the Pacific Fleet of the United States, Rear Admiral W. H. Sutherland,* the latter promising to take him to Panama under his protection, under the promise that he would not return to Nicaragua and that his forces would be disarmed.' The Minister of Foreign Relations also addressed a note to the State Department of the American Government informing the department of the active part taken by the American marines. He said for instance: 'Masaya was taken by assault to-day. . . . *The American troops* captured early this morning the town of Coyotepe. Four men of the naval infantry succumbed during the battle. Six were wounded.' On his part Rear Admiral Sutherland submitted his official report to the Navy Department, dated January 8, 1913, in which he made special mention of the conduct observed by the Commanders G. W. Steele, S. S. and M. Major, and First Lieutenants F. H. Conyer and R. W. Simman. The following is quoted from his report: Commander Steele, chief of the California troops, was at the head of the forces in each of the encounters that took place during the short Nicaragua incident, at the Masaya pass, at Granada, Chichigalpa, in Leon and in the assault on the hill of Coyotepe,—and *he was the first to raise the American flag on the top of the hill . . . !* The circular line of battle began its forward march on the run at five-thirty A.M., on October 4, and the reserves followed in the same manner, etc. The position was taken in thirty-seven minutes *and the California colors were the first to be raised on the top of the hill by Leader Kelsow, Master at Arms!*"

The following is a press clipping of that period: "New York, September 30—The statement of a Washington daily, which is considered well informed, with reference to the policy which the State Department is determined to follow in Central America, has caused a great sensation. The newspaper alluded to says that the United States Government frankly intervened in Nicaragua to prevent the triumph of the Liberal revolution, and that if in the future the circumstances should require it, it would intervene in the other Central American countries! That it must not only be understood as opposed to American policy for European nations to have territorial domain in America, but also in the American countries no European political influence or hegemony of whatever nature will be permitted!"

"San Francisco, Cal., Sept. 30th. The daily newspapers of this city as well as those of Oakland and Los Angeles have expressed their opposition to the policy pursued by Taft in the Central American countries, which is characterized as a filibuster highly prejudicial to the honor of the United States, whose history should be respected!" While in the American Senate, in the month of August, Senator Bacon introduced a resolution directing the appointment of a subcommittee of the Senate's Foreign Relations Committee to investigate the invasion of Nicaragua by American marines and to determine under what authority they invaded the country during the revolution! In censuring the policy of the American State Department in this respect, Senator Bacon said: "In my judgment the executive departments of our government have violated the law in employing the Army and Navy of the United States in Nicaragua!"

Among the several American officers who provoked, during the armed intervention of 1912, not only the wrath but the contempt of the Nicaraguans there ranks foremost a certain Lieutenant-Colonel Chas. S. Long, U. S. M. C., who, after having pledged his word that he would respect the convention regarding the evacuation of Leon, Masaya and Granada apparently made no effort to fulfill his promise. And among the several revolting crimes which were committed at that time by members of the American landing forces, the one which caused the greatest sensation was that of Chichigalpa, where a strong detachment of American marines machine-gunned in cold blood about fifty unarmed Nicaraguan policemen in their barracks. Nicaraguan public opinion also claims that when Admiral Sutherland was informed of that crime he did not even pay attention. A similar incident occurred recently with Admiral Latimer who, apparently, did not take any steps to investigate why a group of American marines made their appearance —according to the Managua press—at about nine or ten P.M. in front of the residence of the ex-Constitutionalist Commander Francisco Sequeira, in Chinandega, and shot him and his wife down in cold blood while Sequeira was opening the door of his house to let them in. This utter disregard for the lives of private citizens, and more specially of the lives of defenseless women, on the part of the American marines, both officers and men, stationed in Nicaragua, make me suspect that of the three hundred of Sandino's men who were reported killed during the post-revolution fight at Ocotal, the greater part most probably belonged to the *civil population* of that place. They were killed—incidentally I presume—(as during the bombing and machine-gunning of Chinandega, in February last) by the American fliers or by Captain Hatfield's men, who *silenced the so-called snipers* in the town. For, according to the first cable dispatch, sent by Minister Eberhard himself, Sandino had, if I am not mistaken, attacked Ocotal at the head of only two hundred followers and his losses were reported to consist only of fifty men. I hope that when Congress reconvenes next winter it will take the necessary steps to investigate not only why Admiral Latimer allowed Sequeira and his wife to be murdered in cold blood by his marines, but also why Admiral Sutherland did not take any steps to investigate and punish the massacre of those fifty defenseless Nicaraguan policemen at Chichigalpa, for in both cases the honor of the American Army and Navy is directly involved. These two and several other cases in which, according to Nicaraguan public opinion, the American marines have not lived up to the high moral standard demanded by army discipline and proper regard for international law, remind me of a report published in the New York *Times* of August 23rd, 1927, regarding the American armed intervention in Haiti and Santo Domingo. It was written by the Staff correspondent of the *Times* at Williamstown, Mass., and said among other things: "A bitter controversy was aroused at the Latin American round table of the Institute of Politics this morning by a charge by Horace G. Knowles, former American Minister to Nicaragua, the Dominican Republic and Bolivia, that American intervention in Latin American republics had resulted in the 'slaughter of thousands of their citizens! In each case of intervention,' Mr. Knowles asserted, 'we have been guilty of violating the sovereign rights of neighbors and proceeding contrary to the universally recognized principles of international law. We have imposed our force upon weak, helpless and defenseless countries, and slaughtered thousands of their citizens. We have attacked them when they expected we would defend them. We have used the Monroe Doctrine to prevent sympathetic European nations going to their rescue when we abused them!' When Commander Shafroth broke in heatedly with a demand that Mr. Knowles state facts, the round table leader, Professor Wm. R. Shepherd, interrupted with the assertion that Mr. Knowles was justified in asserting that thousands were slaughtered. Commander Shafroth again demanded that Mr. Knowles be specific when he said that he knew of no greater acts of inhumanity, wrong and outrage committed on any people than the United States had committed upon the people of the Dominican Republic. Mr. Knowles replied that five thousand soldiers had swept over the country, etc. As to the American occupation of Haiti, in 1915, Mr. Knowles explained that once order had been established, the American troops should not have been kept there. He then asserted that a year later 'Representations were made to the Dominicans that the United States desired to establish a protectorate in that country!' Commander Shafroth was specially indignant at a statement by Professor Knowles 'that this country had sent concession hunters, conscienceless and usurious bankers, avaricious capitalists, bribers, commercial tricksters, murderers, soldiers to shoot them, etc.,' to Latin-American countries, instead of teachers, instructors and helpers. 'That characterization of the people of this country is, in my opinion, monstrous,' said the Commander. 'Soldiers are sent there only to preserve law and order. They have no desire to shoot any one. They do not shoot unless law and order have been rendered nugatory!'"

As Commander Shafroth demanded Mr. Knowles to state facts about the American military occupation of Haiti and Santo Domingo, I will take the liberty of furnishing him a few of those facts by translating in a condensed way some incidents mentioned by Mr. Horacio Blanco Fombona in his book "Crimenes del Imperialismo Americano," published by him recently in Mexico City. I would not be surprised if Commander Shafroth knew Blanco Fombona personally for Fombona was not only living in Santo Domingo during its occupation by the American marine forces in 1916, but was imprisoned and tried in November 7, 1920, by the American military authorities for having published in his review "Letras" the picture of a Dominican peasant named Cayo Baez who, according to his own statements and as everybody in Santo Domingo knew, had red-hot machete blades applied to his naked body by order, and in the presence, of Captain Bucklow, U. S. M. C. No sooner had the number of "Letras" with Cayo Baez's picture appeared, than Blanco Fombona was imprisoned by the American military authorities, tried and fined three hundred dollars. While he remained in prison the American military police closed up for good the printing offices of "Letras" and confiscated the numbers of that review in which Baez's picture had appeared. The picture was authentic for Blanco Fombona had obtained it from the records of the Dominican Archbishopric. Referring to this process Blanco Fombona says:

"When Lieutenant Ellis had retired an elderly much decorated brigadier made his appearance. After he had been sworn in the judge asked him if he knew anything about Cayo Baez. He answered affirmatively, adding that it was his special duty to deal with the complaints made against American officers. He further stated that Baez had been burnt by a Dominican called Escoboza. That both Escoboza and Cayo Baez had declared Captain Bucklow had been present while Baez was being tortured. But that Bucklow asserted that he had not arrived until the torture was over. Besides, he continued, Bucklow was not acting at that time as an American but as the Chief of the Dominican National Guard and, therefore, as a Dominican officer. It was not as an American but as a Dominican that Bucklow committed that crime! When asked by the judge if there had been any more complaints about American officers filed with him he added that there had been also one against a captain named Merkel who had committed suicide before he was put on trial." This Captain Merkel, who also belonged to the American landing forces in Santo Domingo, had left (according to Blanco Fombona's book) the town of La Romana one early morning at the head of fifty American soldiers to trail down the rebel leader, Vicente Evangelista, whom the American troops, operating in the neighborhood of San Pedro de Macoris and El Seybo, had not yet been able to capture despite all their efforts.

As soon as Merkel and his men reached the danger zone, he got off his horse, which he turned over to an orderly, and continued on foot because, as he put it, he needed some exercise. Evangelista had, time and again, fooled his pursuers during the three years he had been fighting the American forces of occupation. The farmers in the surrounding country, despite all imaginable threats, remained silent. They persisted in not knowing anything about Vicentico's doings or whereabouts. Several sorts of terrorism were committed to make them talk. But it was all of no use. They would tell nothing. In La Ceja, which is situated in the sector of Magarin, Captain Taylor had the wife of one Pedro Cedeno (who is still living there) hung to a tree and, with his own hand, shot her full of holes in the presence of her little children, who were begging him not to kill her. After the thing was done he fired a couple of shots over the heads of those unhappy children who fled shrieking with grief and fear. Suspecting that the inhabitants of that neighborhood were trying to cover Evangelista's tracks through their persistent silence, the American military authorities decreed (1) that all the farmers and neighbors of that district be reconcentrated immediately in the towns; and (2) that they should take along with them all their belongings. This order was signed by Colonel C. L. Hoppe, Provost Marshal. This was the famous "reconcentration" over again, which General Weyler had decreed during the Cuban revolution, and which the American Government had branded as the crime against humanity which led the McKinley administration to declare war on Spain! However, the American forces of occupation were not loth in applying that same inhuman system in Santo Domingo, in the hope that nobody abroad would know anything about it as Santo Domingo was isolated from the rest of the world not only by the ocean, but also by the strict censorship which they established immediately on the press, the mail, the telegraph, the cables. Every passenger who was going to leave the country was scrutinized. Every ship was examined from top to bottom. According to the order of reconcentration all men, women or children who should be found outside the city limits of La Romana, etc., after the expiration of said decree, were ordered to be shot. Likewise all farmhouses, ranchos and so forth were to be burnt, and all products of the field, be they standing or harvested already, were also to be destroyed at once. All domestic animals which could not be used for the maintenance of the American expeditionary forces were to be shot and incinerated without any loss of time. Consequently, the unhappy rural population, most of whom were destitute, without any means of support or a roof to shelter them during the damp tropical nights, were soon dying by scores in the streets of the towns in which they had been confined by the American military authorities.

When Captain Merkel and his men reached the river Quisibani they met somebody who looked sometimes like a man and then again like a boy sitting on a fallen tree. He seemed absent-minded and never even made a move to run away. One of Merkel's interpreters, who tried to make him speak, could not make head nor tail out of his jargon. Finally the native guide, who accompanied the troop, told Merkel that that individual was a harmless idiot, who was known in the neighborhood as "el loco," or "the lunatic." He was the son of a poor old widow who cared for him like a child. After he and his mother had reached the concentration camp he had probably run away, to return to his favorite place, which was that fallen tree, where he would sit for hours at a time looking at the swift running waters of the river. That seemed to be his hobby. Notwithstanding that explanation Merkel applied his six-shooter to the lunatic's ear, then thrust it into his mouth, lacerating it, and told him through his interpreter, that if he found him again in that neighborhood he would have him shot on sight. When Merkel and his troops were nearing Quisibani on their way back, for they had failed to round up Vicentico, he spied through his field glasses the "loco" still sitting in the same position, on the fallen tree. Whereupon Merkel borrowed a rifle from one of his men and, carefully aiming, made the poor "loco" roll over and over on the ground, with a bullet in the back of his head. One of his eyes was blown out altogether while his brains were oozing through the bullet hole.

On page ninety-six of his book Blanco Fombona refers to the following incidents: After the American forces had disembarked and occupied the city of Santo Domingo, a boy named Gregorio Urbano Gilbert remarked, in a barber shop of San Pedro de Macoris, that if the Americans tried to disembark there, and nobody else should dare to oppose them, he would fight them single-handed. Nobody paid any attention to what he said because they all thought that it was only a boy bragging. Finally two American warships made their appearance and began landing troops, provided with machine guns. These started advancing cautiously over the deserted wharf. The last of them to land was apparently a superior officer. The boy, who had been hiding behind some bales on the wharf, stepped forth and walked straight up to the advancing marines who kept staring at him in amazement, until the officer, just mentioned, walked up to the boy and, when he had almost reached him, Gregorio Urbano Gilbert fired, felling him with his second shot. Immediately the advancing marines deployed in battle formation and started firing at the numerous bales and bags of sugar piled up on the wharf, as well as at the customs house, the steeple of the church and the deserted housetops. Even the warships commenced firing their cannon, while the boy, who had taken refuge behind some bags of sugar, seeing his chance at last, slipped away and succeeded in getting to Montecristo, on the opposite extreme of the island, where he took up a job in a sugar plantation under an assumed name. But he finally was located and brought before an American officer in charge of the American garrison of Montecristo who asked him why he had shot the commander in Mocoris. Whereupon the boy answered tranquilly: "Because, as a Dominican, I considered it my duty to do so, that's all!" Although his trial had taken place within the prison walls and without any witnesses being present, the American officer did not dare to have him shot at once, without previously consulting his superior officer in Santo Domingo City, which saved the boy's life; for in the meantime the news of his capture had been broadcast over the island. But he was sentenced just the same to NINETY-NINE YEARS' IMPRISONMENT!

Another instance of how the American forces of occupation dealt with the Dominicans who dared to stand up for their rights was, according to Blanco Fombona, that of Casildo Santana, a former lieutenant of Vicente Evangelista, who had fallen into the hands of the American military authorities by foul means. This happened in the following way: Seeing that it was useless to try to capture Evangelista by force, the commander of the American forces, which were pursuing him, offered to appoint him governor of the province of El Seybo if he agreed to give up his arms. Evangelista would not listen to his propositions for a long time but as the American commander insisted time and again and, seeing that his ammunition was running low, he finally consented to have a talk with an emissary, who succeeded in convincing him after many efforts of the good faith of the Americans. Consequently Evangelista went with an escort of about fifty men, among whom was also Casildo Santana, to El Seybo, where he was royally entertained by the American officers, who handed him his appointment as governor of that province in the shape of a pompous document to which were attached many seals and signatures. That night Evangelista's escort went to sleep in the local barracks divided into different groups, lodged in separate rooms. Just before dawn several hundred American soldiers sneaked up to the barracks and disarmed them. They also captured Santana and made him face one of the prison walls, probably to keep him from seeing what was going on. To judge by the noise, he rightly suspected that something serious was going to happen. It was not long before he heard, several times, Evangelista's protesting voice, despite the rattling of guns and the loud voices of command in English which finally ended

THE LOOTING OF NICARAGUA

with a discharge. Soon after he was also stood up against the wall where they had shot Evangelista, whose corpse was lying in front of him. Blood was streaming out of several bullet holes in his head, body and legs. Following the sharp order of their commanding officer the soldiers of the firing squad pointed their guns at Santana, who was quietly awaiting death. But somehow or other the bullets were not forthcoming. Then an interpreter stepped forward and told him that his life would be saved if he revealed the place in the mountains where the rest of Evangelista's men had remained in hiding and where they were keeping their surplus guns and ammunition. As Santana persisted in asserting that he did not know, the sham execution was performed several times, with the same result—Santana would not confess. Whereupon, instead of shooting him the American commander sentenced him also to NINETY-NINE YEARS' IMPRISONMENT!

In one of the stories contained in his book, and which has circulated also all over Latin America, Blanco Fombona says: "The American intervention in Santo Domingo has brought to that unhappy, defenseless country peace, that is true, but not a judicial or a moral peace, but a peace imposed on its people by means of machine guns. Among the many incidents which have occurred in that country during that peace figure also the ones which I am going to mention now. I wish to state also that I can vouch for the veracity of my statements by means of documents whose authenticity cannot be put in doubt, as well as by information which I received from eyewitnesses whom I know to be absolutely dependable. There is the case of Cayo Baez, for instance, who by order and in the presence of Captain Bucklow was tortured by a

Dominican bandit called Ramon Ulises Escobaza, by applying to his body in numerous places machete blades which had been heated to a red-hot point in an improvised hearth. Fearing that if Captain Bucklow ever suspected that he had made any revelations about the torture to which he had been submitted by him, he might have him tortured over again, worse than before, he kept silence and hid away in his little farmhouse, covering up carefully the marks of his wounds, of which he would certainly have died if a woman, who happened to pass the place where Bucklow and his men had left him for dead, had not picked him up and cared for him until he recovered. Escobaza and two other Dominican bandits by the names of Telesforo Cabral and Ramon Antonio Modesto, who were being used and protected by Captains Bucklow, Knotchel and Wright—the American military commanders of that district—were finally caught and dragged before a Dominican tribunal, accused of blackmail, assault, etc. Cayo was also summoned. Seeing that he was under the protection of a Dominican court of justice and that people whom he knew to be all right were not afraid of accusing the accomplices of the above-mentioned American captains, he told his story and, lifting up his shirt, showed to the judges and the public the scars left on his body by the red-hot machete blades. At the sight of those undeniable proofs the presiding judge exclaimed with indignation that it was almost an injustice to condemn the three bandits while those others who were guilty of such a crime remained outside the reach of the Dominican law. The three Dominican bandits were sentenced and punished, but their employers, Captains Bucklow, Knotchel and Wright went scot-free because the Dominican jurisdiction did not reach the American forces of occupation.

In the records of the Court of Appeals of Santiago de los Caballeros, on pages 208, 224 and 225 of the book of sentences, the sentence can be found from which I took these data on March 3, 1920. It was signed by Juan D. Prez, President, Francisco Rodriguez Volta, Augusto Francisco Bido and Antonio Edmundo Martin, judges, as well as by Silvio Silva, secretary. I am keeping a copy of this sentence! It contains clear proof that Captain Wright, while conducting fifteen prisoners from Salcedo to Moca, where his superior officer had ordered them to be sent in order to assure himself that they had been really tortured, divided the prisoners into two groups, one of them with the nine individuals whose bodies showed the scars of the tortures they had been submitted to. These he sent ahead with a Dominican sergeant of the National Guard with instructions to have them shot on the road, near a place called Palmarito. On passing Palmarito the sergeant failed to execute the order. Captain Wright, who was following him with the remaining six prisoners, on seeing that the sergeant had not complied with his wishes, hurried on until he caught up with him and threatened that, unless he obeyed his order, he would have him shot also. He told him to go ahead enough only to keep out of sight. Somehow or other, however, the sergeant, probably in his consternation, did not go far enough and had those nine unhappy fellows shot down in sight of the remaining prisoners, among whom was also a woman by the name of Rita Campos, the mother of one of the victims. Captain Bucklow had ordered, a little while before, another Dominican sergeant, near San Pedro de Macoris, to torture, by means of red-hot machetes, another peasant whom he suspected of being in connivance with the rebels. That sergeant, however, refused energetically to obey his order because, as he said, he was not an assassin or a hangman. Whereupon Bucklow had him arrested and, after applying the torture to him also, shot him down and, summoning the village heads of the neighborhood, pointed out to them the sergeant's corpse with the remark: 'Look at what will happen to all those who disobey my orders!'

"Abraham Hoffis, a Syrian who had been living for some time in Santo Domingo, was saved from death in a really miraculous way by escaping to San Pedro de Macoris just in the nick of time from the claws of Captain Taylor, who had been looking for him in order to do away with him in the same way in which he had killed a friend and fellow countryman of Hoffis', to whom he had applied both the torture of water and of fire. These tortures were unknown to the Dominicans until the soldiers of liberty and civilization arrived on their island. As the thing came about because Hoffis had applied for protection to the French Minister, Taylor was transferred to Santo Domingo City and was not allowed to return to that section of the country where he had committed innumerable crimes. That was all the punishment he got. The American military men used to call him 'typhus,' or 'consumption,' on account of the devastation he caused wherever he went. I saw him myself at Macoris one night, drunk, threatening and provoking the people in the streets and in the cafés. Merkel was another American captain of the type of Taylor and just as bad as he, who was terrorizing also, at that time, the district of Macoris. He also committed several crimes, such as his cold-blooded murder of the wife of Pedro Cedeno. The American commander, whose duty it was to investigate the crimes of Taylor and Merkel, sent Merkel to San Pedro de Macoris, presumably as a punishment. Notwithstanding this he allowed him to resume military operations, although with the admonition that he would have him severely punished if he dared to commit any more *unjustifiable* crimes! Merkel promised to behave. However, no sooner had he arrived at the sugar plantation of Las Pajas, where about thirty peons were busily engaged in the fields earning their wages by the sweat of their brows, than he had them mowed down with machine guns, without leaving one alive, and sent in a report to the commanding officer that he had had a fight with a band of rebels, some of whom he had killed. Unfortunately for Merkel the manager of the plantation, who was also an American, filed a complaint against him, whereupon he was taken prisoner to Macoris, where he committed suicide a few days later. If I were to tell all the crimes which the American forces of occupation committed in the republic of Santo Domingo, I would have material for several volumes! I also wish to state that my book, 'Crimenes del Imperialismo Americano,' does not contain any of the crimes revealed by several other authors, such as Jacinto Lopez and Isidro Favela. One of the most atrocious incidents, which I have not yet mentioned, is that of Hato Mayor, which was one of the districts which suffered most under the tyrannical rule of the American forces of occupation. There even the druggists had to report to the American officers—unless they wanted to get shot—everything they sold, even every prescription, stating the name of the buyer or of the party for whom it was bought. On June 7, 1917, an eighty-year-old man presented himself at the drug store of José Maria Fernandez with a prescription issued by a physician called Guillermo Sanchez. The medicine was intended to heal some wounds. He said that he had to take it at once to El Salto, where the patient was waiting for it. That patient was his own son. The American officers immediately suspected that those medicines could only be for the rebel leader Vicente Evangelista. So they had the old man summoned and forced him to confess that such was the case by having him kicked clear over the plaza, where he was immediately hung to a tree and his body riddled with bullets. A man by the name of Perales cut the rope and the old man's corpse, tied with a lariat to a horse's tail, was dragged all over town as a warning. Major Davis, who was well known at Macoris and its vicinity, witnessed the performance, which he had staged himself, from the steeple of the only church in town. Of course, not all the American officers who have been in Santo Domingo have behaved like bandits. Yet there has been among them such a large percentage of criminals (facinerosos) that they have considerably hurt the reputation of the American Army. Besides, there is also something which is hard to explain in their conduct, if viewed from a moral standpoint. Whenever an American officer has committed a crime the first thing his superiors are wont to do is to hush it up, or to try to prove his innocence, for fear perhaps that if they disclosed the truth it might hurt the honor of the American Army. Every time an investigation is started, the people of Santo Domingo know beforehand that it will always end with the acquittal of the accused officer. Pictures of Cayo Baez showing the scars of torture on his body are circulating everywhere. There is hardly a Dominican or foreigner—be he a tourist or a traveling salesman (except the Americans of course)—who does not take one or several of them along with him as a souvenir. But they do not circulate except behind the backs of the American Military authorities because it would be dangerous to show them."

Among the written testimony contained in Blanco Fombona's book is also the following extract taken from a letter which Monseigneur Nouel, Roman Catholic Archbishop of Santo Domingo, addressed to the American Minister: "It cannot be denied that the people of Santo Domingo have witnessed on more than one occasion, during political upheavals, unjust persecutions, attempts against individual rights, and summary executions, but they have never before known anything like the torture of water or of fire, the strangling rope, the hunting down of men in the sabanas as if they were wild animals, nor the dragging of an eighty-year-old man at the tail of a horse all over the plaza of Hato Mayor!"

Referring to the way the American forces of occupation exercised their control in the Department of Public Works, Blanco Fombona claims among other things that said Department got to be famous not only on account of the numerous filtrations which took place there but more particularly so because of the manifest incapacity of its personnel. On a certain occasion (he states) an American was appointed director of the Department. He resolved, however, at the last moment, not to accept the job. But as his appointment had been already signed and he happened to have a nephew with the same name as his, he had himself supplanted by his nephew who did not know the first thing about engineering. The American officer in charge of the National Commissary Department in 1918 and 1919 allowed six big import firms, without any valid reason, to fix the price on sugar and rice to suit themselves. This irregularity was reported to the military governor, Thomas Snowden, but he did not pay any attention. Last year, with the pretext of economical difficulties, even the public schools were closed!

According to Blanco Fombona (page 89), "the White House is strangling all those Latin American governments who oppose the expansion of American Imperialism!" Here is an example. The Dominican-American Convention of 1907 prescribes that the Receptor turn over on the first of every month to the Fiscal Agent of the Loan the amount of one hundred thousand dollars, while the rest of the customs receipts collected during the previous month is delivered to the Dominican Government to be employed in the amortization of the Loan, or for the purchase or sale of bonds, etc. According to that treaty the United States have the right to receive only the stipulated amount of one hundred thousand dollars to be derived from the Customs House, which is the only source of national revenue affected by said treaty. Notwithstanding, the Receptor General not only has kept the remnant of the Customs House receipts which belonged to the Dominican Government, but has actually disposed of the product of all internal revenues of the country by force. To prove the veracity of this statement I will reproduce the following letter which was addressed by the Receptor General C. H. Baxter to the Secretary of Finance and Commerce of the Republic of Santo Domingo:

"I beg to inform the Department of Finance and Commerce that the Receptor General of the Dominican Customs Houses received to-day, Friday, June 16, 1916, by cable, the following instructions from the Negociado de Asuntos Insulares. By request of the

State Department the Receptoria will assume from now on the control of all the finances of the Dominican Government, inclusive of the collection of all internal revenues, as well as of all expenditures to be made by the Dominican Government. Following those instructions the Receptoria has assumed in the meantime the control, etc." And as Mr. J. M. Jimenez, Secretary of Finance and Commerce, objected to that flagrant abuse on the grounds that it was contrary to the treaty of 1907 between Santo Domingo and the United States, the American military authorities on the island took over the control of the Dominican finances by sheer force, which means with the help of their bayonets!

"The Republic of Santo Domingo," continues Blanco Fombona, "has paid religiously its debt; or rather, the American Government, which controls its Customs House has been very careful to collect every penny that was coming to it. According to the aforementioned Convention of 1907 the Dominican Government binds itself to amortize its outstanding bonds whenever there is a superavit in its budget. As long as the Dominicans themselves were running their government this stipulation had been religiously fulfilled. But the American military government which has been imposed by force on Santo Domingo has failed to do likewise. It is using the superavit for everything except for the amortization of Santo Domingo's debt. A certain Dominican nationalist paper which had asked the American military authorities why they, who had taken over forcibly the control of the Dominican finances, did not live up to the obligations stipulated in said treaty, was promptly threatened in all sorts of ways for having dared put such a question. The Dominican Loan will be paid up automatically by 1923. This prospective solvency of the Dominican finances is seemingly being viewed with disgust by the Washington administration. How is that possible? Santo Domingo without owing a cent to the United States? That will not do! It would mean that the pretext for occupying the island would eventually cease. It would be unpleasant to have to take off the mask of the 'creditor.' It is preferable to absorb the Republic by calling it a 'bad payer.' Consequently the American military government, despite all the efforts imaginable of the people of Santo Domingo to prevent it, contracts in the name of Santo Domingo a new loan of ten million dollars. Already in the *Official Gazette* of Santo Domingo appears a new executive order exacting that the total amount of the interests of said debt be deducted in advance from said loan. The American officer, a certain Mr. Mayo, who is acting as Secretary of Finance of Santo Domingo and whom the Dominicans accuse insistently of having enriched himself during the four years of American military occupation, has already left for the United States to contract the loan. What is the use of the Dominicans trying not to owe a red penny to the United States? The United States is generous enough to lend that beggar republic by force ten million dollars!"

It has been proven time and again that the last resource of Dollar Diplomacy to keep in control of a country's finances when it has been told to move on, consists in forcing said country at the last minute and as its condition *sine non qua,* to contract with them A LONG TERM LOAN, GENERALLY THROUGH, BUT IN ALL CASES GUARANTEED BY, THE WASHINGTON ADMINISTRATION.

This procedure, which is practically equivalent to

the peonage system, only applied to nations instead of to individuals, has been resorted to by Dollar Diplomacy whenever it has succeeded in sinking its talons into the finances of no matter which of the Latin-American republics, more particularly in Central America and the Antilles,—in Cuba, Haiti, Santo Domingo, Panama, El Salvador, etc., and, finally also in Nicaragua, where, taking advantage of the impending American armed intervention, the Dollar Diplomats had Adolfo Diaz borrow quickly another million dollars and give them the priority rights over any loan contracted by Nicaragua for the period of five years! This immoral system of keeping a financial hook permanently in those unhappy countries has been practically sanctioned and legalized by former President William Howard Taft who, according to Senate Hearings on Foreign Loans (page 86), is quoted as saying: "While our policy should not be turned a hair's breadth from the straight path of justice, it may well be made to include intervention to secure for our merchants and our capitalists opportunity for profitable investments which shall inure to the benefit of both countries."

I hope that the preceding information and more particularly that furnished by Sr. Blanco Fombona, may interest the United States Congress sufficiently to start, as soon as possible, a thorough investigation not only of the American armed intervention and military occupation of Santo Domingo, but also of Haiti, since the way the American military government has acted in Santo Domingo seems to have been, from what I have heard, only child's play when compared with the conduct of the American landing forces in Haiti.

I hope also that when Mr. Horace G. Knowles, former American Minister to Nicaragua, shall meet

Commander Shafroth again in the Institute of Politics of Williamstown, Mass., he may be able to furnish that gentleman some of the facts he so ardently desires to hear about the blessings of American armed intervention in Latin America; and, more particularly, about how the American landing forces have been "protecting the lives and interests of the Americans" resident in Santo Domingo.

Chapter XV

Double Jobs for Correspondents — Something About the New Loan — A Repulsive Farce About a Crucifix — Pertinent Remarks by Carleton Beals, S. Guy Inman and Senator Shipstead — The Terrific Slump in U. S. Trade With Latin America — Something About Hatred and a Few Suggestions for Its Cure.

DESPITE the good care which Consul Hueper, Mr. Bornemann and Miss Somarriba, who was in charge of the local hospital, were kind enough to dispense during the few days of rest which I took in that town, I was really glad when at last I arrived at Managua; for I was still very ill with the tropical fever which had seized on me in the jungle. So much so that, instead of going to an hotel, I accepted the kind invitation of Mrs. Maria de Uebersetzig to be her guest. She was a charming hostess, indeed. Of German descent, she has lived for many years in Managua, where everybody respects her very much because of her generous disposition. She is the widow of former Consul Uebersetzig, an ex-German regular army officer, who organized the Military Academy of Managua in the days of President José Santos Zelaya. At her home I had the pleasure of meeting, among other notables, Mrs. Panchita Leal, one of the matrons of the town as well as some very important political personalities such as Congressman Dr. Ramon Romero. Romero ranks among the foremost leaders of the latter-day Nationalist movement in Nicaragua, which has drawn the line between the honest, orderly and sincerely patriotic elements in both the Conservative and Liberal parties, and the venal and ruthless professional politicians of the Estrada-Adolfo Diaz-Chamorro-Moncada-Sacasa school in both parties; who have always catered, either directly or indirectly, to Dollar Diplomacy at the expense of Nicaragua's honor and independence. I also met at Doña Maria's home Dr. Nicolas Osorno, Capt. Lieut. W. Leissner, formerly of the German Navy, Mr. Edgar E. Bahlke, Mr. William Asche, representative of Blohm & Company at Maracaibo, as well as my old friend, General Samuel Santos, who had arrived in the meantime from Guatemala. During those days I went to Granada to visit Mr. Alejandro Marenco, who ranks among the great patriots of Nicaragua; and, combining duty with pleasure, I also accepted the kind invitation of Professor J. W. Schoenberg, the noted German scientist—whom I had met first when he was a German officer with us in Turkey—to visit the famous Masaya volcano. This is the volcano which had so potent a lure for the Conquistadores who mistook its boiling lava for molten gold. I spent some time, too, in the agreeable company of my Venezuelan countryman, Colonel Espinetti, who owns practically every moving picture theater in Nicaragua. The local press, both Conservative and Liberal, received me very well. My good intentions were taken for granted, especially by *El Comercio,* directed by Mr. José Maria Castrillo and *La Noticia,* whose managing editor is Mr. Ramon Aviles.

In Managua I also met Mr. Crampton, temporary representative of the United Press. The American Customs Collector, Mr. Ham, and his second, Mr. Lindberg, were representing the Associated Press. It surprised me very much that the Associated Press in Nicaragua should be represented by men who were practically subordinate officials of the State Department and, therefore, of Secretary Kellogg.

Among the various topics which were widely discussed at Managua in those days was General Sandino's idea about the way the Nicaraguan controversy ought to be settled. According to his opinion, which was broadcast afterwards by the press, the Canal of Nicaragua should not be built exclusively with American capital, but with fifty per cent Latin-American capital; while the remaining fifty per cent—which should include the three million dollars already paid by the American Government to Diaz and Chamorro —should be contributed by whatever nations might want to participate in the construction of the canal. That way, the people of Nicaragua would not have to fear for their independence; and they would incidentally be able to crisscross their country with railroads and heavy truck roads built with their share of the Canal revenues. This would seem to be not such an unintelligent idea for a "bandit" and an "outlaw," as Secretary Kellogg has chosen to brand General Sandino. It is a pity that there is no genuinely Latin-American newspaper of any importance in New York to take up Sandino's idea.

Another problem which was also stirring up quite a cloud of dust in Nicaragua at that time was the million-dollar loan which had been contracted in March by Dr. Zavala, financial agent of the Diaz administration, and the representatives of the Guarantee Trust Company and of J. and W. Seligman and Company of New York. *The Nation,* of New York (in Vol. 125, No. 3239), explains that monstrous loan in the following way:

"They are now engaged in proving that the three hundred Nicaraguans whom American marines and bombing planes murdered on July 17 were 'bandits.' That is the immemorial habit of imperialist usurpers —the British called the Boers bandits and the Irish republicans mere gunmen; the French called the heroic Riffians bandits, and doubtless the ancient Egyptians applied similar names to the armies they defeated. It does not alter the fact that American marines ought not to be doing police duty in Nicaragua, and that Latin-American hearts from Cape Horn to the Rio Grande beat in sympathy with any Latin who fights the Yankee invasion of a Latin country.

"If, however, the authorities in Washington are sincerely interested in tracing down large scale oppression, we suggest that they turn their attention to a document signed more or less at their own suggestion on March 31st last—between Dr. Zavala, financial agent for the American-aided Diaz régime in Nicaragua, and representatives of the Guarantee Trust Company and of J. and W. Seligman & Company of New York. It compares favorably, to be sure, with the usurious loans recently made at Los Angeles by leaders of the Better American Federation and the best local banking circles; but as government financing we have never seen anything to equal it.

"This extraordinary contract to begin with, opens a six-per-cent credit of one million dollars for the period of one year, which may under certain conditions be extended for another six months. Of course no one would ask a bank to lend the money that belongs to its depositors without securing good collateral. In this case one may feel sure that no depositor will complain—the bankers have taken all Nicaragua has—serape, sombrero, sandals and shirts. Two months before the negotiations of this loan the

THE LOOTING OF NICARAGUA

Nicaraguan Congress had voted certain emergency taxes—an export tax on all coffee up to sixty-five cents per one hundred pounds; a fifty-per-cent increase on customs duties on tobacco, wines and liquors; a twelve-per-cent increase in other import duties. All these were mortgaged to the bankers as collateral for this credit.

"But this was not all. As further collateral the bankers put a mortgage on fifty per cent of the surplus of the national treasury revenues. (Fifty per cent had similarly been mortgaged to New York bankers in 1917.) And since Mr. Diaz, even with American marines to do his police work for him, is unlikely to have a surplus, the bankers went further still. They put a mortgage on all the capital stock of the National Bank of Nicaragua, an American corporation with a paid-up capital of three hundred thousand dollars and a worth of twice that, and on all its dividends. They went still further. They added a mortgage on the entire capital stock of the Pacific Railways of Nicaragua, which, efficiently managed by the J. G. White Corporation, associated with the Seligmans, is worth more than the total amount of the credit extended by the bankers!

"According to the former Nicaraguan Consul General in New York City, the bankers were not satisfied with this. The deposits of the bank and the railroad in Canadian and other banks, said to total more than four hundred thousand dollars, were transferred to New York City for the benefit of the Credit Givers. (One wonders whether the money which the bankers lent to Nicaragua was actually the Nicaraguan money which they had transferred from other coffers to their own.) And then they capped the climax. They included in the contract an agreement which substantially said that they would not only mortgage half Nicaragua for their million-dollar loan but would furthermore spend the money for Nicaragua. They explained frankly that the money would be used primarily to equip, arm and maintain the Diaz soldiers (this some one may have hoped, eventually making it unnecessary for American marines to uphold that tottering régime). Money for other purposes will be released only upon approval of a special committee of three, two of whom are Americans! One of these Americans is the American Manager of the Bank of Nicaragua; the other is the American High Commissioner. Now the office of High Commissioner was instituted, we understand, in connection with the financial plan of 1920—drawn up by the Nicaraguan Government with another consortium of New York bankers. As then, the Secretary of State of the United States appoints the High Commissioner, who, nevertheless (probably to avoid difficulties with the law), is not considered an official of the Department of State, the Department of State insists on this finedrawn distinction between *appointee* and official; but in any case, the net result is *that the bankers use a government appointee as their agent and representative in Nicaragua.* The contract is long and contains more serfdom for Nicaragua. Among other things it provides that for five years the two New York banking houses have an option on all Nicaraguan financing.

"Here, we submit, is an interesting case to study for any government official seriously interested in the problem of oppression in Nicaragua. It would be an excellent thing, indeed, if the Department of State would give this matter its serious attention, and inform the public upon the result of its cogitations.

For this kind of oppression concerns the American people as a whole far more profoundly than the effort of a bare-footed army to support itself on a jungle countryside where an American planter happens to have a small property. It was, we take it, to this loan that Mr. Hoover referred when, last spring, he made the unwelcome remark about loans for unproductive purposes, which Mr. Kellogg so bitterly resented. Such loans, which, made with State Department approval, involve the utilization by bankers of State Department designees, involve us in a constant risk of bloody intervention. Suppose Nicaragua should seek to finance herself from other banks, violating its agreement with New York bankers; suppose it should seek to spend some of its amply secured credit in ways of which the High Commissioner, named by the State Department, did not approve—what then? More work for the marines!

"Bankers have often complained that they are unjustly accused of shaping State Department policy. Sometimes, they say, *the State Department begs them to make loans to help its previously determined policies.* By an incredible series of blunders the State Department is now committed to maintaining Adolfo Diaz in office as its puppet president of Nicaragua. Surely no sane business man would want to risk money on so feeble a character as Don Adolfo. *Is the State Department of the United States itself responsible for this shoddy pawnbroking?*"

Regarding the preceding article from *The Nation*, which is sufficiently self-explanatory, we can see that Dollar Diplomacy has certainly done all it possibly could in Nicaragua to live up to former President William Howard Taft's formula—that the Monroe Doctrine "may well be made to include intervention to secure for our merchants and our capitalists opportunity for profitable investments"! To judge by their way of handling the Nicaraguan problem, both Mr. Coolidge and Mr. Kellogg seem to share former President Taft's extraordinary opinion in regard to how to trample on the rights of small and defenseless nations and how to treat the international treaties which were made for their protection. Haiti, Santo Domingo and Nicaragua can vouch for that. The American people do not know—so crafty are Dollar Diplomacy's press agents—that while General Pershing was leaving for Europe, in 1917, at the head of two million American soldiers to fight Germany, because the "Huns" had violated the rights of a weak nation, Belgium, and treated an international treaty, for Belgium's protection, like so many scraps of paper, another part of the American Army, stationed in Haiti, Santo Domingo, Nicaragua, etc., had been engaged in doing things which rank no higher in the scale of honor and humanity.

The Dollar Diplomats and their cronies in the American Government are, no doubt, clever money makers; but they seem to ignore the fact that in the same proportion in which they have been piling up millions, at the expense of the blood of small and defenseless nations, they have been also piling up pyramids of hatred and future troubles for the United States. There are certain natural laws of equilibrium and stability which do not permit any nation to constitute itself the financial arbiter of the world. Sooner or later the crash is bound to come, as, during the World War, the principle was established that the capital of the enemy countries invested abroad shall be liable for the moral and financial damages caused by their respective governments. It is hard telling

THE LOOTING OF NICARAGUA

who would turn out to be the loser in the long run if England, or no matter who, should form another powerful coalition, this time against the United States. Such a coalition would find the ground already well prepared. Dollar Diplomacy has attended to that in a masterly way, indeed!

A few days before I left for Guatemala and the United States, I was very much amused by a picture published in a Managua paper, representing José Maria Moncada pinning the cross of peace on the breast of Admiral Latimer. This cross, as I was told by Doña Maria Uebersetzig, was a small golden crucifix which Moncada had purchased in a German jewelry store and from which he had had the image of Christ filed off. Though Moncada's purpose was not reverence, yet those, who regard the Christ sacredly, can be glad that even His gilt image was not included in this repulsive spectacle. I heard at that time that arrangements were being made to dispatch several platoons of the new Guardia Nacional, the American officered native constabulary, which had not been even recruited yet, to help the American marines in the Segovia and Jinotega mountains fight General Sandino. In a special cable from Balboa C. R., published by the New York *Times* of August 28th, I read among other interesting information "that according to General Feland the only duty remaining for the Marines in Nicaragua was to police the country and to train the native constabulary, etc." I wonder why Dollar Diplomacy, which has been in absolute control of Nicaragua's money bags for the last seventeen years, has not attended to that before instead of allowing its puppet governments, since 1909, to recruit their armies by every species of cruelty even from among the female population of Nicaragua. I presume that the reconvening of Congress next winter and Sandino's and Salgado's patriotic attitude have had probably something to do with all that hurrying and scurrying all of a sudden! Let us hope at any rate that the new, American-officered Nicaraguan constabulary may not be recruited, as in Santo Domingo and Haiti, from the bandit class to be commanded by individuals of the type of Bucklow, Knotchel, Wright, Taylor, Davis, etc., who have left such memories in Santo Domingo; unless the State Department wants the people of Nicaragua to rise again and again. For there will not be any real peace in Nicaragua, Central America and the Antilles as long as those people are not entirely left alone to work out their own salvation.

I will conclude with the following extracts taken from some recently published articles in *Current History* by three American observers whose words can be depended on. These are Mr. Carleton Beals, Mr. Samuel Guy Inman and Senator Henrik Shipstead:

"Recently the clamor against *Tio Sam* (Uncle Sam)," says Mr. Beals, "has become increasingly loud and bitter. The Union of Central and South America and the Antilles (UCSAYA), headquarters in Mexico, is actively spreading propaganda in favor of an all-Latin American boycott against American goods, a propaganda which has found considerable echo. At the last Pan-American trade congress, the South American delegates bitterly attacked our tariff schedules and threatened to turn to Europe. Ugarte thunders to Latin-American youth from his retreat in Niza his old 1912 slogan, 'Latin America for the Latin Americans.' Isidro Favela, ex-Secretary of Foreign Affairs under Carranza, declares that the United States is allied with the *Nicaraguan traitors,* and all

Latin-American peoples should mourn because their governments have been unconcerned over the *brutal and imperialistic outrage* perpetrated. Blanco Fombona of Venezuela lifts his voice accusingly. Dr. Alfredo Palacios organizes the Congress of Ibero-Americano youth in Montevideo, declaring that 'we have nothing to do with the United States except defend ourselves from the claws of its great capitalists.' The Salvadorian editors, denouncing the United States, have petitioned their government to withdraw recognition of Diaz in Nicaragua. In recent months *El Cosmos* of Colombia, the *Journal de Brasil*, *La Nacion* of Argentina, *Excelsior* of Mexico, *El Imparcial* of Guatemala, *El Diario* of Costa Rica, *El Mundo* of Cuba, in short, practically every leading newspaper of Latin America has carried articles sharply critical, even openly bitter. From the Rio Grande south, old hymns of hate against the Colossus of the North have been dug up to be resung at public gatherings. But not with lyric addresses or hymns of hate will the eighty million people to the south of us ultimately emerge from a semi-colonial status to adult nationhood. Obviously, we cannot hope to control politically, or even economically, let alone ideologically, any appreciable extent of Latin-American territory. Emerging nationality and participation in a common racial culture, spread over a larger contiguous area than any homogeneous group of peoples in the world, will ultimately tip the balance."

Financially, too, the countries to the south of us will achieve independence. At the Third Pan-American Congress, Mr. Hoover, advocating loans for purely industrial purposes, declared (*New York Journal of Commerce,* May 3, 1927): "The need of Latin-American countries will be found to be only temporary and in the course of time they, too, will come to be exporters of capital. We may take it as a certainty that with the upbuilding of the economic structure each American State will in turn, at some time, begin to produce that surplus which will, when converted into capital, relieve it of the necessity of external borrowing."

To this Mr. Inmans adds his views, as follows:

"Latin-American suspicion of the Monroe declaration began only with the Mexican War, when the United States took about half Mexico's territory. It continued because of the unwise *braggadocio* of many of our statesmen concerning our 'manifest destiny'; was augmented by the Spanish-American War when the Philippines and Porto Rico came under the Stars and Stripes, and Cuba had her sovereignty limited by the Platt Amendment, and was still further increased by American military movements in Panama, Haiti, Santo Domingo, Nicaragua and Mexico. The most recent maneuvers of the marines in Nicaragua have aroused a perfect storm of protest, the like of which has never been known before. The Monroe Doctrine, therefore, stands to-day in the eyes of the Latin Americans as one of the principal dangers that threaten their sovereignty. Instead of 'America for the Americans' our Southern friends generally believe that the doctrine now means 'America for the North Americans'; instead of its being a protection from Europe they believe that it means a protectorate by the United States. Although many of our own statesmen are pointing to the noble unselfishness of the United States in its 'big brother' attitude of protecting Latin America from Europe, Latin America is inclined to betake herself to Europe and to the League of Nations for protection against the United States. The matter is well illustrated by extracts from Mr. Hughes' definition of the doctrine and Latin-American criticism of it. In an address in Minneapolis on August 30, 1923, Mr. Hughes said: 'As the policy embodied in the Monroe Doctrine is distinctly the policy of the United States, the government of the United States reserves to itself its definition, interpretation and application.' How this address was received in Latin America is typified by the following extract from an article of Jesus Semprun, published in a number of the most important reviews of Latin America: 'If in tropical America there were a powerful nation conscious of its duties, of its situation and of its dangers, Mr. Hughes' discourse would inevitably plant a *casus belli* . . . for that which Mr. Hughes declares is that the United States will intervene . . . that whenever it likes it will occupy by force American territories which it desires; it will enforce on other peoples the necessary obedience to carry out its own designs, to foment its own interests and to impose its unquestionable economic and political sovereignty in the New World!'

"Europe has no longer a Holy Alliance made up of the absolute monarchs, formed for the suppression of a few weak republics of America. There are nearly as many republics in the other parts of the world as there are in America, and governments like that of Great Britain give as much opportunity of registering popular opinion as do republics. Not only has Europe the League of Nations but she has the Locarno Treaties and conferences which, if they do not always settle problems, at least bring publicity which makes impossible to-day the scheming of the old Holy Alliance. So, also, the Latin American countries, far from considering unity for the purpose of resisting Spain and

Portugal, to-day often turn to Europe for spiritual aid and political inspiration, while they talk much of a Latin-American League of Defense against the United States. Most of them are in the full current of the international organization.

"The original Monroe Doctrine definitely stated *that there should be no intervention by one government in the affairs of another.* During the last quarter of a century, however, that doctrine has been changed by the United States, since we have intervened many times in the affairs of the smaller Caribbean countries. Those acts of intervention have never been submitted to Congress in spite of the fact that some of them have exercised military control with the suppression of all civil government. In Santo Domingo such a situation continued for eight years! The modern way to intervene, if such a serious step is absolutely necessary, is by joint action of several nations. It is a most significant fact not often referred to by the admirers of Mr. Roosevelt that though he began the policy of intervention in Santo Domingo, he stated several times during his trip to South America, that if intervention became necessary in America in the future it should be a joint affair between the United States and other American nations. Just as the rest of the world has come to international organization through which it will settle its questions, so must we in America. Certainly the enlightened opinion of the United States does not wish to use our great power to force our will on our neighbors. Even if we wish to we cannot do it much longer without coming into violent contact with Latin America and the League of Nations group. The only way out is through joint action."

Senator Shipstead comes sharply to the point with these statements:

"The Monroe Doctrine is dead, and has been dead for many years. It lived only as long as its original spirit was followed. At the present time, instead of maintaining financial protectorates over our sister republics in Latin America, it would be more correct to say that we are holding them under a form of military and financial dictatorship. These various military and financial dictatorships have been imposed upon the Latin-American countries under successive administrations and by the force of American arms. Instances could be multiplied indefinitely. Any well-informed American citizen is now aware that our present Latin-American policy is frankly one of economic aggression involving political dictatorship. It is still covered by the name of the Monroe Doctrine, but it has nothing in common with that doctrine as originally enunciated. In the case of the Monroe Doctrine we must do one of two things: Either we must abandon the idealism of the Monroe Doctrine altogether, acknowledging frankly what our acts are in Latin America, and accepting the consequences both at home and abroad; or we must revive the idealism of the Monroe Doctrine, cleave to it in deeds, as in words, and make our acts square with our professions. It is a moral issue of first proportion. But moral issues work themselves out in practical results. The question before us is—can we afford in dollars and cents to pursue our present policy in Latin America much longer? Has Dollar Diplomacy really gained in terms of national gain? It undoubtedly has paid well for a few interests and individuals. But does all that actually pay to the general commercial enterprise of a nation? The following statistics for 1925 and 1926 taken from the monthly summary of the Department of Commerce go to show that it *does not!* Total amount of exports to Latin America:

(1925) $407,849,726
(1926) $350,585,124
Difference, 14%

"Thus, granting that the activities of the State Department and the employment of the United States marines have brought profits to perhaps a score of our leading industrial and financial interests, what is the gain to the general business of the country, to the merchants, manufacturers and farmers who have to work without the special services of the Federal Government in their behalf? Their lot seems to be to bear in taxation a share of the expense of a policy which benefits only a privileged few, which netted a loss in trade of fifty-seven million dollars, or fourteen per cent of our total exports to eight of our sister Latin-American republics, in the calendar year just closed. These are serious figures. Are we not killing the goose that lays the golden eggs in Latin America? The moral issue cannot be evaded. An unconscious boycott of American goods, based on growing enmity, is obviously beginning to operate in Latin America. And every day that our present hypocritical Latin-American policy goes on, we are losing prestige in the field of international relations; every day we are gaining the increased enmity of all the American continent outside of our borders. The time may come when we shall need friends in the Western Continent, and elsewhere in the world!"

It will take true statesmanship, patience, and good will to eradicate the seeds of enmity which have been so lavishly sown in the fast-germinating tropical soil of Latin America. The old saying "good lover and

THE LOOTING OF NICARAGUA

good hater" applies pretty widely to the Latin American. No generalization about any race is strictly true, nor applicable to all its individuals; but, allowing even for large exception, it can be said that Latin Americans care less about the dollar than their northern neighbors. There are sound reasons for this general difference between the two peoples. One of these reasons is the sun. In North America, that is, in the United States and Canada, excepting only a few territories, man grows his food with some difficulty, and his good or poor crops affect, in a degree, all his brethren of the industrial centers. Therefore his food, and the dollar which is more or less governed by his food, influence his thoughts, his pleasures, his emotions, the more because hazard and doubt attend them. In Latin America sun and soil produce food for man in luxurious abundance. Nature's generous storehouses, the climates of both lowland and highland in their separate fashions, the glory of sun and moon, the flaming beauty of the landscape, all these react still, as for over four centuries they have reacted, upon a people whose ancestors also were children of the sun—the Andalusian for instance, the Saracen, and, more recently, the Maya and the Inca; to none of these did the crop and the dollar ever have to mean what they have to mean in Maine and Dakota. Therefore, quite logically, a passion, an ideal, or a hatred can seem of more importance to a Latin American than a shipment of cheap canned goods from the United States. This sounds somewhat farfetched, even jocular, but it points a moral. It is not wise to arouse hatred in a race which can afford to foster it.

Let us consider some of the possible avenues for that hatred. There is the League of Nations, which includes Latin America. As yet, there has been no *concerted* action there by the Latin-American members of the League in regard to the oppressions of the United States. But feed the fires of hatred only a little more, and that mass action will develop; to use a high tariff, probably, as its effective weapon. Then, looking a little farther into the future, we can see the probable diverting of Latin-America's commerce from the markets of the United States to those of Asia and Europe. China looms up as the greatest competitor. Already Chinese capital is behind large syndicates in India, Java, Sumatra, trafficking in silk, coffee, metals, though these syndicates bear European names. That an awakened China, branching into modern industries on a large scale—which her millions of cheap laborers will enable her to do—will seek to buy the necessary raw material and to sell her finished products in Latin America is geographically assured. How will the United States meet that competition? With high wages in the United States and low wages in China, the Chinese merchants will be able to undersell the American merchants in any market. And sentiment, which is really a powerful element of Latin-American psychology, will not be engaged on the side of American business! Already, with no new powerful competitor of the United States in her markets, Latin-America had reduced her once friendly commercial exchange with the United States—as Senator Shipstead points out—by fifty-seven million dollars at the close of the year 1926. Fifty-seven million dollars in one year! This reduction does not hurt the companies who hold concessions under the puppet presidents installed by the United States State Department. It only injures legitimate trade. Therefore the Dollar Diplomats go on merrily with their program of loot, bloodshed and terrorization. They will have taken out their billions—always efficiently aided by the State Department and the American Military forces—before the big crash comes. They care no more about future injury to America than they care how many conscript women were killed yesterday, or mutilated, for the sake of their friend, Adolfo Diaz, who assures to them the best parts of the fatted calf. The looter, the bandit, is seldom a true patriot!

But is it not high time that the American public—and, in particular, the commercial and industrial classes—demand in no uncertain tone that the State Department cease dry-nursing these bandits and look seriously to the welfare of the nation, whose honor it represents and whose international interests it has specially under its care? Two reforms would seem to be immediately necessary: first, the elimination from the State Department and the Army and Navy of those individuals who have "business" connections with concessionaires in Latin America; and, secondly, a thorough house-cleaning by those newspapers and news agencies whose correspondents in Latin-America have, also, such business connections as make their correspondence of doubtful value to say the least.

To restore the faith of Latin America in the honesty and justice of the United States one step should be taken without delay. The long term clauses in loan contracts, which compel the debtor country to remain in debt and paying interest for years—in defiance of their will and their ability to pay up—should be annulled. It is certainly an immoral and arbitrary procedure to force a man or a nation into that degrading position. This is one of Dollar Diplomacy's favorite devices in Latin America and the Antilles. Furthermore these loans should not be guaranteed, as they are, by the United States Government. Borrowing and lending money is a business transaction. Let business be business, but not politics.

All concessions in Latin America, especially in Central America and the Antilles, should be subject to revision by the governments of those countries; to make them comply with the law, in case they have been granted illegally—as is too frequent—by Dollar Diplomacy's own puppet presidents. The Government of the United States should not intervene in any issue of this sort. In the case of annulment, the concessionaires should be refunded their expenditures and should be given a reasonable compensation. Arbitration should be the final resort in case of serious dispute. These fake Claims Commissions, consisting of two citizens of the United States and one citizen of the Latin-American country involved, should be done away with. No American armed forces should ever be landed on the soil of a sovereign and independent Latin-American republic to "intervene." If intervention should be necessary it should never be undertaken by the United States alone but in conjunction with two Latin-American powers.

Thirdly, as I have said before in these pages—as well as in public addresses—throughout all Latin America, and possibly especially in Nicaragua and the other Central American republics, there are rich, and easy, opportunities for Americans who are willing to prosper in legitimate business. And the honest business man wins friendship and respect not for himself alone but for his nation.

There is another point, perhaps it is purely a moral one, which I would like to raise for consideration by the people of this country. Wherever Dollar Diplomacy and marines have held sway, as in Nicaragua,

Santo Domingo, etc., government schools have disappeared and the revenues, once used to support them, have been diverted to the benefit of clerical establishments. This is one of the most disastrous results of the influence of the United States in Latin America and the Antilles. A curious anomaly is presented, surely, by the spectacle of the United States—which is so largely Protestant, or at least non-Catholic, and which has the public school as one of the pillars of her social system—using her money, and her armed power, to strengthen the Dark Ages substratum which lingers in the structure of the Roman Catholic Church. Like most modern Catholics, both in America and elsewhere, I believe in secular education. It seems to me that the American public school is perhaps the most satisfactory example America has given to the world of the efficiency of Democracy in quickening the human faculties and preparing them for intelligent living. Are Americans really content to be the chief assisting agency in barring thousands of poor Nicaraguan and Dominican children from education? That is what it means, because the few parochial schools do not enroll the children of the poorer classes. It is *their* fate to grow up to be ignorant helpless *peones,* sweating and half-starving under the lash of the concessionaires. That, of course, is the purpose of closing the public schools. All powers of darkness, whether founded on money or on superstition, need an ignorant populace to exploit; otherwise their power vanishes, like clouds dispersed by the sun. This, the sectarian, aspect of "Intervention" is of the gravest moment to the United States. Inevitably the present policy, if continued, will breed religious strife inside her boundaries. As the mass of non-Catholics in America begin to understand how the old colonial system of the Roman Church is supported and solidified by American capital, by the American State Department and by American armed forces, they will become indignant. There will be bitter recriminations between Protestants and Catholics in this country; and intolerant acts will be committed which will fan slumbering fires into fury. Has not the conflict between State and Church in Mexico already sounded echoes in the United States—in the press, in state legislatures, in Congress and the Senate and from a thousand pulpits? Can any American deny that religous bigotry has raised its head in this nation and let the whir of its rattles be heard? Then does not serious peril threaten the internal harmony of this Republic, and increase in menace, as the American political policy in Central America and the Antilles becomes more and more involved with the political and economic policy of Rome in those countries? History has made us sadly wise regarding the durability, as well as the violence, of the hatreds which spring from religious controversy.

Neither Catholics nor Protestants in the United States understand, apparently, how the modern Latin American regards this question of the Church. We do not (as some Protestants seem to wish) love our ancient Faith less than did our fathers; nor are we (as many Catholics in the United States seem to fear) on the verge of Atheism and Hell. But we are resolved that our churches shall be autonomous to a large extent and that our spiritual counselors shall be, like ourselves, native sons imbued with our own ideals, lovers of our countries and patriotic laborers for the welfare of our masses. For the Latin American of the educated classes there can be no peace, nor true content, while he sees the masses of his countrymen ground under the heels of Dollar Diplomacy, marines and a foreign priesthood; all working together for the enslavement of his compatriots and the ruin of his homeland. We value our spiritual bond with Rome and with the Catholic Church all over the world. Our contest is with that alien hierarchical circle which—having gained sufficient power in the realms of politics and education, particularly—exploits our countries as spiritual colonies in the same manner in which Spain once exploited them as imperial colonies; i.e., never for our benefit, but always for Rome's. This question is to the forefront in all our republics to-day; and it would appear to be one in which the United States obviously ought not to mix even indirectly (as she is doing now), if only for the sake of peace and brotherhood within her own borders.

But my plea to North Americans is to look farther yet, beyond the limits of self-interest. Indubitably, awakening Asia rises on the skyline as a great, probably the greatest, commercial power of the near future. It is a truism of history that the world's great traders spread their cultural ideas with their commerce. Social and political systems have been modified and changed by vast economic invasions. Americans of both continents should remember that the very ideals underlying our western democracies will be menaced in that day to come. We need to put up a solid front from the Arctic to Cape Horn for the protection of future generations as well as our own.

Sources of Information

American Federation of Labor—Associated Press, New York *World,* October 13, 1927.
— Report of Proceedings of the Fourth Labor Congress.
Arguello, H. O.—Letter from Puerto Cabezas, February 10, 1927.
— Letter from Puerto Cabezas, February 19, 1927.
— Letter from Puerto Cabezas, March 20, 1927.
Aviles, Rivas—Battle of Zaguna de Perlas, *Diario Moderno,* Managua, June 6, 1927.
Beals, Carlton—Finis Coronat Opus, *The Nation,* Vol. 125, 1927.
— Latin American Nations' Failure to Attain Unity, *Current History,* September, 1927.
Bejarano, José Miguel—Secretary Mexican Chamber of Commerce of the United States, Inc., Dollar Diplomacy in Nicaragua, *The Tanager,* July, 1927.
Bolanos, G. Aleman—Antecedents about Dr. Sacasa's Political Career, the *Excelsior,* Guatemala, July 15, 1927.
— Detailed written account of J. M. Moncada's political history.
— Detailed written information about the Irias Expedition to the Pacific Coast, etc.
Borah, Senator Wm. E.—Speech at the Jewish Congress, Washington, D. C., February, 1927.
Brooks, William S.—New York *Times,* March 5, 1927, March 29, 1927, and April 19, 1927.

Carter, C. B.—The Kentucky Feud in Nicaragua, *World's Work*, July, 1927.
Cuyamel Fruit Company—Letter from El Gallo, December 28, 1926.
Encyclopedia Britannica—See articles on Nicaragua and other pertinent topics.
Escamilla, Juan—De Puerto Cabezas a Managua, *La Noticia*, June 9, 1927.
Feland, Gen.—New York *Times*, August 28, 1927.
Fombona, Horacio Blanco—Crimenes del Imperialismo Americano.
Hardy, J. H.—Letter from La Barra, March 3, 1927.
Inman, Samuel Guy—The Monroe Doctrine as an Obsolete Principle, *Current History*, September, 1927.
Knowles, Horace G.—Knowles Arouses Politics Institute, New York *Times*, August 23, 1927.
Latimer, Admiral—Proclamation at Managua, May 10, 1927.
Lindsay, Corporal Wm.—Written announcement at Matiguas, May 19, 1927.
Lovos, Vicente—Letter to Captain Kattengell, February 25, 1927.
MacPherson, L. G.—Letter from La Barra, March 2, 1927.
Moffat, Thos. P.—New York *World*, July 25, 1927.
Moncada, J. M.—Proclamation at Managua, May 5, 1927.
— Utterances during a banquet given at Gen. Feland's residence in Managua, Guatemala press, July, 1927.
National Citizens' Committee on Relations with Latin America—Circular of May 9, 1927.
Nogales, Rafael de—Four Years Beneath the Crescent, *Scribner's*, 1926.